Praise for *Feedback to Feed*

MW00786134

"Leading learning meets specificity! Tepper and Flynn take t
change we know—feedback— and comprehensively break it do
grounded in theory and practice. Treat *Feedback to Feed Forward* as a master cookbook. Look
for what you need and delve into it with a connoisseur's appetite."

—Michael Fullan, Professor Emeritus,
OISE/University of Toronto

"Teachers are starving for effective feedback—feedback they can actually use to take next
steps in their teaching and their students' learning. Grounded in research and the authors'
years of experience, *Feedback to Feed Forward* provides an indispensable guide for instructional leaders in how to use an instructional framework, collect a variety of evidence, and
analyze impact on student learning—all in the service of providing teachers with objective,
growth-oriented, and actionable feedback. Practical and accessible, the book combines a
compelling vision for instructional leadership focused on student learning with authentic
examples, data collection tools, and concrete strategies that anyone who supports teachers,
regardless of the level expertise, can apply immediately to their own practice."

—Nancy Love, Author of *The Data Coach's Guide for
Improving Learning for All Students*

"*Feedback to Feed Forward: 31 Strategies to Lead Learning* is a must-read for practicing school
leaders whose roles have rapidly evolved over the past several years. Tepper and Flynn have
masterfully unpacked the essential elements of effective supervision and evaluation that
supports teachers in improving their practice. In this practical guidebook, the authors focus
on the practices of instructional leaders who have become leaders of learning in their
schools. As the result of years of work supporting schools and districts who have struggled
to implement new systems of educator evaluation, they have seen firsthand the need to
support school leaders in developing a new set of core skills and strategies to confidently and
effectively lead learning in their schools. In order for school leaders to feel comfortable
immersing themselves in teaching and learning every day, they need ongoing professional
learning and support to develop the skills for effective observation and direct feedback that
promotes growth, improves teacher practice, and results in student learning."

—Sara J. Barzee, Chief Talent Officer;
CT State Department of Education

"I love how versatile and practical the content of this book is! No matter what evaluation
rubric or method you use, this process of data collection, connecting the data to the rubric,
and setting a course of action leads to meaningful feedback that teachers can immediately
implement in their classroom practice. Tepper and Flynn create a system of support to help
administrators through every stage of the evaluation process. Whether readers are new to the
process or have been conducting evaluations for years, they can connect to where they are
and can easily determine next steps for themselves throughout every chapter. The authors
provide guidance that supports leaders in fostering a climate that cultivates a collaborative
and reflective approach to growth and development through the evaluation process."

—Alisha L. DiCorpo, Assistant Superintendent;
New Milford, CT

"*Feedback to Feed Forward: 31 Strategies to Lead Learning* gives me a whole new way to think about classroom observation by elevating this very common practice to a strategic, purposeful, and scientific professional development tool! It is a book so full of strategies, information, guidance, and tips to improve my work that I will read, re-read, and study it continually as I hone my skills of observation and feedback to promote teacher growth. With regard to my work as an observer of classroom instruction, this book enabled me to answer the three highlighted questions, "Where am I going? How am I going? Where to next?" Tepper and Flynn provide a clear, step-by-step way to think about and perform observations for the purpose of defining what I am actually looking for, seeking evidence of it while in the room and using that evidence to craft actionable feedback for a teacher."

—Amy Bruce, Principal,
West Ridge Elementary; Thornton, CO

"One of the best books I have read regarding evaluation practices. In my almost 13 years as an administrator I have always known that feedback and discussion after the evaluation were important but now I have a better understanding of how to address very specific aspects. Looking at the big picture in a way that breaks it down into four categories was incredibly helpful. While it feels overwhelming to think about doing all of these things in one evaluation, since it is a new approach for me—now that I know better, I must do better. I have been practicing some of my learning while reading the book with one of my teachers and the first time I went in I didn't know who was more nervous, her or me! However, there was a sense of excitement knowing that I was gaining skills to be a better evaluator, which in turn will produce better teachers and more engaged learners! This is a process that will take time, but taking the first step has opened a whole new door for me in improving my evaluation process!"

—Chris deNeui, Principal,
Central Elementary School; Nevada, IA

"Tepper and Flynn, and the principles that they so comprehensively elaborate upon in this book, are most responsible for my professional growth as a teacher and leader. These tenets have built my leadership capacity on a myriad of levels: from effectively collecting evidence during a classroom observation to giving effective and actionable feedback to teachers. This text will quickly rise to the top and become a *tour de force* in the world of educational leadership."

—John Mastroianni, K–12 Music Department Chair,
Director of Bands; Canton, CT

Feedback to Feed Forward

To every instructional leader who strives to transform teaching and learning each day.

Feedback to Feed Forward

31 Strategies to Lead Learning

Amy Tepper and Patrick Flynn

CORWIN
A SAGE Publishing Company

FOR INFORMATION:

Corwin

A SAGE Company

2455 Teller Road

Thousand Oaks, California 91320

(800) 233-9936

www.corwin.com

SAGE Publications Ltd.

1 Oliver's Yard

55 City Road

London EC1Y 1SP

United Kingdom

SAGE Publications India Pvt. Ltd.

B 1/I 1 Mohan Cooperative Industrial Area

Mathura Road, New Delhi 110 044

India

SAGE Publications Asia-Pacific Pte. Ltd.

3 Church Street

#10-04 Samsung Hub

Singapore 049483

Publisher: Arnis Burvlkovs
Development Editor: Desirée A. Bartlett
Editorial Assistant: Eliza B. Erickson
Production Editor: Tori Mirsadjadi
Copy Editor: Tina Hardy
Typesetter: C&M Digitals (P) Ltd.
Proofreader: Rae-Ann Goodwin
Indexer: Beth Nauman-Montana
Cover Designer: Anupama Krishnan
Marketing Manager: Nicole Franks

Printed in the United States of America.

Library of Congress Cataloging-in-Publication Data

Names: Tepper, Amy, author. | Flynn, Patrick W., author.

Title: Feedback to feed forward : 31 strategies to lead learning / Amy Tepper and Patrick Flynn.

Description: First edition. | Thousand Oaks, California : Corwin, [2018] | Includes bibliographical references and index.

Identifiers: LCCN 2018006757 | ISBN 9781544320229 (pbk. : acid-free paper)

Subjects: LCSH: Teachers—Rating of—United States. | Teaching United States—Evaluation. | Teacher effectiveness—United States. | Observation (Educational method)

Classification: LCC LB2838 .T45 2018 | DDC 371.14/4—dc23
LC record available at https://lccn.loc.gov/2018006757

This book is printed on acid-free paper.

18 19 20 21 22 10 9 8 7 6 5 4 3 2 1

Contents

Visit the companion website at
resources.corwin.com/feedforward for downloadable resources.

Preface

Welcome to the first day of the rest of your life! You are holding a handbook we believe all leaders should own, and we are pleased it is has made its way into your hands. Every day, we work to support leaders just like you—peer observers, teacher leaders, coaches, administrators—and have come to recognize that you all need help in your work to lead the teaching and learning in your classrooms and buildings. We know teachers need support not just from an evaluator but from a leader of learning who provides feedback that feeds forward, and teachers need it—yesterday. And we know that to make a difference for our teachers and students, instructional leaders must shift from inspecting instruction to impacting practices through high-quality observation and feedback.

Leaders need the skills and strategies to do this—to conduct comprehensive observations, analyze lessons for effectiveness, and develop high-leverage action steps that will change practices and outcomes, yet they are not receiving enough professional learning or leader preparation to be able to do so. This gets us up every day and has driven our vision as career educators—a vision of making a difference for our leaders and teachers and the students they serve.

This book was created to be your "how-to" guide. What clearly sets it apart is the inclusion of comprehensive explanations of standards, descriptions of discrete core skills, and outlining of strategies to ensure that leaders—regardless of experience—are able to directly apply improved observation and feedback practices. We provide you with explicit think-alouds, strategies, and authentic lesson examples from the field through each step of the process so that this book will serve as a comprehensive learning tool for leaders in all roles and experience levels.

It is clear to us that this book will not just be helpful; it is long overdue. We expect you will feel the same as you read, unable to put it back on your shelf. You will find that the strategies and skills outlined chapter by chapter are immediately transferable, the moment you leave the office and enter a classroom. We know this because this book has been developed from our coaching and work every day, all year, with instructional leaders just like you. As a result of reading this book, we expect readers to be better prepared to do the following:

- Recognize the role and responsibilities of an instructional leader as an agent of change focused on the learning and the learners.

- Utilize district evaluation systems and instructional frameworks to leverage growth and increase objectivity.

- Understand the essential components of high-quality teacher feedback to promote growth, defined by three core competencies, a set of six standards, and 21 discrete skills.

- Define effective instruction and engagement.

- Effectively collect evidence during a classroom observation to develop impactful feedback.

- Analyze/focus observation and feedback on teacher impact on engagement and student learning.

- Determine evidence-based areas of strength on which to build areas of challenge and determine actionable high-leverage next steps.

- Promote teacher reflection.

Beyond this, a critical purpose of the book is to also provide a broader context to

- develop the capacity of teachers and nonevaluating support staff to observe, analyze for effectiveness, reflect, debrief, review artifacts, and develop solutions with peers or in professional learning communities; and

- build district internal capacity and develop measurable system-based learning designs and solutions.

Although it took us one year to write this book, it has been in development for over six years through our hands-on embedded training with a mix of rural and urban schools, including over 58 Connecticut districts, the State Departments of Education in Connecticut and New York, and school districts and communities in Louisiana and New Jersey, including Newark public schools. Through our work with nearly 1,000 instructional leaders and through completion of over 8,000 classroom observations, we have come to recognize how to support our leaders of learning in a meaningful and impactful way.

Anyone who supports teachers in any capacity or who supports or trains instructional leaders will benefit from the skills and strategies presented. This is also written for those currently enrolled in or just completing leadership preparation programs. For district decision makers and professional learning providers and designers, you too will find value. You will be able to utilize the recommended practices, processes, and standards to assess current support and develop aligned, systems-based, embedded professional learning.

You will begin your journey in Chapter 1 with the research supporting the need for a shift in practices. The standards you will encounter in Chapters 2 and 3 represent foundational skills necessary for success in the remaining four chapters, so we recommend that all readers move through the chapters and strategies in the order presented, regardless of your experience level or years observing in classrooms. Within each chapter, you will encounter strategies and steps that are often most effective when followed sequentially and with fidelity. There is no quick fix or shortcut to this work. Teaching practices and student outcomes will be impacted tenfold by your time and dedication to the strategies we suggest.

The last chapter provides examples and next steps for district and systems planning in which, above all, we suggest a collaborative, team-based approach. Engaging with colleagues, teachers you support, and/or as a whole district through a book study, coupled with collegial conversations and classroom visits, will create a shared vision of effective instruction and focus on learning.

In each chapter you will find an essential question and stop and think questions that will allow you to reflect on your own practices. These also open the door for rich discussion within your team. And finally, to aid the reader, you can access online resources to support each chapter at **https://resources .corwin.com/feedforward.**

This book was not written to be read in one sitting. It will take patience and stamina as you work to master the 31 strategies. Put the book down periodically and go try out a new strategy. Ask yourselves, "How did that go?" We are hoping you work through each chapter by placing stickies and highlighting text for rereads, revisiting sections as you practice new strategies, and sharing your learning with your team—and most importantly, that you come to rely on this book as you grow in your instructional leadership, finding it never rests on your shelf for very long.

—Amy and Patrick

Acknowledgments

First and foremost, we want to acknowledge the many leaders, coaches, and teachers we have come to know through our work over the past 25 years. We never would have been able to write this without you. We know we exhausted many of you with our stamina for talking instruction for six hours straight, our ongoing questioning, and forgotten break times at each and every training. But know that your dedication to your students and passion for your own learning continue to inspire us. Every one of your challenges and aha moments taught us about what leaders need to be able to support teachers and to provide feedback that feeds forward.

We must thank the amazing Michael Fullan. Your lightning-quick mind supplied us with the title of our book in 22 seconds—all over chicken wings and lamb meatballs while at a table with our other hero Andy Hargreaves. Thanks to each of you for showing an interest in two new writers.

We are grateful for the friends who provided feedback throughout the process, especially Dr. Jordan Grossman, one of our earliest believers and first readers; Maureen Armstrong, our favorite librarian and tyrant grammarian copy editor, who taught us the ins and outs of the "em dash"; and our rock, Amanda Van Blaricom, who poured through the pages as a new learner and tirelessly readied the manuscript for printing.

We never would have finished without Rocky's Aqua, Shanks Waterfront, and Water's Edge Restaurants—your breathtaking New England shoreline views and endless calamari provided much needed inspiration on long writing days. Thanks for letting us occupy a table for seven hours at a time. Siesta Key Beach, thanks for sharing your sunsets with us after hours of editing draft after draft under our umbrella.

Of course, we thank our ever-patient family members and friends (even though some said we were writing a *boring* book), who we rarely saw during the year-long writing process. And, for Bobbi, who won't get to read it but would have loved it.

Finally, Amy would like to acknowledge Dr. Frank Fuller who taught her early on what leadership looks like. Thank you for seeing who I could be.

Patrick would like to recognize Dr. John Chubb, who provided him with countless opportunities to define himself as a leader over an all too short a period of time. Your conviction and commitment to American education for *all* will forever be an inspiration.

Many thanks to Corwin for your support and allowing us to share our vision and passion with many.

Publisher's Acknowledgments

Corwin gratefully acknowledges the contributions of the following reviewers:

Donna Fong, Clinical Instructor and Field Supervisor
Lamar University Department of Educational Leadership
Beaumont, TX

Shelly Allen, Clinical Instructor and Field Supervisor
Lamar University Department of Educational Leadership
Beaumont, TX

Ray Boyd, Principal
West Beechboro Independent Primary School
Beechboro, Western Australia

About the Authors

Amy Tepper has served as a teacher, administrator, and program director in various K–12 settings and startups that include virtual, homeschool, blended, and public schools. She held the position of executive director of a Sylvan Learning Center, opened an alternative 6th- through 12th-grade school in Okaloosa County, Florida, and later was actively engaged in Florida high school redesign and career education reform, providing technical assistance across the state. Amy had the opportunity to collaborate with a team of parents to develop the Ohana Institute, an innovative blended school, focused on global citizenship and discovery learning, serving as director in its first year. As a consultant, she provided instructional and administrative coaching at an international school in Panama before joining ReVISION Learning Partnership in 2013. Amy has since completed countless classroom observations through work as a peer validator, evaluating practices in Newark and New Haven schools, and in providing embedded, ongoing support for instructional leaders and teachers in the areas of high-quality observation, feedback, and teaching and learning across Connecticut.

Patrick Flynn has worked as a teacher, teacher leader, curriculum director, and executive program director in K–12 settings in over 11 different states. As the executive director of high schools for Edison Schools and the chief academic officer for Great Schools Workshop in Sacramento, California, Patrick worked with building and district administrations in nine states to implement systemic high school reform. He has provided professional learning in the areas of transformational leadership, performance management systems, standards-driven instruction, and data-driven decision making. Patrick is founder and executive director of ReVISION Learning Partnership, providing professional development and support to districts and educational organizations in Connecticut, New York, New Jersey, and Louisiana since 2010. He has led several school improvement initiatives in rural and urban settings and supported school reform internationally in the United Arab Emirates with the Abu Dhabi Education Council. He has presented nationally and internationally, including as a keynote speaker at the Forum on Big Data at the Tianjin University of Technology, in Tianjin, China. ReVISION Learning is highly sought after for its leadership in providing the highest quality professional learning opportunities for teacher, administrators, and district personnel.

What does it mean to lead learning?

↳ LOVE!

Before you are a leader, success is all about growing yourself. When you become a leader, success is all about growing others. —Jack Welch, former GE chairman and CEO

Leading growth for all those who work in school environments is an immensely challenging job as it calls for us to become teachers of teachers, leading learning for adults and students alike. Major changes in education over the past five years have sparked a resurgence of 30-year-old conversations highlighting the positive impact of school leaders on the effectiveness of teacher practice and subsequent student outcomes (Flath, 1989; Schmidt-Davis & Bottoms, 2011). Research by the Wallace Foundation (2013) reiterates an "empirical link between school leadership and improved student achievement" (p. 3) and "is second only to classroom instruction among all school-related factors that contribute to what students learn at school" (Leithwood, Seashore Louis, Anderson, & Wahlstrom, 2004, p. 5). Principals and school administrators are

✳ school leadership is 2nd only to classroom instruction

experiencing increased levels of responsibility for leading teachers in their work in providing a high-quality education for all students.

Among their chief tasks, leaders are responsible for supporting teachers in setting clear goals for instruction and ensuring the allocation of resources to do so, as well as managing and leading the development of curriculum, monitoring unit and lesson plans, and conducting evaluations as essential requirements of the job. At no other time in the history of education have such specific policies focused on instructional outcomes that clearly define the need for improved instructional leadership practices in our schools. What we do know is that this type of work requires not only specific training but also ongoing support. The administrators with whom we work are building the structures and managing their time not only to support teachers through professional learning but also in finding ways to *lead* the learning in classrooms.

The role of the school administrator in most current systems can be broken down into three core categories:

- School Manager: handling all aspects related to the building, buses, and budget

- Stakeholder Supporter: creating a positive climate for parent, student, and staff interaction and encouraging voice

- Instructional Leader: leading the teaching and learning

Often, administrators are engaged in the first two roles driven by task and driven by policy for the third. While the first two roles are significant and necessary to the well-being of a school culture, the role of "instructional leader" requires engagement in activities that directly impact student outcomes (Flath, 1989), such as observing classroom instruction, reviewing performance goals and progress, communicating with teachers, implementing professional learning, attending team meetings, and providing impactful feedback. Whether it is due to environment, systems designs, or challenging time issues, sometimes these activities fall by the wayside, though we know they are essential to increasing levels of teaching and learning in our classrooms. Realities of a day in the front office and demands beyond all three of the necessary roles outlined continue to pull administrators away from a focus on classroom excellence. "The life of most school leaders is interrupt driven" (National SAM Innovation Project [NSIP], 2018).

It is our belief that leading learning should become the primary focus of a principal's job, time, and effort, as this role provides the opportunity for principals to speak directly to an instructional vision for students and the instructional strategies we know are effective for meeting that vision

(DuFour, 2002; DuFour & Marzano, 2011; MET Project, 2015; Wallace Foundation, 2013). This need for instructional leadership in our schools is not simply an American educational concern but a universal one. The Organisation for Economic Co-operation and Development (OECD) reports that reviewing international systems of educator evaluation has validated that clearly there is

> a need to reinforce the pedagogical leadership skills of school directors as their role in many countries still retains a more traditional focus on administrative tasks. The objective is that school leaders operate effective feedback, coaching and appraisal arrangements for their staff and effectively lead whole-school evaluation processes (OECD, 2013).

Finding Time to Lead Learning

Studies show the typical percentage of time a building leader at the elementary level spends on tasks that seemingly are related to teaching and learning, such as observation and feedback requirements, can be up to 28 percent and sometimes higher at the secondary level due to additional administrators (Costa, 2014; Horng, Klasik, & Loeb, 2009; Lavigne, Shakman, Zweig, & Greller, 2016).

A closer examination of these studies, however, reveals that a majority of this time is being spent on activities that do not directly impact student learning. Some of the findings include the following:

- A study from Stanford showed that on average, principals spent only about 8 percent of the school day in classrooms. Only about half that time was dedicated to "day-to-day instruction tasks," such as observing or coaching teachers (Horng et al., 2009).

- The "largest non-value added category in the studies we reviewed was the category of logistics [such as scheduling/calendar]. Of 535 samples of the 4,844, or 11 percent of all samples in one study, [data] revealed that time was focused on the daily operations and management of the school community, again, having little direct impact on teaching and learning" (Costa, 2014).

- An international study of 13 countries, including the United States, showed that while principals "devote a lot of time to developing and promoting their schools' educational goals and monitoring teachers' implementation of those goals in teaching . . . less time is given to giving advice to teachers about questions or problems with teaching" (Loveless, 2016)—the known strategy that impacts practices.

Though "Instructional Leader" is one of the three primary functions of a building administrator, making the 28 percent seem logical, to truly lead learning these observation and feedback efforts should encompass more than one third of a leader's time. This is not to suggest that the activities beyond the classroom are not important or necessary. Nor is it suggested here that the burden of addressing issues of time rests solely on the shoulders of an individual leader, as principals of regular public schools reported spending an average of 59 hours per week on the job.

While 28 percent of the leader's time is committed to what we might call instructional leadership activities, what will it take for that to increase, allowing leaders to commit to more while ensuring that this time is quality time? One may argue that dramatic changes to the system must be made for this to be possible. In almost all studies reviewed, researchers and authors suggested that "district and state leaders may consider how school principals could benefit from additional supports, such as adding an assistant principal to the administrative team or providing leadership coaching" (Lavigne et al., 2016, p. 8).

However, we know the reality for most is not as simple or feasible as adding another person. Many of the administrators with whom we work want to—and are finding the time to—engage more frequently in those activities that serve to lead learning. It is possible! The Wallace Foundation recognized this and invested in a time-management analysis and restructuring process that recaptures an average of 27 days in the first year of implementation for a leader (NSIP, 2018).

How do administrators find the time?

First, they carefully consider the following:

- How they *opt* to use their time. (When is it in their control? How are they choosing to use their time?)

- How they create efficiencies for themselves. (Are they using organized time-management systems, processes, and protocols?)

- How they use strategies to ensure instruction is occurring at its highest levels in classrooms. (What are they doing to engage in effective observation and feedback practices?)

They also know this is not a quick fix. We polled the many instructional leaders we know who are successfully leading the learning in their buildings and found several common effective practices. How can you:

1. Make visiting classrooms a priority, even if it is just for 10 minutes at a time and only includes a few teachers during a given week.

2. Communicate a message to everyone on your staff, your parents, and your students that supporting instruction is your number one priority.

This allows you to help them see why you will be out of your office or "unavailable."

3. Examine your use of time, conducting your own time study to determine what tasks and responsibilities are keeping you from observing teaching and learning. Discern what is or is not in your control and be realistic.

4. Work with what is in your control first, as a high frequency of emergency parent meetings and out-of-building training will require longer range solutions. In your building, investigate the response protocols for events such as discipline issues, unannounced parent visits, and incoming emails. Also, determine what can be accomplished when students are not in the building.

5. Work with your assistant and clerical staff. These individuals hold a critical role in ensuring your success. Parents, teachers, and students must learn to schedule appointments and not expect immediate attention or answers. Your assistant can guard against the "I just need to see her for a minute . . ." "But it's urgent . . ." situations.

6. Consider what your assistant is telling parents when you are not in your office; is it, "I'm sorry; she's not at her desk again" or "Today she is out visiting classrooms"? Think about how your assistant is helping you categorize and filter high-priority emails, issues, and calls, handling smaller issues.

7. Find time to attend professional learning communities (PLCs) and department, grade-level, or data team meetings to talk about teaching and learning occurring in the building.

8. Show your team your commitment to lead learning by ensuring you meet with every teacher you observe, even if it is only for a short time. This will require high-quality observation and feedback skills even without the benefit of pre-observation meetings and 30 to 40 minutes of evidence collection.

From the field . . .

Christine Baldelli, principal, and Cheryl Milo, assistant principal at New Fairfield Middle School, raised expectations at their school for both themselves as leaders and for their teachers. They go beyond evaluation policies associated with observation and feedback and work to consistently observe in classrooms each month. They manage their time around a dedication to the teaching and learning in their building, balancing their administrative responsibilities and following a schedule.

(Continued)

(Continued)

The secret to their success lies in five key areas.

1. ***Priorities:*** *We preblock times one month ahead for certain days and certain periods for classroom walk-throughs (paying attention to periods 1, 2, and 3), so you get out at different times for 5 to 10 minutes. We are challenging ourselves this year based on last year. We use a walk-through form for tracking and set goals based on it, so we visited 100% of classrooms by October 1. It is important to have a schedule and commit to it.*

2. ***Management of schedule:*** *If "Instructional Time" is on our calendars, anyone who has access knows not to touch it. And unless there is a fire, you stick to it. Parents know phone calls and emails are answered before school or after 3:30 p.m.*

3. ***Management of roles:*** *As principal and assistant principal, there is no separation. We each just handle what's going on if one is out in classrooms. We come together as a team. We don't say, "My assistant does all of the PPTs," or "The principal handles all parent calls." We split things down the middle as best we can.*

4. ***Finding time to talk about teaching and learning:*** *Teachers will come down and ask us for feedback. We may also bump into a teacher in the hallway to start a dialogue. During data rounds/meetings, we can mention certain students and specific strategies we observed. As we are writing reports, we also share our feedback to receive each other's input.*

5. ***Determining teacher needs:*** *Because we are out in classrooms, we know what our teachers need (such as in designing professional development for them). As a result, we can drive the direction of the training and allow for differentiation. The more we know about what's going on in the classroom, the better we can address what they need. You also have to know your curriculum. If you don't know what they are teaching and why, you don't know what's supposed to be going on. We also attend trainings with our teachers. Christine attended the NGSS training with them, "so I know the expectations when I am observing and meeting with them. They [teachers] know I am more vested. If you see it in the classroom, you can make connections from training."*

> **Stop and Think:** What keeps you from engaging in tasks related to the teaching and learning in your building(s)? What strategies do you use/could you use to find more time to do so?

Christine and Cheryl are constantly mindful not just of the quantity of the tasks in which they are engaged but of the quality of those activities. Their classroom visits are focused on targeted practices, concerns, and growth areas related to their school goals (such as increasing discourse, inquiry, and personalization). For them and for all instructional leaders, it is not the walking through that matters.

> Simply walking through classrooms without a unifying theory of action that both focuses the walkthrough and promotes critical assessment of the collected information is unlikely to inform efforts to raise student achievement. Students have a better chance of achieving when school leaders spend their time using the information they gather . . . rather than simply collecting it. (Moss & Brookhart, 2015, p. 15)

That is the fundamental purpose of this book—for you to enhance your skill set in how to collect the necessary information and then how to use it to promote growth. It is to provide a pathway and guidebook for educators to lead learning in its truest sense. Supporting teachers and students as learners through improved observation and feedback is the most impactful leadership practice affecting teachers, and it drives the instructional vision. In this book, we will provide practical strategies, tools, and examples from extensive fieldwork that can be applied directly to classroom visits and feedback cycles, helping you reshape your supervision and evaluation practices.

Rethinking Evaluation

Hong Kong Professor Kai-Ming Cheng noted, "successful evaluation will help teachers think about students, and unsuccessful evaluation will make them think about themselves and their career" (Walker, 2013). Improvements have been made in accountability measures and evaluation systems since Race to the Top; however, schools everywhere "are not necessarily making full use of teacher evaluations as opportunities for teachers to grow" (Rosen & Parise, 2017). In the face of the Every Student Succeeds Act (ESSA), state policymakers are revisiting the state-by-state, end-of-year results of performance and practice measures associated with educator evaluation. A review of 2016 results showing an average of 93 percent of teachers rated as Proficient or above in

20 states reinforces that "new evaluations systems . . . have not consistently resulted in greater differentiation among teacher performance ratings" (Kraft & Gilmour, 2017, p. 242) and continued effort needs to occur to ensure teachers are fairly and accurately evaluated.

We know that the design of most educator evaluation systems in the United States are partially at fault, as they align themselves with current federal and state guidelines. These guidelines are heavily weighted toward an inspection model of accountability, with only marginal attention paid to primary mechanisms that we know effectively promote growth and improved professional practice. What ended up accompanying the introduction of these systems was training that ensured evaluators were successful in checking things off a list, tracking test scores, tagging evidence, and filling out forms. These skills took precedence over insight, reflection, coaching, growth, and a focus on gains in student readiness for the future. These realities ensured compliance but did not build the potential for continuous improvement of student success (MET Project, 2015).

What if, instead . . .

- The foundation of educator evaluation was built and implemented on a framework of growth, instead of inspection of practice?

- Supervisor training was designed to support the development of an instructional leader instead of just an observer of classroom practice?

- The focus of observation became what, how, and if students were learning, instead of just whether or not teachers "performed" at proficient levels?

Evaluators need to learn strategies that safely blur the lines of supervision and evaluation—acting on a combination of those practices supports student achievement—as opposed to only monitoring and managing teacher practice. "The purpose of supervision should be the enhancement of teacher's pedagogical skills with the ultimate goal of enhancing student achievement" (Marzano, Frontier, & Livingston, 2011, p. 2). Nearly 300 Teachers of the Year were surveyed and "fewer than half of respondents (49%) indicated that their observers were well-trained in conducting classroom observations" and "forty-two percent (42%) of respondents perceived their evaluation system as focused primarily on 'getting a score or rating' rather than on professional growth" (Goe, Wylie, Bosso, & Olson, 2017, p. 2).

Kim Marshall (2013) defined supervision as "observation and coaching" and evaluation as "summative end of year judgments" (p. 20) and asserted the following.

At its best, the supervision and evaluation process has five core functions:

1. **Appraisal:** Getting an accurate sense of the quality of instruction

2. **Affirmation:** Retaining and further developing teachers in the top two categories

3. **Improvement:** Coaching and supporting development of teachers in the bottom two categories

4. **Housecleaning:** Dismissing teachers who are still not effective after a reasonable chance to improve

5. **Quality Assurance:** Being able to honestly tell parents and other stakeholders that every child will have good teaching in every class-room every year

We want to build leaders' capacity for all five. "Done well, the process is an important contributor to continuously improving teaching and learning. Done poorly, it under-challenges effective teachers and allows mediocre and ineffective practices to continue" (Marshall, 2013, pp. 21–22).

Leading Change Through Educator Evaluation

Leading in a time of change is challenging, and now, more than ever, our teachers need knowledgeable and effective instructional leaders with whom to collaborate as they navigate new standards and expectations. Observation is at

FIGURE 1.1: EFFECTS OF SUPPORT AND CHALLENGE ON TEACHERS

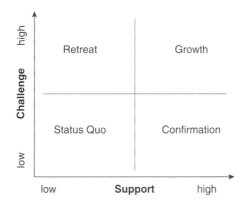

Source: Courtesy of ReVISION

the heart of the work leaders must be prepared to carry out to lead learning for both their staff and the students they serve. Instructional leaders can successfully navigate the waters of change by blending supervision and evaluation to support teachers, but they must be mindful of key principles in the process. Figure 1.1 is representative of Sir Michael Barber's work with McKinsey Global Education (Barber & Mourshed, 2007) and his ideas on teacher development, showing an important dynamic between levels of challenge and support. Optimal growth occurs when both levels increase in equal amounts over time.

Unfortunately, traditional holistic evaluation models have often fallen short in challenging teachers and thus have resulted in stagnant scenarios:

- Teachers feel **confirmed** because they have received *"satisfactory"* ratings (which in many cases are overinflated).

- Or even worse, teachers feel no need to change, seeing new initiatives as trends that will come and go, maintaining the **status quo** because they have received no useful feedback at all about their teaching.

- With the arrival of new curriculum and rigorous student learning standards, such as Common Core, and new accountability measures, such as the use of rubrics with new expectations focusing on instruction *and* outcomes, teachers are presented with significant challenges. These same teachers often are not provided the explicit related professional learning or support required for success, or in many cases, even basic understanding. Situations such as these can and do generate anxiety, mistrust, and **retreat,** causing a breakdown in leader/teacher relationships and resulting in some teachers leaving the field.

"All good leadership is a judicious mixture of push, pull, and nudge. This is a sophisticated practice. It's a combination of nonjudgmentalism, not being pejorative about where people are at the beginning, combined with moving them forward" (Hargreaves & Fullan, 2012, p. 39).

Quality instructional leaders must leverage what is known about change leadership and employ rubrics not only to analyze and evaluate teaching practices but to target specific professional development needs to promote professional **growth.** Always keep in mind that high-quality leaders are teachers of teachers. Would we set our students on a path of rigorous learning tasks with challenging expectations for shared responsibility without ensuring they would be successful? Don't we take the time to model, explicitly teach, monitor, and adjust?

Leaders must "unwrap" performance standards with teachers to help them gain significant clarity about expectations (support), encourage teachers to self-evaluate (challenge) to determine their most pertinent areas of growth, analyze teacher practice in action (challenge), and respond by providing resources and nurturing a growth-minded school culture and climate (support). Finding the balance between **challenge** and **support** in education is where leaders can ensure clarity of direction and purpose and drive new levels of learning for both teachers and students.

However, the established system and the implementation of that system currently generate minimal impact on teacher practice, professional learning, and student outcomes. If we are to see the pendulum swing,

- Those who generate policy must strongly acknowledge and apply what we have long known about change leadership.

- We must consider the way in which we are building capacity of those leading the change.

Stop and Think: How do you challenge, yet support, your teachers?

Core Assumptions About Current Practice

Initially, in the process of shifting teacher evaluation policy and practice, decision makers and policymakers, along with professional learning providers, falsely assumed the training they were providing to administrators would increase the capacity to coach, lead learning, and impact student outcomes. As we have the opportunity to witness the realities and results of those assumptions every day (see Tables 1.1–1.3), it has become clear to us why current evaluation and supervision practices are still leading to confirmation, status quo, and even retreat, and why the related training requires new thinking and revision.

TABLE 1.1	CORE ASSUMPTION 1

Assumption #1: That administrators, based on preparation programs and training they received, would be able to apply the skills they learned to observation in the classroom.

Reality: As we work with administrators in observation practices, we watch as many enter the rooms, find a seat somewhere in the back (and often remain), and begin to furiously script notes or tap at breakneck speed on a computer keyboard. When we ask them about these methods, most simply say, referring to the training they have received, "when we observe, we need to script everything that is said and seen so that we have a preponderance of evidence for rating the teacher." However, with this method, the observer becomes a spectator or court reporter.

Additionally, we find that with existing training or preparation, there is an issue of transfer. When video-based training is used in isolation, observers do not or cannot always successfully apply essential strategies when observing in the classroom (such as how to interact with students).

When observers recognize the value and role of purposeful evidence collection and develop the necessary related strategies and skill sets, they understand how feedback to a teacher will result in more than just a regurgitated script (from the scripting method) or a summary (from the limited notetaking/interaction methods). This is complex work but critical to our efforts in providing teachers with a sense of how instruction is engaging students in the learning and, ultimately, what those students have learned.

TABLE 1.2	CORE ASSUMPTION 2

Assumption #2: That administrators, based on preparation programs and training they received, would be able to analyze the observed practice of a teacher against a set of teacher performance standards and determine the potential impact on students.

Reality: Instructional frameworks, or rubrics, are invaluable tools that serve to:

- Define effective practice.
- Provide look-fors for observations.
- Establish clear standards and expectations.
- Provide leverage for growth and action steps.

Yet we are finding that leaders are still developing a deep understanding of indicators, attributes, and differences between performance levels, not having had an opportunity to engage in a high-level deconstruction of effective teaching and learning outlined by the framework. This can result in inaccurate ratings, subjective feedback, frustration on both the leader's and teacher's part, and diminished trust. The lack of depth of knowledge leaves observers unable to utilize the instrument effectively or efficiently to promote growth in a region or school.

Ultimately, observers need professional learning, that they have not necessarily received, on how to use their most valuable tool—the framework—to leverage growth, build a teacher's understanding of effective practice, or promote reflection about expected practices. Without this, teachers are left with little understanding of how evidence is collected related to the learning in their classrooms or how/why they were given a specific rating.

W. James Popham (2013) asserted that feedback should be about "a teacher's instructional ability. [The] dominant factor to be employed in appraising a teacher should be a teacher's effectiveness in promoting worthwhile learning" (p. 28). But are the findings about effectiveness being conveyed to a teacher? Are leaders successfully promoting reflection, building a teacher's accuracy in self-perception, and impacting instructional practices? We came to recognize there was a belief about the leader's capacity to provide feedback after an observation—Assumption #3 (Table 1.3).

TABLE 1.3	CORE ASSUMPTION 3

Assumption #3: That administrators, based on preparation programs and training they received, would be able to provide feedback that would directly impact teacher effectiveness.

Reality: Though administrators receive training to watch instruction and provide a rating, there has been little to no direct support to build their capacity to go beyond conveyance of the number score or a summary. However, even when evaluators accurately select performance levels, it does not mean teachers are receiving feedback that ensures new learning. This is compounded by the fact that potentially less-than-impactful feedback is provided only two to four times during a typical school year.

When we assume evaluators are effectively collecting evidence, analyzing impact on learning, and utilizing the framework (Assumptions #1 and #2), and they are in fact *not* doing or *not able* to do these things, the realistic picture is this:

- Teachers are not leaving feedback meetings or reading feedback reports understanding their ratings.

- Observers are unable to determine high-leverage coaching points that

  - are realistic and attainable next steps for a teacher;

  - impact and/or connect multiple aspects of instruction (such as establishing a clear learning target to then determine clear criteria); and/or

  - impact a high number of students.

- Teachers are not recognizing from the feedback their effectiveness or what to do next or differently.

- Teachers are unable to reflect on their own practices or next steps.

We have many opportunities to observe teachers in feedback meetings or sit with them as they read a written report. They often bring pads into the meetings, holding a pen throughout, waiting to write down a new idea or next step. Yet many leave having never written a thing. We have watched teachers, when provided with written feedback, scan the report searching for the rating, or before an administrator can begin a feedback meeting, ask, "What was my overall rating?" Before meetings, we have asked leaders to provide an example of one thing the teacher was trying since the last meeting, and they are unable to tell us. The reality is that the process is generally not resulting in any significant changes in practice.

Simply stated, "an effective evaluation system should help teachers teach better" (Marzano & Toth, 2013, p. 14).

> **Stop and Think:** What are the current realities of your evaluation system? What assumptions were made about leader readiness and capacity in the creation of it?

Feedback as the Common Thread

It is clear that no impact on practice and performance can be had without routine and formative feedback, and, rightly, feedback for growth should be at the heart of educator evaluation (Hattie, 2009). Feedback that feeds forward—especially within an educator evaluation model—is best defined as information provided by an evaluator regarding a teacher's performance related to a set of standards that supports professional growth and the capacity to impact student success. When delivered through the application of evaluation systems, feedback can provide not only the opportunity for collaborative learning and reflection but also a forum for developing targeted professional growth plans—a true blend of evaluation and supervision.

More than ever, for leaders to apply Barber's approaches to teacher development, they need guidance and support as they take on the challenge of blended supervisory and evaluative roles, engaging in work that will ensure meaningful teacher performance reviews. Every element of policy and structural design of supervision and evaluation, as well as corresponding professional learning, should reaffirm and realign to this goal.

Studies of the principles of performance improvement (Killion, 2015; MET Project, 2015; Stone & Heen, 2014) clearly demonstrate the high impact of quality feedback on teachers.

1. Leaders cannot assume experience or tenure will serve as a determining factor in student outcomes. "In the absence of useful feedback, most teacher performance plateaus by their third or fourth year on the job" (MET Project, 2010). Impactful feedback can ensure teachers continue to climb higher.

2. Teachers' greatest improvement occurs early in their careers, contrary to our thoughts about a 10,000-hour rule. One study found that close to half of the gains in teacher growth and learning are realized during the first few years of teaching (Clotfelter, Ladd, & Vigdor, 2007). Think about how high-quality feedback could accelerate that growth in those early-career learning years. In fact, several studies (Tschannen-Moran, Woolfolk Hoy, & Hoy, 1998) found that teachers—especially early-career professionals—*want, require,* and *desire* feedback.

Through our work and through numerous classroom observations, we have developed a fundamental set of guiding principles (see Table 1.4) that support the necessary shift from a system of evaluation based on inspection and assessment to one of continuous cycles of improvement through quality feedback, self-reflection, reviews of practice, and aligned professional learning. We live by these guidelines in the work we do to support instructional leaders, helping them to build environments of trust and autonomy for teachers and staff through feedback for growth.

TABLE 1.4	REVISION LEARNING (RVL) GUIDING PRINCIPLES
Multifaceted Feedback	Feedback must be based on routine observation of practice, reviews of artifactual evidence (both teacher- and student-produced), and collegial dialogue.
Formative Feedback for Summative Assessment	Feedback must be formative, providing ongoing support on performance and practice and encouraging specific areas of growth toward end-of-year teacher and student expectations.
Cycles of Continuous Improvement	Feedback must inform professional learning to build coherence with clear through-lines between district/region, school, and individual goals, and the central mission, vision, and purpose of the organization.
Autonomy and Ownership Through Individual and Group Reflection	Feedback must lead to a climate of ownership through ongoing self-reflective practice, perpetuating continuous improvement toward organizational objectives, and increased collective efficacy.
Observer Capacity	Feedback must be provided from a qualified instructional leader as observer capacity is a chief influence on teacher success.

A Shift From Summary to Analysis

We have come to discover, in our review of different types of feedback reports and through our observations of leaders' conversations with teachers, that not all feedback is equal. There is a wide variance in what teachers receive in terms of depth, clarity, and usefulness. Often, the leaders who author written feedback do not see the value in the report, believing it is only conversations that can result in great changes. We agree on the power of verbal feedback; however, it is the processing and crafting of the report and the production of a learning tool (the focus of this book) that prepare a leader for such an impactful conversation. Regardless of the forms, teachers require more than a summary, narration, or list of events, as this practice is generally reinforcing the inspection model. They require an analysis of learning, which serves to align evaluator practice with a growth model. But what does analysis of learning look and sound like?

While we will go into the differences in greater depth in Chapter 4, let's be clear on what we mean by a "summary of events" and an "analysis of effectiveness," as this differentiation in quality represents the foundation of our work.

In the following feedback examples, the leader has determined the observed lesson met the "Proficient" performance level after observing an elementary language arts lesson. While you are reading, consider what is being conveyed to a teacher through the feedback.

Summary

Teacher implements purposeful strategies that lead to critical thinking and uses a balance of support and challenge to help students advance their learning.

Teacher uses think-aloud: "I am going to reread and use sticky notes to mark the setting, character, and plot. Oooh, I just read the problem and know this part is important to the plot."

Teacher models completing Story Element Chart and states, "When I write about the character I need to be specific and use his name."

Teacher asks questions: "What parts of the story are included in the plot?"

Analysis

Students were asked to locate elements of "Trickster Tales" in their texts to construct an understanding of a new type of story in the folktale genre. Because the teacher conducted a close reading through a think-aloud, modeled steps for the task, and checked for student understanding before they left the carpet, most students were able to successfully follow the same steps at their desks. Eight of twelve students began reading and correctly noted on stickies evidence of the story elements. Because the teacher modeled her thinking around specific qualities of characters in a trickster tale and students worked with leveled texts, all of those eight could explain to the observer characteristics that made their trickster tale different. Also contributing was the fact that this was a consistent process for analyzing genres all year as evidenced by the chart referenced in the mini-lesson, which students were able to explain later to the observer.

Stop and Think: What did you notice about the quality of the two types of feedback?

Shifting From Summary to Analysis

By comparing the two examples, it should be clear which type of feedback best supports teachers. Through our work with instructional leaders and teachers, we have arrived at five key reasons for the need to shift from feedback that summarizes events to that which provides an analysis of the impacts of instruction.

Reason 1: Realign the Focus to Teaching *and* Learning

Not so long ago, classroom visits focused solely on inspecting *teacher actions*. Did he or she orient students to the right page number? Did he or she show enthusiasm? Did he or she amplify student responses? We had not considered how those actions actually affected students nor had we examined the learning that was occurring as a result. Our evaluation instruments and purpose for walk-throughs revolved around completing a checklist or inspecting a classroom for expected practices. We never considered the following:

- Did the students in fact turn to the right page and begin working productively?

- Were the students showing equal or greater enthusiasm for the topic or impending inquiry?

- Did the teacher's statements or questions allow students to think deeply or advance toward mastery of the objective? Most importantly, how did we know?

Did you notice in the previous example of a summary, the focus was only on teacher actions?

When Amy was trained as an evaluator, she was required to use a type of instrument for evaluation that focused solely on teacher actions (shown in Figure 1.2), which required an observer to insert hash marks next to items describing teacher behaviors. The focus on the use of the instrument in the preliminary training and during the year was accuracy of the counts. Feedback meetings with her teachers included the total number of tally marks for each category.

Since then, however, it has become clear to most that the *learning* occurring in our classrooms should be the focus of observation, evaluation, and feedback (Marshall, 2013; Popham 2013).

Reason 2: Change the Goal of Feedback to Growth

After an administrator visited a classroom, teachers received a completed version of a tally sheet like the one in Figure 1.2 (e.g., number of times he or she amplified or oriented students), and more recently, a list of evidence

FIGURE 1.2: OBSERVATION CHECKLIST

3.0 INSTRUCTIONAL ORGANIZATION AND DEVELOPMENT					
1. Begins instruction promptly					1. Delays
2. Handles materials in an orderly manner					2. Does not organize materials systematically
3. Orients students to classwork/ maintains academic focus					3. Allows talk/activity unrelated to subject
4. Conducts beginning/ending review					4.
5. Questions: academic comprehension/ lesson development	a. Single factual (Domain 5.0)				5a. Allows unison response
	b. Requires analysis/ reasons				5b. Poses multiple questions asked as one
					5c. Poses nonacademic questions/ nonacademic procedural questions
6. Recognizes response/amplifies/ gives correct feedback					6. Ignores student or responses/expresses sarcasm, disgust, harshness
7. Gives specific academic praise					7. Uses general, nonspecific praise
8. Provides for practice					8. Extends discourse, changes topic with no practice
9. Gives directions/assigns/checks comprehension of homework seatwork assignments/gives feedback					9. Gives inadequate directions on homework/no feedback

Source: Florida Department of Education

(T: "quote"; S: "quote") or a narrative of events witnessed. Conversations revolved around a recitation of these lists, causing feedback to have little impact on teacher practices or student outcomes. When looking at the following sample, consider how the feedback after an observation of a math lesson would or would not contribute to the growth of the teacher. For this lesson, the leader has selected a "Developing" rating:

> The teacher occasionally communicated clear learning expectations to the students. This was evidenced by student responses. These included a student responding by stating that the shape was 2 D.
>
> The teacher asked: "Is that flat or would it be a solid?" The student responded: "Flat."
>
> The teacher then said: "Can you hold it in your hand?" The student said: "Yes." Which helped him to understand the meaning of 3D.

Though the observer included student actions, the feedback does not answer *how* "this was evidenced by student responses" and only lists the teacher's and student's quotes; therefore, the teacher has no understanding of why the practice *was not effective*. Observation and feedback can and should drive growth and development (Clark & Duggins, 2016; Marzano & Toth, 2013).

Reason 3: Move Toward Promoting Reflective Practice

Until recently, building administrators have been viewed as reporters of what was observed, and teachers were the receivers of the information. As administrators shift from managers to instructional leaders, every conversation with a teacher and opportunity to provide feedback can promote reflective thinking. When leaders provide an analysis of effectiveness, they are essentially modeling or providing a "think-aloud" for teachers to utilize every day in their own practices. Leaders are guiding teachers to focus not just on teaching but also on learning, helping them determine their own impact on student outcomes every day. Through this shift, teachers no longer have to wait for a report but can engage in their own processing and self-assessment of effectiveness, known strategies that allow for goal setting and improved practice (Marzano, Frontier, & Livingston, 2011), which serve to increase efficacy (Goddard, Hoy, & Hoy, 2000).

Look back at the previous sample. If the teacher is essentially only receiving the rating and this feedback, how can he or she use the leader's statement as a model for reflection?

Reason 4: Ensure Fair and Accurate Performance Evaluations

There have been sweeping changes in instructional frameworks utilized for evaluation in districts/regions across the country and outside of the United States, which now include the additions of new language, expectations, and attention to student outcomes. To "rate" a lesson, evaluators must conduct an analysis of those outcomes. In many cases, they cannot accurately determine how the lesson exemplified a particular performance level found in framework indicators or attributes without doing so.

Consider this "Proficient" description from an indicator related to engagement: "Employs differentiated strategies, tasks, and questions that cognitively engage students in constructing new and meaningful learning through appropriately integrated recall, problem solving, critical and creative thinking, purposeful discourse and/or inquiry. Uses resources and flexible groupings that cognitively engage students in demonstrating new learning in multiple ways" (Connecticut State Department of Education [CSDE], 2014).

> **Stop and Think:** Do you have a similar indicator or attribute on your own rubric? What type of analysis does it require on the observer's part?

In this example, notice a "Proficient" rating can only be determined through extensive deconstruction of the teacher's use of each of the instructional methods and through an analysis of the *impact* of those on the level of students' engagement and understanding.

Without an observer conducting a detailed and thorough dissection of the effectiveness of the practices, a teacher can potentially receive inaccurate or inflated ratings. If we are using an instructional framework as a backbone to leverage growth without accurately recognizing and conveying what is or is not effective practice, the tool is rendered no more useful than the checklists of the past, leaving teachers frustrated. Let's consider another feedback sample provided to a teacher after an observation that leaves a teacher wondering how and why he received a particular rating:

```
Rating: Developing

The strategies/task/questions did not lead students
to construct new and meaningful learning. The use of
resources and or grouping failed to promote active
engagement or support new learning.

The lesson did not provide a review of the "attributes"
of the lesson @ the onset after the opener.
```

Clearly, some key findings are missing. To accurately rate this attribute and support the claim about practice, the evaluator must conduct an analysis of the effectiveness of all observed strategies, tasks, questions, groupings, and resources to determine if and how the teacher cognitively engaged the students and advanced learning through these. Without this—and without then explicitly supporting and conveying those findings—the fairness and accuracy of the rating can be called into question.

Reason 5: Determine High-Leverage Coaching Points

If observers have not collected comprehensive evidence, they cannot effectively analyze how a teacher's choices are affecting a majority of students. Beyond inaccurate ratings, this also puts observers at risk of providing inaccurate or irrelevant coaching points. Comprehensive evidence collection and analysis of instructional practice will ensure leaders determine and/or promote teacher reflection about the most impactful next steps. While this will be addressed further in Chapter 5, it is important to remember throughout this chapter that the ultimate goal in providing feedback is to change practice and student outcomes through attainable, specific, and high-impact next steps.

So what does it take to develop the type of feedback aligned to these five key reasons for the shift?

Core Skills for Observation and Feedback

Teachers require a leader with whom they can collaborate to promote daily improvements in instruction through honest feedback about the learning being experienced by students within classrooms (DuFour & Marzano, 2011). In this same manner, every educational leader charged with implementing the complex work of improving teacher effectiveness deserves support for their own professional development and learning around the essential skills needed to effectively lead learning. Leaders and those who support those leaders must invest in their own growth in applying the core skills required to observe teacher practice and construct high-quality feedback.

Stop and Think: What core skills do instructional leaders require to effectively supervise and evaluate teaching and lead learning?

As we seek to transform teaching and learning, new expectations and practices in instruction and educator evaluation require new skills on the part of evaluators and leaders. The MET project studies that began in 2009 offer a growing body of research to support our understanding of the impact observation and feedback are having on classroom practice and student outcomes. In the MET Project (2014) study, "Building Trust in Observations," researchers concluded that expectations should ensure "trustworthy observations are consistent, unbiased, authentic, reasonable, and beneficial" (p. 1), driven by "clear and explicit rubrics, comprehensive training, monitoring, and assessment" (p. 2). The researchers argued that training needs to include learning about the rubric and how to use it; raising observers' awareness of their own biases and ways to counter those during observations and developing their skills through explicit instruction, modeling, and practice scoring; and modeling and training in how to provide postobservation feedback (p. 4).

The report suggested that the skills and knowledge associated with accurate observations include the following:

- Learning to watch.

- Taking and organizing good notes.

- Scoring accurately with the rubric.

- Providing feedback.

The 2013 MET Project report, "Ensuring Fair and Reliable Measures of Effective Teaching," reminds us that "teachers need to know that they are being observed by the right people with the right skills" (p. 18).

Core Competencies

Chapters 2 through 6 are organized to address these very elements of observer and supervisory practice within three critical core competencies that serve to build capacity to lead learning:

1. Effective **observation and evidence collection**

2. Explicit **analysis of effectiveness** of instruction evidence

3. Development of **high-quality feedback**

Indicators of Practice

We have broken these competencies down into six indicators or standards of practice to guide the work of evaluators and instructional coaches. The chapters ahead will delve into each of the indicators and corresponding discrete skills, ensuring leaders walk away with immediate and practical methods for implementation in their schools. Though we promote the use of evaluation to lead growth, *anyone* who supports teachers will benefit from the explicit strategies and suggested steps in each chapter.

Remember, just as in our classrooms, standards provide a framework of expectations and guide practice of key skills. The six standards of evidence-based observation and feedback are housed within our ReVISION Learning Supervisory Continuum and serve as the backbone of our learning design for observers. Through this, we can measure the quality of feedback and leverage growth, and we *can* support leaders in the development of those skills necessary to ensure they can deliver feedback that feeds forward.

Twenty-One Core Skills

In the spring of 2017, we introduced 21 core skills in alignment with the core competencies and the six standards of practice. For each of the core competencies, we have identified seven skills that must be mastered (see Table 1.5). These skills are presented in detail and in alignment with the standards in each chapter, allowing you to use the book as a guide to work toward proficiency in each. Visit **resources.corwin.com/feedforward** to view the full RVL Supervisory Continuum and Core Skill overview.

TABLE 1.5 RVL SKILL OVERVIEW

3 Core Competencies	Observe and Collect Evidence	Analyze Effectiveness	Provide Written/Verbal Feedback
21 Core Skills	Unpack a Rubric	Analyze Objectively	Recognize Research-Based Strategies
	Describe Look-Fors	Analyze Evidence	Build on Instructional Strengths
	Identify Types of Data	Determine Student Engagement Levels	Scaffold Next Steps
	Collect Qualitative Evidence	Determine Impact on Engagement	Review for Objectivity
	Collect Quantitative Evidence	Determine Impact on Learning	Compose Feedback
	Collect Evidence of Student Engagement	Determine Performance Levels	Create Clear Connections
	Observe Objectively	Craft a Claim	Develop Reflective Questions

What's Ahead?

As you turn to Chapter 2, you will begin to build your capacity in the first core skills and will be introduced to the first set of the 31 strategies—addressing Assumptions #1 and #2 along with the MET suggestions. You will find processes for the foundational step of your journey to lead learning—building a deepened understanding of your framework and increasing your capacity to use that framework to not just collect aligned and required evidence but to leverage growth. Chapter 3 provides you with explicit strategies for use of time in a classroom during a lesson for *purposeful* evidence collection grounded in the framework.

As you head into Chapter 4, we are addressing Assumption #3, as we move to one of the most challenging steps in the process: analyzing collected evidence to determine effectiveness of instruction. We provide you with authentic examples of "think-alouds" from classroom observations along with explicit step-by-step guides for organizing that evidence. The chapter leads you through a process for determining cause-and-effect relationships that occur during a lesson and provides thinking frames that enable you to accurately select and support performance levels. The tools and resources offered increase your capacity to provide direct and explicit connections for a teacher (and promote teacher reflection) about the impact on student engagement and thinking and movement toward mastery of a learning target or deeper understanding.

Chapters 5 and 6 focus on the discrete skills associated with designing and delivering high-quality feedback that feeds forward (also related to Assumption #3). Through explicit examples from authentic observations, observers will develop the understanding of how to determine, convey, and/or promote reflection about areas of strength (effective practice) and growth (less-than-effective practice). Readers will collect strategies to develop high-impact next steps, with a total of 12 strategies in these two chapters.

It has become abundantly clear that instructional leaders need an entirely new skill set that requires much more than the typical training models most states or districts/regions offer. Therefore, in Chapter 7, we provide examples of professional learning designs from several districts/regions that demonstrate a dedication to the support of their instructional leaders. What is unique about our work is that we have applied the research and literature alongside administrators to formulate policies and structures of educator evaluation and training within districts/regions. In other words, actual applied practice and the resulting outcomes have informed the design of policy at the local level. These districts/regions made no assumptions about what their leaders could or could not do relative to the core competencies, indicators and skills, and dedicated time and resources to provide necessary professional learning.

If you are holding this book, you are on your way to learning the type of day-to-day strategies the instructional leaders with whom we work are using to provide feedback that feeds forward. We are glad you are on this journey with us. Take out your highlighters and stickies; the work begins on the next page.

How can you use an instructional framework to improve observation and feedback practices?

We have the opportunity to work with new and veteran leaders and a common thread always emerges—all need to better understand the instructional framework—and this is where we always begin. We have found that regardless of years of experience of the leaders in our groups, they have never engaged in a deconstruction of their framework to the level we advocate. We often hear the following:

"I am wavering between performance levels."

"Evidence fits in multiple places."

"I don't know what I am looking for."

"Teachers look right at the labels/performance levels and shut down."

You may have said any of these at some point as well and will find that the strategies in this chapter address these challenges. Leaders share with us that engaging in the process has dramatically changed their understanding of the expected teaching and learning for their region or district, so don't skip this essential step and your first six strategies.

> **From the field . . .**
>
> *Developing a common understanding of the rubric and shared protocols to collect evidence has allowed my administrative team to facilitate evidence-based observations and provide meaningful feedback to our teachers. Before our work to develop a shared vision for effective instruction and deepen our command of the rubric language, our district evaluators struggled to collect the right evidence. Most of us were trained to script what we observed in the classroom as a passive observer, presenting that information back to the teacher in limited conversation. We were missing out!*
>
> —Cheri Burke, Assistant Superintendent

The importance of the use of an instructional framework to define practice in the classroom has garnered much attention. Commercial frameworks such as Robert Marzano's Teacher Evaluation Model (Learning Sciences Marzano Center, 2017; Marzano, 2007) and Charlotte Danielson's Framework for Teaching (The Danielson Group, 2013) have provided direction as supervisors and teachers sought to define quality instructional practices that would result in increased student learning. Regions, states, and countries invested both time and dollars to ensure that supervisors and teachers had well-researched and descriptive standards of teaching practice that could be used to guide their instruction and professional learning. Those who were most successful took the time not only to adopt but to deconstruct the teacher performance standards of practice inherent in these frameworks to generate a shared vision to guide practice in every classroom.

It is shared vision that drives feedback that feeds forward, as through careful examination and interpretation of the expected teaching and learning you become more accurate in your assessment of classroom practice and student outcomes. This understanding influences observation and evidence-collection practices that will result in more explicit feedback provided to a teacher. Teachers can themselves then learn to "use comprehensive frameworks throughout the school year to collect data related to their teaching, reflect on their practice, and identity specific instructional strategies they can work on to improve their repertoire of skills" (Mielke & Frontier, 2012, p. 10). This drives a teacher's ability to accurately perceive effectiveness related to teaching and learning, increasing self-efficacy.

Stop and Think: You might have unpacked your new framework the year it was introduced. Who engaged in this process? To what level? How long ago? What steps were taken to ensure teachers understood the framework expectations?

Ensuring that instructional leaders possess the skills to unwrap and uncover the expectations defined within an instructional rubric to accurately assess the levels of practice is the fundamental purpose of RVL 1.A, the first standard of six of the ReVISION Learning Supervisory Continuum. Take a few moments to review the descriptions in Figure 2.1. Notice in the "Proficient" level there are three critical areas necessary for high quality feedback related

FIGURE 2.1: RVL STANDARD 1.A

ReVISION Supervisory Continuum				
Domain 1: Evidence-Based Observation	**Beginning**	**Developing**	**Proficient**	**Exceptional**
A. Evidence cited is directly tied to the appropriate indicators of practice and accurately represents the levels of performance.	Evidence of teaching practice is often misaligned with the appropriate performance indicators. Evidence of teaching practice is not associated with levels of performance. Little to no connections have been made between teaching practice and performance indicators.	There is some evidence of teaching practice that is aligned with the appropriate performance indicators and levels, there are numerous instances where it is not. Some evidence of teaching practice is associated with levels of performance. There are some/ a few connections that are made between teaching practice and performance indicators.	Most evidence of teaching practice is aligned with the appropriate performance indicators and levels. Most evidence of teaching practice is associated with levels of performance. Most connections are made between teaching practice and performance indicators, some of which are clear and explicit.	All evidence of teaching practice is aligned with the appropriate performance indicators and levels. All evidence of teaching practice is associated with levels of performance. There are clear and explicit connections made between all teaching practice and performance indicators.

to this standard: that the observer's evidence is aligned with the framework indicators, the evidence is associated with levels of practice, and connections are clearly made between those. Based on your feedback, teachers need to understand how and why you chose a performance level and how that relates to your instructional framework. Hattie (2007) established that feedback should answer the following for the receiver:

- Where am I going?

- How am I going?

- And where to next? (p. 86)

Proficiency in standard RVL 1.A ensures that your feedback addresses current practice by answering this question for a teacher: "How am I going?"

Skill Set for Building Understanding of a Framework

In Table 2.1, consider some of the most common challenges leaders encounter related to RVL 1.A.

TABLE 2.1   RVL 1.A COMMON CHALLENGES
Misaligned evidence
Inaccurate selection of performance ratings
Observer not calibrated with the group or norm
Performance level not supported or clear
Evidence just listed without connections to the indicator
No clear claim about instructional practice

Think for a moment as to what a teacher might experience upon receiving feedback that contains an element mentioned in this list of challenges.

In this chapter, leaders will learn to do the following:

- Develop strategies to deconstruct an instructional framework and the standards of teacher performance.

- Develop strategies to determine look-fors to improve observation and feedback practices.

- Understand how to craft a claim statement about instruction and student outcomes that allows for formative learning after each observation.

Table 2.2 outlines five core instructional leader skills related to the first standard of the ReVISION Learning Supervisory Continuum.

TABLE 2.2	SKILL SET FOR RVL 1.A
Core Skill	**Description**
Unpack a Rubric	Analyzing an instructional framework in order to uncover intent and the meaning of specific terms and phrases
Describe Look-Fors	Identifying and aligning specific observable behaviors of an educator's instructional practice and student interaction to distinct indicators on a framework
Determine Evidence Relevancy	Understanding how to classify and organize collected evidence to determine significance and alignment against a framework or expectations
Determine a Performance Level	Aligning collected evidence from an observation to the correct indicator or performance level on a framework
Craft a Claim Statement	Making a claim about instructional practice that is supported by evidence and aligns to indicators on a performance framework
Create Clear Connections	Connecting evidence to the framework indicators

Deconstructing Your Framework

For decades, much has been written about the influence of expectations on student performance. What students believe about what is expected of them typically results in achievement that aligns to those expectations (Bandura, 1977; Dweck, 2006; Howard, 1992; Rosenthal & Jacobsen, 1968). Research also supports the assertion that students are more apt to align their actions to expectations when they are clear about what is expected of them (Moss & Brookhart, 2012). Similarly, research in effective job performance evaluation reveals that understanding what is expected of us leads to improved performance regardless of age or profession (Danielson, 2007; Glickman, 2008). Thus, the impact of a leader's capacity to use those expectations to inspire his or her staff to perform at their very best is paramount to the success of any school or organization.

Regardless of the rubric you use, the strategies in this chapter are most effective when followed comprehensively and sequentially. Though you may be a veteran administrator or have been evaluating teachers for years using your framework, stick with us! Remember, it is important to take the time to work through these strategies for yourself and—more importantly—for your team and your teachers. You may uncover layers you did not know were there. The first step in deconstructing your framework is to build a shared understanding of the practice known to be most effective in generating student achievement and success. How a leader uses that shared understanding to build a common vision for instructional practice in his or her building can make the difference between truly leading learning and ineffective, meaningless support.

Our friends in New Milford Public Schools unpacked their rubric years ago upon initial rollout. However, they have made it a renewed priority after recently deepening their own understanding of key indicators. The administrators are taking advantage of opportunities across a school year to build their teachers' and coaches' understanding of effective teaching and learning through new levels of deconstruction of the framework. Using strategies outlined in this chapter, they have planned the following:

- At staff meetings, the literacy coach will be leading teachers through selected indicators aligned to current trends noticed during walk-throughs.

- High school administrators will be working to calibrate department chairs' understanding of performance levels and look-fors for observations, unpacking attributes aligned to the school goals and building professional learning for department meetings each month.

- Elementary teams will meet to unpack critical attributes monthly.

- As an ongoing step, leaders will take the time to build teacher knowledge during all individual feedback meetings, pulling claims from rubric language, using the framework as a reference during the conversation, and further clarifying unclear phrases or ratings together.

The overarching process for unpacking a rubric individually or with your leadership team or teachers includes six core strategies.

Strategy 1: Understand the structure

To maximize the use of any tool or resource, one must become familiar with how it is designed. Understanding the structure of your tool will save time and create efficiencies and will also enable you to support teachers in their understanding of the tool.

Through the examination of some common elements of quality rubrics, we can provide you with an understanding of some initial steps in this process.

Overarching Intents

Figure 2.2 shows a snapshot from a rubric that outlines the structural elements of this state's framework and the standards of practice translated into a set of expectations both in and out of the classroom. Your framework may

FIGURE 2.2: RUBRIC AT A GLANCE

CCT Rubric for Effective Teaching 2014 – AT A GLANCE	
Evidence Generally Collected Through In-Class Observations	**Evidence Generally Collected Through Non-Classroom/Reviews of Practice**
Domain 1 — Classroom Environment, Student Engagement and Commitment to Learning *Teachers promote student engagement, independence and interdependence in learning and facilitate a positive learning community by:* 1a. Creating a positive learning environment that is responsive to and respectful of the learning needs of all students. 1b. Promoting developmentally appropriate standards of behavior that support a productive learning environment for all students. 1c. Maximizing instructional time by effectively managing routines and transitions.	**Domain 2 — Planning for Active Learning** *Teachers plan instruction to engage students in rigorous and relevant learning and to promote their curiosity about the world at large by:* 2a. Planning of instructional content that is aligned with standards, builds on students' prior knowledge and provides for appropriate level of challenge for all students. 2b. Planning instruction to cognitively engage students in the content. 2c. Selecting appropriate assessment strategies to monitor student progress.
Domain 3 — Instruction for Active Learning *Teachers implement instruction to engage students in rigorous and relevant learning and to promote their curiosity about the world at large by:* 3a. Implementing instructional content for learning. 3b. Leading students to construct meaning and apply new learning through the use of a variety of differentiated and evidence-based learning strategies. 3c. Assessing student learning, providing feedback to students and adjusting instruction.	**Domain 4 — Professional Responsibilities and Teacher Leadership** *Teachers maximize support for student learning by developing and demonstrating professionalism, collaboration and leadership by:* 4a. Engaging in continuous professional learning to impact instruction and student learning. 4b. Collaborating to develop and sustain a professional learning environment to support student learning. 4c. Working with colleagues, students and families to develop and sustain a positive school climate that supports student learning.

Connecticut State Department Of Education
HOTLINE 860-713-6868   5   sde.seed@ct.gov   SEED

© CSDE 2014

Source: Common Core of Teaching (2014), Connecticut State Department of Education

contain such a resource, and this type of overview quickly allows you to deter-mine overarching intents or a classification system within the tool. Yours may also contain a structure of "domains" as broader fields or categories of teaching practice that are often subdivided into "indicators" of teaching.

Stop and Think: What are the broader fields or categories within your rubric? What indicators exist in your rubric that are best assessed through an observation in the classroom?

If your school, region, district, or state has developed a rubric to support the implementation and measurement of your standards, you will sometimes find, within each domain or indicator, short summaries, phrases, bullet points, and/or small statements of intent commonly referred to as attributes. Notice in Figure 2.3 the statements under the title of each domain, such as, "Teachers implement instruction to engage students in rigorous and relevant learning and to promote their curiosity about the world at large by . . . ." This is then followed by interconnected indicators.

The attributes are typically accompanied by performance descriptions within a 4- or 5-point rating scale that outlines the associated teaching practice or student behavior/outcomes across multiple levels. These are often catego-rized as "Beginning," "Below Standard," or "Basic," to reference the lowest level of performance, and "Highly Effective," "Innovating," or "Exemplary," to describe the highest levels of performance. Notice the framework in Figure 2.3 is structured as a *progression* of performance levels, with "and" between the "Proficient" and "Exemplary" levels. This also occurs in the rubric in Figure 2.4, where performance is progressive across every level.

You will see that while the language of rubrics may differ, often the same components exist. For example, while Connecticut may use the terms "indi-cators" and "attributes," Colorado uses the terms "quality standard" and "elements" to organize the expected practices. What is most important is to understand how *your* specific rubric is designed to support your use in pro-moting teacher growth.

Stop and Think: How are your framework performance levels catego-rized? What are the perceptions or connotations of those in your district/region or system?

FIGURE 2.3: RUBRIC DESIGN EXAMPLE 1

	3: Instruction for Active Learning			
Indicator 3c	*Teachers implement instruction to* **engage students in rigorous and relevant learning** *and to* **promote their curiosity about the world at large by:** Assessing student learning, providing feedback to students, and adjusting instruction.			
	Below Standard	**Developing**	**Proficient**	**Exemplary**
Attributes				*In addition to the characteristics of* **Proficient,** *including one or more of the following:*
Criteria for student success	Does not communicate criteria for success and/or opportunities for students to self-assess are rare.	Communicates general criteria for success and provides limited opportunities for students to self-assess.	Communicates specific criteria for success and provides multiple opportunities for students to self-assess.	Integrates student input in generating specific criteria for assignments.
Ongoing assessment of student learning	Assesses student learning with focus limited to task completion and/or compliance rather than student achievement of lesson purpose/ objective.	Assesses student learning with focus on whole-class progress toward achievement of the intended instructional outcomes.	Assesses student learning with focus on eliciting evidence of learning at critical points in the lesson in order to monitor individual and group progress toward achievement of the intended instructional outcomes.	Promotes students' independent monitoring and self-assess, helping themselves or their peers to improve their learning.
Feedback to students	Provides no meaningful feedback or feedback lacks specificity and/or is inaccurate.	Provides feedback that partially guides students toward the intended instructional outcomes.	Provides individualized, descriptive feedback that is accurate, actionable, and helps students advance their learning.	Encourages peer feedback that is specific and focuses on advancing student learning.
Instructional Adjustments	Makes no attempts to adjust instruction.	Makes some attempts to adjust instruction that is primarily in response to whole-group performance.	Adjusts instruction as necessary in response to individual and group performance.	Students identify ways to adjust instruction that will be effective for them as individuals and results in quality work.

Source: Common Core of Teaching (2014), Connecticut State Department of Education

FIGURE 2.4: RUBRIC DESIGN EXAMPLE 2

QUALITY STANDARD III
Teachers plan and deliver effective instruction and create an environment that facilitates learning for their students.

Basic	Partially Proficient	Proficient (Meets State Standard)	Accomplished	Exemplary

ELEMENT H: Teachers use appropriate methods to assess what each student has learned, including formal and informal assessments and use results to plan further instruction.

Basic	Partially Proficient	Proficient (Meets State Standard)	Accomplished	Exemplary
THE TEACHER: ○ *Involves students in monitoring their learning.* ○ *Assesses learning outcomes appropriately.*	. . . and **THE TEACHER:** ▫ Implements appropriate strategies for assigning grades. ▫ Evaluates student performance based on multiple measures. ▫ Includes documentation of student progress toward mastery of state content standards in assessment plans.	. . . and **THE TEACHER** *provides actionable, timely, specific and individualized feedback about the quality of student work to:* ○ **Students.** ▫ Families and significant adults. ▫ Other professionals who work with students. ○ *Teachers' students to use feedback to improve their learning.*	. . . and **STUDENTS:** ○ *Self-assess on a variety of skills and concepts.* ○ *Articulate their personal strengths and needs based on self-assessment.* ○ *Effectively use formal and informal feedback to monitor their learning.*	. . . and **STUDENTS** *assume ownership for:* ○ *Monitoring their progress.* ○ *Setting learning goals.* ○ *Applying teacher feedback to improve performance and accelerate their learning.*

○ Professional Practice is ***Observable*** during a classroom observation.

▫ Professional Practice is ***Not Observable*** during a classroom observation.

Source: Colorado State Model Evaluation for Teachers Rubric courtesy of Colorado Department of Education (2017)

Strategy 2: Understand the connections

No matter the design of your framework, the important step to take after you have reviewed the basic structure is to determine the overarching meaning or big picture of each domain, indicator, and/or attribute. To help walk you through this process as you examine the intent of your rubric, let's look at Figure 2.4 again and the overarching intent of a *Quality Standard* and *Element*.

As you review, you will notice that the element can be organized around two core ideas for teachers, with assessment at the center.

- How the teacher plans for and implements assessment methods to allow students to monitor their own progress and set learning goals

- How the teacher is using multiple measures to formally and informally assess and provide feedback that accelerates learning.

As you explore elements of the basic structure, you need to think holistically about expected practices versus seeing each of the actions as isolated steps to complete or check off. Element H within this quality standard focuses on a teacher's assessment practice and how formal and informal data are used to support student learning. The first connection to be made is to understand that effective planning is essential to meet a "Basic" level of performance, while "Proficiency" in feedback practice in this indicator requires the teacher to react in the moment throughout a lesson, sometimes regardless of careful planning. This element necessitates that the observer not only gather information as the teacher asks questions, monitors, and confers, but also determine how the teacher's planning is impacting understanding of student needs.

Before you even begin using a rubric to observe and analyze instructional practice in action in the classroom, you need to be sure that you are clear about why a particular practice is considered important and essential to student success, in isolation and as it connects to other practices/indicators. For example, teacher success in Element H relies on a clear and specific learning objective, which resides in another standard. Your goal in applying our Strategy 2 is to ensure that you, and ultimately your teachers, recognize the essential practice for meeting proficiency or higher.

In the next strategy, you will begin to consider the research intrinsic in your teacher performance standards. Engaging in thinking about the research will further develop your understanding of the overarching intent and interconnectivity of the practices just introduced in Strategy 2.

> **Stop and Think:** How have you analyzed your rubric to determine the intent of each of the performance standards you use to assess teacher effectiveness?

Strategy 3: Understand the research

"In-depth knowledge in areas that extend beyond instructional practice is also required in conducting proper evaluations and providing adequate feedback.

Some of these include:

- *Expertise in the area being evaluated (curriculum, instructional strategies, classroom management, etc.)*

- *Knowledge of educational evaluation theories and methodologies*

- *Expertise in pedagogy, content, and pedagogical content knowledge."* (California Teachers Association, 2012, p. 21)

These expectations from the California Teachers Association reinforce why we have built one of our strategies to revolve around understanding the research of your instructional framework. To provide effective feedback, you must develop your capacity to support teachers in implementing those strategies we know have the greatest impact on learners. Regions, states, and countries recognize this importance, and many now insert language directly into the performance levels of the expectation related to research. Let's look at how Colorado (bottom example) and Australia (top example) did this (Figure 2.5). Notice the difference in Australia's structure and that the "Lead" level sets an expectation for teachers to evaluate the effectiveness of strategies using research about how students learn, while Colorado identifies research-based strategies as being a "Basic" requirement for meeting Element C.

Fundamentally, McKay (2013) reminded us, "to engage teachers in learning, school leaders need to understand the nature of learning and how it occurs" (p. 43). The shift for many from building managers to instructional leaders has been stressful, with new expectations as to what *you* should know about teaching and learning. Though much has fundamentally stayed the same (Piaget, Dewey, Vygotsky, et al.), much has significantly changed. We are not advocating that you become experts in every aspect (unless, of course, this is what you desire!). However, to become an instructional leader who creates real change and growth, you need more than a surface understanding of core essentials. Further, it is important to know where our students are headed. Ask yourself this: What kinds of jobs will they have? What will they be able to contribute to their

FIGURE 2.5: EXAMPLES OF RESEARCH LANGUAGE

STANDARD 1 KNOW STUDENTS AND HOW THEY LEARN				1
FOCUS	**GRADUATE**	**PROFICIENT**	**HIGHLY ACCOMPLISHED**	**LEAD**
Understand how students learn	1.2.1 Demonstrate knowledge and understanding of research into how students learn and the implication for teaching.	1.2.2 Structure teaching programs using research and collegial advice about how students learn.	1.2.3 Expand understanding of how students learn using research and workplace knowledge.	1.2.4 Lead processes to evaluate the effectiveness of teaching programs using research and workplace knowledge about how students learn.

Basic	Partially Proficient	Proficient (Meets State Standard)	Accomplished	Exemplary
ELEMENT C: Teachers demonstrate a rich knowledge of current research on effective instructional practices to meet the developmental and academic needs of their students.				
THE TEACHER: ○ *Incorporates evidence-based strategies into lessons*.	. . . and **THE TEACHER:** ▫ Makes connections between student data and research-based practices.	. . . and **THE TEACHER:** ○ *Individualizes instructional approach to meet unique needs of each student*.	. . . and **STUDENTS:** ○ *Embrace new and unique ways of learning as they are introduced through research-based lessons*.	. . . and **STUDENTS:** ○ *Apply skills and knowledge learned in the classroom*.

Sources: Australian Professional Standards for Teachers (top) retrieved from NSW Education Standards Authority (2018) and Colorado State Model Evaluation for Teachers Rubric (bottom) retrieved from Colorado Department of Education (2017)

communities? What kind of world will they live in? What instructional practices will meet their needs based on this understanding?

Stop for a moment and review your own instructional indicators. You might notice the effective and exemplary descriptions reflect critical skill sets, dispositions, and behaviors along with the recommended teacher strategies to ensure students are college- and/or career-ready in a changing world.

> **Stop and Think:** Did your country, state, district, region, or school create a profile of a graduate, answering what students need to know and know how to do upon leaving your K–12 system? Does the framework include these skills and dispositions?

Marzano, Danielson, or anyone who worked to design your instructional framework utilized key elements of "research-based strategies," integrating the need for a focus on

  a. learning communities and expectations;

  b. relevance and connections;

  c. cognitive demand and construction of learning; and

  d. student demonstration of learning.

Most likely, related research-based strategies are integrated into the design of the "Proficient" and "Exemplary" descriptions and expectations (or directly stated such, as in Figure 2.5). Remember, within these ratings, generally you will find clear descriptions and look-fors of effective teacher practices, often along with the desired student outcomes.

Look through Table 2.3 as an example of how to organize your thinking around research and the big-picture goal of observation and feedback. This provides you with a guide with four key areas of instructional practice for your evidence collection, development of feedback, and conversations with teachers. Regardless of the purpose or duration of your observation, your attention during a lesson should always remain broad, keeping the four areas shown in the table in mind. An example of supporting research has been included in the last column for each area, but as you know, there are volumes written on each individual topic alone. Chapter 3 will further explore how to use this frame to help you collect related evidence, and in Chapter 5, you will learn how to use this research to better understand and cite areas of growth and strength for a teacher after a lesson. In addition, you will have the opportunity to self-assess your understanding of more specific critical research areas.

> **Stop and Think:** What research has been the basis for the development of your rubric? Which of your indicators highlight specific research-based strategies and what is your understanding of those strategies?

TABLE 2.3	THE BIG PICTURE	
Key area	What you might want to understand based on research	What the research says
Environment	How does a positive learning community impact learning? How can a teacher foster growth mindset and grit?	*"As soon as children become able to evaluate themselves, some of them become afraid of challenges. They become afraid of not being smart"* (Dweck, 2006, p. 16).
Purpose	Why is it important for all students to understand the day's learning purpose? Why should learning be relevant? What is the role of connections in the learning process?	*"Learning targets have no inherent power. They enhance student learning and achievement only when educators commit to consistently and intentionally sharing them with students"* (Moss et al., 2011, p. 69).
Process	Why is it important to build student-centered lessons? What does it mean to engage students? What does rigorous instruction or engagement look like? How does engagement impact learning? How do students construct new learning?	*"To gradually release responsibility is to equip students with what they need to be engaged and self-directed learners"* (Fisher & Frey, 2014, p. 161). *"We must give students supports that they can hold on to as they take the lead—not just push them onto the path and hope they find their way"* (Fisher & Frey, 2008, cited in Cappello & Moss, 2010, p. 44).
Understanding	How could students be asked to apply or use the new learning? Why is formative assessment important? How does actionable feedback impact learning?	*"The world doesn't care what you know. What the world cares about is what you do with what you know."* —Tony Wagner *"Assessment for learning is about eliciting that productive response to assessment results from students every time. It can produce winning streaks for all students"* (Stiggins, 2007).

Strategy 3 not only opens the door to connections that exist across your rubric as described in Strategy 2; it also raises your awareness of those elements of the rubric that may be unfamiliar or challenging to you as you prepare to observe in the classroom.

Unpacking Expectations

Strategy 4: Identify challenging phrases

Have you ever been in the situation where you were reading education-based materials and an acronym, phrase, or word was dropped in by the author and you needed to immediately open up a Google search to find out what it meant? If you have been in education even for a short time, more than likely you can respond yes to this question. Literature and materials in the education field are often an alphabet soup of acronyms, systems, and approaches, and the jargon can mean different things depending on the person's interpretation.

Knowing this, you should expect that in your rubric exists several phrases or concepts that may be challenging to understand. Designing rubric performance levels is a complex art and science, so these are hard to avoid. These phrases require further clarification and development of a common understanding across your team, school, and region/district. Strategy 4 is designed to help you engage in a review of your rubric so that before you work with teachers, you clearly understand elements that may lead to confusion and possibly even disagreement. It is highly recommended that you engage this strategy with a peer or a group of peers and eventually with the teachers you serve.

So what do we mean by "challenging" phrases? Look at the examples of critical aspects of effective instruction from Danielson's Framework for Teaching (The Danielson Group, 2013). Which words and phrases jump out at you as potentially confusing, open to misinterpretation, or challenging to define?

> "Outcomes are differentiated to encourage individual students to take educational risks."

> "Outcomes represent high expectations and rigor."

What do we mean by educational risks? What do we all consider to be high expectations? How do we define rigor? Those words and phrases can have different meanings to different people. This may be dependent on the education preparatory program you completed, literature you have studied in your professional development or, potentially, even the local, regional, or national vision for these practices.

Challenging phrases can take on many forms. You may have also noticed words like "some" or "most" in your rubric, such as in

> "The teacher relies on a single strategy or alternate set of materials to make the lesson accessible to most students though some students may not be able to access certain parts of the lesson and/or some may not be challenged" (Ohio Department of Education, 2015).

Or qualitative phrases like

> "Uses incentives wisely" or "Uses mediocre methods to check for understanding" (Marshall, 2011).

It is critical for you to first *isolate* which phrases and words may be challenging within your rubric. Notice if the designer has offered some assistance with these, such as in Marshall's addition: "e.g., thumbs up/thumbs down" as a "mediocre method." These are helpful, but as a team, you want to determine and then work with teachers to understand why this method is not considered effective (related to your work with research-based strategies).

Danielson (The Danielson Group, 2013) provides examples for "high expectations" and "educational risks": "Some students identify additional learning" or "The teacher encourages students to set their own goals; he provides them with a taxonomy of challenge verbs." However, her list ends with "and others . . ." as she recognizes these are just a few examples.

After locating the phrases, you and your team should determine what research, literature, and knowledge about effective teaching and learning will best support you and your teachers' understanding of the related practice represented by the phrase. Regardless of the framework you are using, you will generally find similar terms or phrases related to key components of instruction or service delivery. Beyond the examples above, some of the most common challenging phrases from rubrics include the following:

- Advancing learning

- Engagement/cognitive or intellectual engagement

- Appropriate challenge/level of rigor or challenging

- Clear objectives/clear sense

- Learning expectations

Read on to see an example of a leadership team's development of a common definition of "cognitive engagement" based on the following attributes:

> Employs differentiated strategies, tasks and questions that cognitively engage students in constructing new and meaningful learning through appropriately integrated recall, problem-solving, critical and creative thinking, purposeful discourse and/or inquiry.
>
> Uses resources and flexible groupings that cognitively engage students in demonstrating new learning in multiple ways, including application of new learning to make interdisciplinary, real world, career or global connections (CSDE, 2014).

"cognitive engagement"

Cognitive engagement is synonymous with student investment in learning. When students are cognitively engaged, they are clear about the purpose of the learning activity and the approach with which they are attempting to construct knowledge. Cognitive engagement requires that a learner put forth fruitful effort constructing or applying new learning on tasks with a cognitive demand and a willingness to persevere when faced with challenging tasks and concepts. It also implies that the learning is deep and meaningful, as opposed to students simply appearing busy and on task. Teachers want students to not just silently grapple with rigorous tasks but also to interact with peers and a variety of materials to help them process information and come to a deeper understanding of content and/or learning processes.

- You might find you can also use nonexamples to begin or add to this process. For example, "cognitive engagement" is *not* compliance. Looking at nonproficient rating language can also help you see it is *not* solely recalling or repeating rote information.

- You can also look in the rubric language for defining characteristics. For example, look back after the phrase "cognitive engagement" in the indicator description; you will see and determine it *includes* "critical thinking," "purposeful discourse," and "real-world connections."

You may find unpacking one phrase leads to the need to unpack another, such as "purposeful discourse" (as a characteristic of cognitive engagement). While some of the phrases you identify are not necessarily unfamiliar, they often conjure up different ideas about the related classroom practice and/or result in different interpretations. These differences in understanding are what you seek to eliminate as you plan and prepare to support your teachers through feedback about their classroom practice. At **resources.corwin .com/feedforward** you will find additional examples of defined challenging phrases.

> **Stop and Think:** Which phrases in your own rubric have been consistently challenging to you, your team, and/or your teachers? How can you build understanding of these?

The work of discussing and defining these phrases can serve as an excellent professional learning or faculty meeting activity with your staff and can help build trust as you engage in your classroom observations.

Strategy 5: Identify key levers

Determining a Performance Level

Paying close attention to the differences between performance levels and ratings, known as key levers, is an important step in deconstructing a rubric. The deep understanding of these will help you see how behaviors and actions differ from, say, "Unsatisfactory" to "Progressing" to "Proficient" to "Exemplary" (such as in Table 2.4), allowing you to accurately select ratings. In addition, this understanding helps clarify the practice for the teacher so that he or she may utilize descriptions during planning and self-reflection ("Where am I going?" and "How am I going?"). Making clear distinctions between levels of practice is one of the more difficult tasks for new evaluators or those new to a framework. Sometimes, the distinction between practices outlined in levels of performance can elude the evaluator, as those differences are reflected in just one word or in a handful of short phrases. Review the performance levels of the sample indicator in Table 2.4 with attention to how the descriptions differ along the progression.

TABLE 2.4 INDICATOR FOR KEY LEVERS

Unsatisfactory	Progressing	Proficient	Exemplary
Little to no evidence of checks for academic understanding, missing nearly all key moments, and/or only checks for understanding of directions. Does not get an accurate reading of the class's understanding from most checks.	Sometimes checks for academic understanding but misses several key moments and/or mostly checks for understanding of directions. Gets an accurate reading of the class's understanding from most checks.	Consistently checks for academic understanding at almost all key moments to determine pace of the lesson and whether or not key steps or concepts need to be discussed further before moving on. Gets an accurate reading of the class's understanding from almost every check.	Checks for academic understanding are seamlessly embedded in the lesson to determine pace and whether or not key steps or concepts need to be discussed further before moving on. Gets an accurate reading of the class's understanding from every check.

Source: Dallas Independent School District, 2014

Notice that the first difference resides in how often the teacher checks for understanding during a lesson. There are several important words and phrases that help you differentiate between the levels, such as "Little to no," "Sometimes," and "Consistently." These represent the key levers. Moving on, you will see that the "Proficient" description includes "checks for academic understanding" and "gets an accurate reading of the class's understanding" at critical points in the lesson, while the "Progressing" level includes "mostly checks for understanding of directions." In this instance, the key lever lies in the quality and focus of the checks and if the teacher is assessing learning. These lever examples highlight an important distinction and offer a way for an observer to clearly determine performance levels.

What is often challenging is when the difference is based on a quantity versus a quality measure. Notice in the Dallas example, it is quantity of a *teacher action*. However, you might need to address quantity of *student outcomes/behaviors*. For example, remember our earlier example from the Ohio rubric: "**. . . accessible to most students though some students may not be able to access . . .**"? (We will explore in greater depth strategies for collecting evidence aligned with these types of quantity measures in Chapter 3.)

What is generally clear in most rubrics, however, is that they have been designed to include not only quantity and frequency measures but also quality and onus of control toward the students and/or elements of collegial/peer support between each performance level. Taking time as an instructional leader to identify these levers will ensure accuracy in rating, providing a deeper level of clarity about how the evidence collected reflects each performance level.

Many instructional leaders find that writing directly on a rubric provides the best option for dissecting each rating within an indicator (see Table 2.5).

TABLE 2.5   KEY LEVERS ANNOTATION

Beginning	Developing	Proficient	Exemplary
Does not clearly communicate learning expectations to students.	Communicates learning expectations to students and sets a general purpose for instruction, which may require further clarification.	Clearly communicates learning expectations to students and sets a specific purpose for instruction and helps students to see how the learning is aligned with Common Core State Standards.	Students are encouraged to explain how the learning is situated within the broader learning context/curriculum.

Source: Common Core of Teaching (2014), Connecticut State Department of Education

In this example, it is important to recognize there is a clear pattern related to the practice in the classroom. The key levers in this example reflect the

- level of clarity of the purpose and expectations,
- depth or specificity of the purpose and expectations, and
- student role (from no understanding to complete understanding).

From this examination of the rubric, your documentation of the trends might look like this:

- The "Beginning" level: when the teacher does not clearly communicate the learning expectations.

- The "Developing" level: when the teacher communicates the learning expectations but the purpose is general, causing students to need clarification.

- The "Proficient" level: when the teacher has clearly communicated the purpose, it is specific, and the teacher's communication of the purpose causes students to see how learning is aligned with standards.

- The "Exemplary" level: when the teacher is encouraging or designing the class instruction so that students are explaining the purpose.

A completed annotated rubric like the ones in Figure 2.6 on the next page can serve as a valuable resource for a leader.

We highly recommend engaging in this level of deconstruction with your leadership team and then with your teachers. Visit **resources.corwin .com/feedforward** for examples from group discussions and a method for examining key levers across a domain.

Describing Look-Fors

Strategy 6: Engage in the *behavioralization* process

The final strategy in deconstructing your framework combines and reinforces all of the steps from Strategies 1 to 5 into a plan to support your evidence collection during an observation in the classroom. While *behavioralization* is not found in Webster's dictionary, it captures the intent of Strategy 6—to describe the behaviors behind the standards of practice in a rubric and prepare an observer for the assessment of those standards. While it is important to remember that no one modality of collecting evidence of practice should ever be considered enough to support a true understanding of the levels of practice, classroom observation remains the most common and is the focus of the strategies we are providing in this chapter and book.

FIGURE 2.6: ANNOTATED RUBRICS

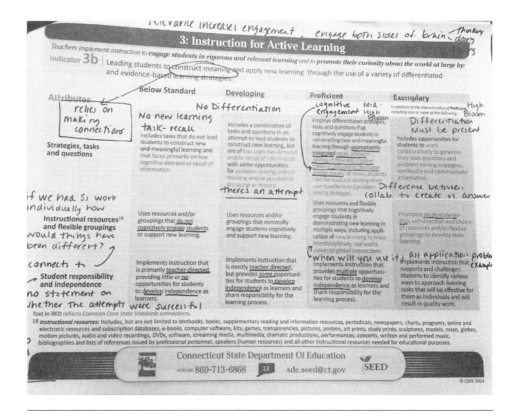

Sources: Regional School District 1 rubric (top) reprinted with permission from Rebecca Gaschel Clark. CSDE 2014 (bottom) reprinted with permission from Linda Scoralick.

Before you begin the process for any teacher performance standard or indicator, be sure to answer the following questions from Strategies 2 to 5:

- What is the overarching intent?

- What are the fundamental research-based strategies?

- What are the challenging phrases in the indicator?

- What are the key levers?

These understandings then allow you to identify more specifically the types of look-fors, evidence to be collected about the teacher performance standard in the classroom, helping you understand and assess the current performance level of the teacher.

Table 2.6 on the next page provides an example of an organizer we use for a single attribute or indicator with leaders and/or teachers:

> Employs differentiated strategies, tasks, and questions that cognitively engage students in constructing new and meaningful learning through appropriately integrated recall, problem solving, critical and creative thinking, purposeful discourse, and/or inquiry. At times, students take the lead and develop their own questions and problem-solving strategies (CSDE, 2014).

The steps are somewhat clear in the organizer, and the evidence is identified along three categories related to the selected indicator/attribute:

Students:

- What student actions, behaviors, or dispositions might you see and hear?

- What are students doing, discussing, asking, and responding?

Teacher:

- What teacher actions, behaviors, or dispositions might you see and hear?

- What can a teacher provide the students (handouts or charts) to help scaffold their experience?

Products:

- What ongoing products, student work, resources, charts, or other items might you see?

Begin with the "Proficient"-level description from the indicator or attribute and complete the organizer, identifying the look-fors that will support your analysis of classroom practice and student outcomes within each of the three categories. You will provide richer, more meaningful feedback for teachers by

TABLE 2.6 · SAMPLE *BEHAVIORALIZATION*

For the indicator studied, write the name of the indicator and attribute below.	Desired Student Outcome/Action	Teacher Action/Scaffold	Artifacts/Resources
Indicator and attribute	Student Outcome/Action	Teacher Action/Scaffold	Artifacts/Resources
	• What student actions, behaviors, or dispositions might you see and hear? • What are students doing, discussing, asking, and responding? • *THINK: Who's doing the work?*	• What teacher actions, behaviors, or dispositions might you see and hear? • *THINK: What has the teacher done to initiate student action so they can do the work?*	• What has the teacher provided the students (handouts or charts) to help scaffold their experience? • What ongoing products, student work, resources, charts, or other items might you see? • *THINK: What could you see in ongoing student work? What could the products/process show?*
3b strategies, tasks, and questions	• Students are actively engaged in the learning activity. • Students are working or talking about open-ended concepts and/or problems using higher level thinking and questioning. • Students are talking to each other about the work. • Students are asking questions of each other. • Students are applying multiple approaches to completing the task, solving the problem, or creating a product. • Students are accessing and processing information in a variety of ways. • Students are not just utilizing recall skills. They are analyzing, evaluating, synthesizing, and/or applying knowledge. • Multiple students are responding to teacher questions (not one student being called on at a time).	• Ask questions that extend the learning and encourage students to analyze, examine, or synthesize. • Prompt students to clarify their thinking, i.e., "What makes you say that? or "Tell me more." • Present lessons to the whole group that are brief and multisensory. • Provide tiered work to meet the needs of the various levels. • Have students turn and talk instead of calling on one student at a time. • Refer students to tools and strategies when they are stuck.	• Graphic organizers • Work that has been revised • Individual notebooks • Tiered task sheets • Anchor charts that are referred to explicitly • Individualized copies of whole class materials • Checklists to monitor work completion • Verbal prompt cards/charts • Written directions • Manipulatives • Mentor texts • Sketches/diagrams, notebook entries, drafts, written work, annotations, outlines, reports, charts, tables, graphs

building your observation skill set to include student outcomes, actions, and various artifacts related to the teacher performance standard instead of a simple collection of evidence about teacher practice alone.

Engaging in the *behavioralization* process can change mindsets as you and/or your teachers unwrap the teacher performance standards in the rubric. The collaborative deconstruction of rubric language develops levels of trust between teachers and supervisors by helping bring transparency to what is being observed in the classrooms. Completing a *behavioralization* provides a depth of understanding of performance and practice articulated in the rubric and is essential on the part of every leader who is seeking to develop feedback that feeds forward.

Stop and Think: Considering the *behavioralization* process, how might you use this with your peers and with teachers and why?

Using a Feedback Frame

Once you have a clear understanding of look-fors and key levers, you can begin to align your evidence to determine performance levels and to craft definitive statements about the practice and outcomes you observed. To create clear and valid feedback, we suggest the use of our feedback frame, "Claim, Connect, Action," shown in Figure 2.7 below.

FIGURE 2.7: CLAIM, CONNECT, ACTION

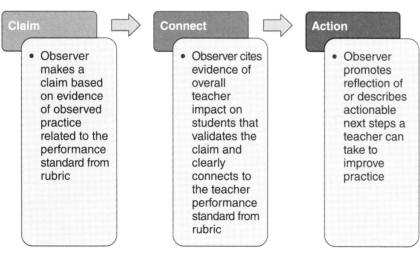

Source: Courtesy of ReVISION

Three steps shown in Figure 2.7 are as follows:

1. Formulate a ***claim*** about teacher practice that is aligned to a framework.
2. ***Connect*** and validate that claim with objective and legitimate evidence from an observation (Chapters 3 and 4).
3. Craft feedback to support teacher growth through action and reflection (Chapters 5 and 6).

As you can see from the list, the full process of creating feedback through the Claim, Connect, Action frame is examined in the next four chapters. The process involves all three of our core competencies: observation and evidence collection, analysis of evidence, and the creation of effective feedback. In the remainder of this chapter, we will explore steps to creating a claim statement that can be directly validated by evidence, ultimately leading to targeted next steps for teacher growth.

Crafting a Claim

Everything to this point in the chapter has been designed to set you on the path to clearly recognize what evidence needs to be collected during an observation based on your instructional framework. At the point of analyzing evidence to determine a performance level, you are setting the stage to make a claim about teacher practice so that your feedback is directly rooted in the observed instructional practice and outcomes.

There are three basic steps to crafting a claim statement, one of which you have already encountered If you have followed the strategies in this chapter:

Step 1: Know your teacher performance standards and what you are expecting

As you apply everything you have learned so far, you are creating a comprehensive understanding of your rubric. As you use the tool and collaborate with peers and teachers, you will continuously grow in your understanding of the standards of teaching practice and how they manifest in the classroom.

Step 2: Align evidence and determine relevance

Determining the relevance of your collected data is a multistep process. Many of the strategies for doing so are explored in greater depth in Chapter 4 as you learn to analyze your evidence, but let's start with some basics first.

Do you find yourself returning to your desk after a 45-minute classroom observation overwhelmed with eight pages of notes? Once you have collected evidence, it is critical that you are able to determine what is relevant and what is not within those notes. At this point in your process, you need to sift through your evidence and consider how what you have collected aligns to particular attributes/indicators. This is often called "coding" or "tagging" evidence to the rubric. (You will see how having a strong understanding of your rubric helps to speed up this process.)

Picture the start of the lesson and the evidence you might collect chronologically. Let's say you want to focus on assessment from an observation, as you read through your evidence on the first two pages of notes between the time stamps of 8:50 and 9:20. You have quotes and miscellaneous pieces of evidence that include the following:

- Teacher quotes for greetings as students arrive.

- Description of teacher routine for collecting homework.

- Teacher quotes of directions given.

- Descriptions of students gathering supplies and transitioning to the new lesson for the day.

- Quotes from teacher introducing the new lesson.

As you sift through your evidence, you do not deem these items to be relevant to the evaluation of assessment methods. However, within the notes during this same time frame, you locate aligned and relevant evidence:

- Nearly half (8/20) of the students incorrectly completed the Do Now.

- Five were not finished when the teacher put the answers on the board (six minutes of work time).

- Teacher checked to see that everyone copied down the correct answers.

- Teacher did not address the misunderstandings, going on with the day's lesson.

Through this data, you are basically working to answer, "What did I see?" related to assessment. Then, as an observer, you want to stop and ask yourself if there is any other evidence you need that you have elsewhere within your notes or importantly, did not collect.

Step 3: Align your evidence to determine a performance level

The next step in your analysis is to ask two questions:

- How does "What did I see" compare to the expected performance outlined in my rubric for ongoing assessment?

- What are the key levers and what evidence will lead me to understand the level of performance?

You have already begun to process these questions in your examination of Strategy 5: Identify Key Levers and through your initial analysis of the evidence in the last step. Once you have examined the relevance (what fits or aligns), you can then determine the accurate performance level.

Let's look again at the evidence collected from the sixth-grade math lesson and how it is aligned and relevant to the assessment attribute shown in Figure 2.8 to move toward selecting a performance level.

FIGURE 2.8: EXAMPLE 1 TO DETERMINE PERFORMANCE LEVEL

	Below Standard	Developing	Proficient	Exemplary
Attributes				*In addition to the characteristics of* **Proficient,** *including one or more of the following:*
Ongoing assessment of student learning	Assesses student learning with focus limited to task completion and/or compliance rather than student achievement of lesson purpose/objectives.	Assesses student learning with focus on whole-class progress toward achievement of the intended instructional outcomes.	Assesses student learning with focus on eliciting evidence of learning at critical points in the lesson in order to monitor individual and group progress toward achievement of the intended instructional outcomes.	Promotes students' independent monitoring and self-assess, helping themselves or their peers to improve their learning.

Source: Common Core of Teaching (2014), Connecticut State Department of Education

Remember the observer's relevant evidence related to assessment:

- Nearly half (8/20) of the students incorrectly completed the Do Now.

- Five were not finished when the teacher put the answers on the board (six minutes of work time).

- Teacher checked to see that everyone copied down the correct answers.

- Teacher did not address the misunderstandings, going on with the day's lesson.

In this lesson, nearly 50 percent of the students were not able to complete the assigned task, and because the teacher did not "**elicit evidence of learning at critical points**" in the lesson, the observer cannot make a claim about the practice from the "Proficient" description. The teacher did monitor, but the evidence characterizes this assessment as checking to see if students had copied the correct answers, which is aligned to the rubric language of "**limited to task completion and/or compliance.**" Therefore, the evidence validates the fact that the teacher "**Assessed student learning with focus limited to task completion and/or compliance rather than student achievement of lesson purpose/objective**" as described in the "Below Standard" performance level.

For a sample of notes taken during an observation and then organized, visit **resources.corwin.com/feedforward**.

Let's look at another lesson example, beginning with a sample attribute you have seen about "instructional purpose" (see Figure 2.9).

FIGURE 2.9: EXAMPLE 2 TO DETERMINE PERFORMANCE LEVEL

Indicator 3a	*Teachers implement instruction to **engage students in rigorous and relevant learning** and to **promote their curiosity about the world at large by:*** Implementing instructional content for learning.			
	Below Standard	**Developing**	**Proficient**	**Exemplary**
Attributes				*In addition to the characteristics of **Proficient,** including one or more of the following:*
Instructional purpose	Does not clearly communicate learning expectations to students.	Communicates learning expectations to students and sets a general purpose for instruction, which may require further clarification.	Clearly communicates learning expectations to students and sets a specific purpose for instruction and helps students to see how the learning is aligned with Common Core State Standards and/or other appropriate Connecticut content standards.	Students are encouraged to explain how the learning is situated within the broader learning context/curriculum.

Source: Common Core of Teaching (2014), Connecticut State Department of Education

In examining the "Proficient" and "Exemplary" performance levels, you are provided clues from the rubric as to what appropriate, aligned, and relevant evidence might be:

The teacher has

> **"communicated the learning expectations,"** and **"clearly presents the instructional content**."

These actions all lead to students who can

> **"explain how the learning is situated within the broader learning context/curriculum**."

If you had observed an 11th-grade civics lesson in which students were required to demonstrate their understanding of using text evidence to support an argument about the need for laws in society, you would look through your collected evidence to locate data to determine what you saw, which may include the following:

- Quotes from the teacher communicating why text evidence is needed to support an argument.

- Quotes from students explaining the learning expectation.

- The number of students who could explain the learning expectation.

- Responses to observer questions about the importance of laws in society.

After determining what you saw, analysis of your evidence against the described expectations of practice and resulting outcomes begins with asking yourself this:

> "How does 'What did I see' compare to the expected performance outlined in my rubric for ongoing assessment?"

Based on this indicator and the "Proficient" and "Exemplary" descriptions, we expect that the teacher will communicate the learning and that students can and will explain the learning and context.

Then, as you examine what you have identified, you can ask this:

- "What are the key levers and what evidence will lead to understanding the level of performance?"

Remember, the key levers between the "Proficient" and "Exemplary" performance levels for this attribute include differences in practice, such as the following:

- The teacher is "clearly communicating learning expectations" versus the "students are explaining" the learning.

- The teacher is "clearly" and "logically" presenting content versus "challenging students to extend learning."

The key levers in this example represent a significant shift to student ownership of the learning in the classroom, and it is important for you to examine your notes for specific ways in which these were evidenced during the observation. This takes a step beyond tagging evidence—which is where many observers fail to truly leverage the information they collect—and allows you to use that evidence to validate a claim about practice for the teacher.

As you grow in your overall observation and feedback practice, you will begin to refine your evidence-collection skills (Chapter 3) and analyze that evidence for impact (Chapter 4), which will also impact your analysis for relevance. The greatest benefit over time is that your capacity to identify in the moment what needs to be collected will improve, leading to less irrelevant or extraneous information.

Step 4: Create your claim statement

This last step involves using the language of the performance level to develop a claim based on the evidence collected once you have aligned the evidence and determined the appropriate performance level. You will encounter the math lesson and assessment again in upcoming chapters, so to practice building a claim, let's start with an easier and common indicator related to routines and transitions. We will review two effective samples of claims after a leader observed a third-grade lesson involving station rotations. The students had been working in a station model each week for the previous four months yet were unclear about what station to visit or what specifically to do at each station. The observer used the indicator language in Figure 2.10.

```
During  the  observation,  the  teacher  inconsistently  estab-
lished  routines  and  transitions,  resulting  in  some  loss  of
instructional time as evidenced by . . .
```

or

```
Though  there  are  some  routines  and  transitions  in  place  and
students  have  a  general  understanding  of  them,  the  teacher
```

inconsistently established station routines and transitions, resulting in some loss of instructional time as evidenced by . . .

FIGURE 2.10: INDICATOR TO BUILD A CLAIM

	Below Standard	Developing	Proficient	Exemplary
Attributes				*In addition to the characteristics of* **Proficient**, *including one or more of the following:*
Routines and transitions appropriate to needs of students	Does not establish or ineffectively establishes routines and transitions, resulting in significant loss of instructional time.	Inconsistently establishes routines and transitions, resulting in some loss of instructional time.	Establishes routines and transitions resulting in maximized instructional time.	Teacher encourages and/or provides opportunities for students to independently facilitate routines and transitions.

Source: Common Core of Teaching (2014), Connecticut State Department of Education

What do you notice about the difference between the claims? Both are effective, but one may be considered more positive than the other. Selecting the best approach is determined in large part by the professional and personal needs of the teacher. Knowing how a person gives and receives information (i.e., is the individual more directive in his or her personality or does he or she require directives that include praise?) should guide your articulation of the claim statement (Chapter 6). The observer's next steps would be to include aligned evidence in a "Connect" section to support the claim.

These examples would then be followed by clearly identifying the quantitative and qualitative data collected during the observation that validate the claim, such as duration of time for rotations, description of students' movement, their actions upon arriving in the station, and their responses to your questions. (You will learn more about types of evidence in Chapter 3.)

Stop and Think: How have you communicated the level of practice to support your teacher's formative development? How does that compare to the claim process outlined here?

Bravmann (2004) identified a summative evaluation as one that focuses on "endpoint measurement only and omits the very aspects of assessment that enable us to attain positive outcomes" through ongoing formative feedback. The fact that teachers have been left with summative analysis and not necessarily formative evaluation is the very reason why we must be able to turn our evidence into a claim based on the language of the rubric. Instructional leaders must look to inform teacher growth every time they are observing in the classroom, making each time a formative and developmental opportunity.

Final Thoughts

The strategies and skills related to RVL 1.A lay the foundation for all of the other work ahead to improve your observation and feedback practice. Establishing clarity for yourself and others of the expectations based on your rubric is a fundamental function of your instructional leadership and ensures accurate and aligned formative feedback for teacher growth. Once you are clear about the expectations for teaching and learning, you begin to understand the evidence of teacher practice and student outcomes you need to collect during an observation and can work to build that understanding with your teachers.

In this chapter, you explored the first five strategies of effective observation and feedback through deconstruction of your framework:

- Unpack the standards of teacher performance and practice the country, state, region, district, or school has selected as compulsory and/or essential to demonstrating teacher effectiveness.

- Describe look-fors aligned to quality observation practice that support understanding of learning, not just teaching.

- Accurately select the performance level associated with your indicators through the identification of key levers.

- Analyze collected evidence to support understanding of relevancy and alignment to indicators.

You also explored the steps to:

- Craft a claim statement that allows for formative learning after each observation.

Remember, you can access support resources at **resources.corwin.com/ feedforward.**

Chapter 3 will ensure that you recognize the types of evidence available to you as an observer during a lesson, which you will then use to support your claims and select performance levels. The next chapter will also provide you with a set of strategies for effective and efficient collection methods of that evidence as you will be introduced to our second standard: **RVL 1.B: *"Qualitative and quantitative evidence cited in feedback is aligned, appropriate, and facilitates targeted growth and improvement."***

How can you collect evidence in the classroom to improve feedback?

3

Classroom observation can cause your head to spin when you are unsure of what to collect and how to capture the necessary evidence to determine the effectiveness of the instruction. Have you ever said . . .

"I am overwhelmed trying to collect everything."

"I don't know how to capture what I need."

"I can't write/type fast enough."

"I don't know what to record/collect."

We have come to realize that evidence collection is an art and a science requiring a clear head and nimble feet and the ability to adapt to any classroom layout, instructional structure, or lesson design. Because we want to build your ability to observe in any setting, you will encounter 10 strategies (#7–#16) in this chapter. Don't panic!

It's time to get up out of your chairs!

> **From the field . . .**
>
> *Now that I am using a balance of qualitative and quantitative evidence I've changed the lens through which I view instruction for myself and my teachers. When evaluating a strategy, my qualitative evaluation is enhanced by the addition of quantitative evidence such as, how many students were successful, were engaged in activity, or completed assignment. My feedback has changed from what's good vs. bad to what's effective vs. ineffective. Balanced evidence has made my practice stronger and has translated into written feedback that really lets teachers see what happened throughout their lessons.*
>
> *This more comprehensive understanding of what occurred then makes for fertile ground to talk with teachers. Data such as, "50% of students did not finish their task," crystallizes for a teacher what outcome needs to improve and becomes a benchmark to measure improvement. Our conversations have blossomed into action steps as teachers are better able to understand the changes they can make to improve their practice and student outcomes.*
>
> —Anne Bilko, Principal

Collecting and citing a balance of evidence aligned to an instructional framework are some of the most challenging steps in your journey toward effectively leading learning. As suggested in Chapter 2, the importance of this competency cannot be underestimated, as the quality of the observer's evidence directly impacts the quality of the feedback to the teacher.

Take a moment to review the performance levels related to RVL 1.B in Figure 3.1 on the opposite page.

You might notice across the levels that effective leaders not only collect but *cite evidence with enough specificity.* They ensure both teacher and student evidence is included in feedback, claims about practice are clearly supported, and growth is promoted. In the past, you may have received or provided feedback similar to this example:

```
10:36 - 100% students with eyes on teacher

10:42 - Students chorally respond "No" in response to
teacher question

10:43 - 100% of students with eyes on teacher

10:45 - 100% of students participate in turn-and-talk

10:52 - 100% of students with eyes on text reading
independently
```

FIGURE 3.1: RVL STANDARD 1.B

ReVISION Supervisory Continuum				
Domain 1: Evidence-Based Observation	**Beginning**	**Developing**	**Proficient**	**Exceptional**
B. Qualitative and quantitative evidence cited in feedback is aligned, appropriate, and facilitates targeted growth and improvement.	Evidence cited about teaching practice includes only one type of data. Evidence is not specific enough to validate claims about teacher practice and support teacher growth and improvement.	While the evidence cited is a mix of qualitative and quantitative data, it lacks the alignment and specificity needed to validate claims about teacher practice and support teacher growth and improvement.	The evidence cited is a mix of qualitative and quantitative data. It includes enough specificity needed to validate claims about teacher practice and support some teacher growth and improvement.	The evidence cited is balanced between qualitative and quantitative data and specific facts that provide supportive suggestions and potential benchmarks for teacher growth and improvement.

© 2018 ReVISION Learning Partnership, LLC All Rights Reserved

Stop and Think: What do you notice about this feedback?

Clearly, the observer is collecting detailed evidence, but by citing it in this way, how does the observer help a teacher learn about next steps in the area of engagement? The feedback is only reporting that all were on-task for 16 minutes and this does not feed forward.

In this chapter, leaders will learn to do the following:

- Understand bias related to observation and evidence-collection.

- Review foundations of student engagement and learning.

- Recognize the general types of data available for collection during an observation (and understand what we mean by a "mix" or "balance" of evidence mentioned in Figure 3.1).

- Develop objective evidence-collection strategies, including those for interacting with students about ongoing work and learning during a lesson.

- Understand how the use of evidence in feedback serves to promote teacher growth.

Skill Set for Collecting Evidence

As you read through each section, continue to think about how you can personalize the strategies ahead based on the content areas and grade levels you currently observe. Remember that every lesson will be different each time you step into a classroom, which will require you to remain flexible with the use of the suggested strategies. Common challenges you may encounter are listed in Table 3.1.

TABLE 3.1	RVL 1.B COMMON CHALLENGES

Observer Behaviors:
Scripting only/word-for-word capture
Not knowing how to collect evidence
Not capturing quantitative data
Not circulating the room
Not effectively engaging with students
Taking the environment or preexisting conditions for granted
Lacking concentration or attention during a lesson
In feedback:
Summary or general evidence versus details
Lack of specific evidence of teaching and learning
Lack of quantitative data

Take a few minutes to review the essential skills aligned to RVL 1.B that we will address (see Table 3.2).

TABLE 3.2	SKILL SET FOR RVL 1.B

Observe Objectively	Collecting evidence during an observation without bias with attention to teaching and learning
Identify Types of Data	Identifying the types of data to be collected
Collect Quantitative Data	Determining how and when to collect measurable data during an observation
Collect Qualitative Data	Determining how and when to collect evidence that characterizes what is happening or is in the form of direct quotes
Collect Evidence of Student Engagement and Learning	Determining how and when to collect evidence that clearly demonstrates levels of student engagement and learning
Create Clear Connections	Citing evidence that clearly supports a claim about instruction and promotes growth

Teaching is one of the few professions in which the observation of actual, in-the-moment practice is an essential part of the support, supervision, and evaluation process for its practitioners. In most other fields, this opportunity for review and feedback in process is rare, as a final outcome or product (securing the sale or meeting quarterly targets) serves as the assessment or measurement of success and competency. Because teaching involves the shaping of children's mindsets, dispositions, and thinking, classroom observation provides a valuable opportunity to gather evidence and engage with students as this is occurring. This leads to ongoing impactful feedback that supports and celebrates process versus a focus solely on the outcomes.

It is important to remember that observation is a skill to be developed and practiced. "Systematic observation requires more than just being present and looking around" (Patton, 2015, p. 11). To collect evidence that will result in high-quality feedback, observers need to know what evidence is and what kinds of evidence are relevant and necessary. "The ideal observation captures context, the unfolding of events over time, and critical interactions, and it includes talking with those involved in the activity" (Patton, 2015, p. 27).

Bias in Observation

One consistent challenge for observers is related to a natural inclination toward subjectivity. Instructional leaders strive to engage in evaluation and coaching practices that are transparent, fair, and objective. However, as human beings, this is not always easily accomplished. We bring preconceived notions, judgments, and opinions before and during an observation that can impact the quality and overall objectivity of our evidence collection. Though Chapter 6 delves into objectivity in leaders' evidence review and feedback practices, in this chapter we focus on the notions or judgments we might bring into a classroom or form while we are *observing* a lesson.

Stop and Think: How is it possible for two evaluators to observe the same lesson and leave the classroom with different evidence, conclusions, and/or ratings?

You may have considered that a factor is related to the observers' common understanding of the framework or particular instructional practices (from Chapter 2), but one additional important reason is related to observer bias.

Perhaps you've been on the receiving end of varying statements from student witnesses of the same incident—a missing cell phone or favorite pen, horseplay or bullying on the playground, or an interaction on the bus. Or maybe you have heard stories of witness accounts of a single car accident or traumatic event that were vastly different. Humans who are taking in sights and sounds during events process the information with emotion and/or through life experiences. If we consider Piaget's cognitive theory (1972), we recognize that we vary in the way we organize knowledge and information, and we possess individual mental pictures of the world; therefore, it makes sense that two observers experience an event in different ways. The observers are basically drawing from memories and notions and applying those to the current situation. We assimilate the new information into existing schemas or use existing schemas to organize new information. But how can we minimize this in our work as instructional leaders?

The human brain is a high-functioning computer taking in large quantities of data at incredible rates of speed, working to ensure the processing of the data is efficient. This can result in shortcuts, preferences, or tendencies in our thinking.

Though a complex concept, we can arrive at the conclusion that cognitive bias is a tendency, shortcut, or limitation of our brain that is connected to memories, emotions, or attention that serve to help us address four key functions in our lives:

- **To filter too much information:** We will only notice repetition and confirmation.

- **To make meaning:** We will fill in the gaps and look for patterns using current information.

- **To think and act quickly:** We will assume we are right in our assessments.

- **To store what's needed:** We will generalize. (Benson, 2016)

We can often jump to quick judgments or decisions that result in inaccurate assessments of instructional effectiveness. This can occur before an observer enters a classroom or can be prompted by any number of factors in the moment. "Just about anything an evaluator sees or hears in a classroom might trigger a favorable or unfavorable impression. That includes the styles of speech, dress, and backgrounds of teachers and students" (MET Project 2015, p. 45). Observers will sometimes make sweeping assumptions and forget that "one good element does not equal a good lesson and one bad element does not equal a bad lesson" (Archer et al., 2016. p. 321).

Common Biases

Though there are hundreds of biases that exist, in this chapter you will explore four that will directly impact your ability to observe objectively. The first two are sometimes based on preconceived judgments of personalities or known behaviors outside of the classroom *or* can be triggered based on something we see or hear during the observation.

1. The ***Halo Effect*** is the tendency to make assumptions based on a positive action or characteristic, applying it to everything else the person does.

2. The ***Horn Effect*** can be viewed as the direct opposite—one negative action or characteristic can be applied to everything else.

Before a lesson

Consider how your experiences with teachers throughout a year or over several years can cloud your ability to remain objective before you even arrive to observe a lesson. How do you feel about the teachers who do the following:

- Volunteer for everything, are always the last working in the building each night, bring cupcakes to all faculty meetings, or who will try any new strategy suggested?

- Consistently talk to tablemates during your faculty meetings or are answering emails instead of discussing new strategies, do not honor deadlines, or refuse to make changes in the classroom based on your coaching, thinking everything is just a phase or trend?

We are sure you can picture someone who fits each description and that you immediately felt an emotional or sensory response.

During a lesson

A classroom layout also can immediately cause you to jump to conclusions about a teacher's instructional abilities. Think of how you feel when you see the following:

- The messy or disorganized room: Shelves are spilling over in disarray; papers, trash and broken pencils are on the floor; and/or sloppy anchor charts are posted.

- The appealing room: Lights are dimmed and there are comfortable seating options, classical music is playing softly, attractive charts and motivational posters are hung, and/or shelves and supplies are orderly and labeled.

If you make it past the initial judgments, once the lesson gets started you may experience situations such as this:

- As Ms. C. monitors and provides feedback while students work, Ms. C independently takes pencils out of students' hands and erases their work in their notebooks. This is counterintuitive to what you believe about building student efficacy. It clouds the rest of your observation because you are frustrated by this practice and are seeing the immediate negative reactions on students' faces, thus forgetting to write things down on your pad. (Horn Effect)

Though we have instructional preferences and an understanding of research-based strategies, it is important to remain focused and collect evidence of student mindset and understanding (or misunderstanding) to clearly show the teacher how her actions are impacting their independence and ability to construct new learning.

- After months of coaching, Mr. T. finally began his prealgebra lesson with differentiated work instead of 20 minutes of whole-group home-work review. You are so thrilled that it doesn't matter if the differen-tiation is appropriate or even advancing learning—he made a change! (Halo Effect)

In Chapter 5, we will talk about how critical it is to recognize teacher risk-taking and baby steps in improving practice, but leaders must also remain objective to collect evidence for feedback that supports the question "What's next?"

Additional Types of Bias

3. Halo and Horn Effects are similar to another tendency known as **_Selective Attention_**. Often, we observe lessons with a particular focus or intent, resulting in missed evidence and inaccurate assess-ments. For example, you were so focused on the prealgebra teacher *not* reviewing homework for 20 minutes that you did not collect evidence as to the effectiveness of what he was doing in its place.

4. Closely related to Selective Attention is another common observer tendency known as **_Confirmation Bias_**. "A judgment made during an observation may color how an observer views the rest of the lesson, so that the only other evidence that's noted is that which confirms the judgment" (MET, 2015, p. 40). This results in evidence collection that confirms what you think or expect, possi-bly ignoring evidence that supports the contrary. Often, once you

have made the initial judgment, because you continually seek only support for that, it is difficult to see alternate perspectives or reality. Consider the Horn Effect example of the teacher erasing students' work. You might have only collected evidence of how she was negatively impacting student self-esteem during that lesson or return for later observations looking to confirm that she does not support students and is callous—when, in fact, she cares greatly for them and just needs coaching in feedback strategies.

Stop and Think: Think about your recent classroom observations. What biases did you bring into the work and why?

Strategies to Avoid Bias

Most likely, you could name at least one situation where bias clouded your ability to observe objectively. That's okay! Remember, we are all human. Let's now discuss three strategies for objective observation.

Strategy 7: Develop an awareness

As the human brain is wired to work efficiently, we need to be aware of when we are looking for patterns, taking shortcuts, or tending toward subjective reasoning or thinking. Before you step into a room for an observation, clear your head and remember you are there to support every teacher through accurate and fair evidence collection. When you become aware of your biases, you can begin to develop your own strategies to overcome them. A failure to recognize your own bias is actually a bias.

Strategy 8: Observe with a wide lens

Don't get fixated on one action, student, or aspect of instruction. Though you may be revisiting a classroom because the teacher is trying out a new strategy or tool, it is still important to consider how that one particular practice fits into the context of what we consider to be the "big picture" (from Chapter 2). Remember, this provides a framework for your evidence collection, development of feedback, and conversations with teachers. Your attention during a lesson should always remain broad, with the four elements of instructional practice shown in Table 3.3 always in mind. Ideally, your evidence collection allows you to return to your desk able to answer the related critical questions, even after a 10-minute visit.

TABLE 3.3	THE BIG PICTURE FOR EVIDENCE COLLECTION
Key area	**What you are collecting**
Environment	How are students set up for success in the face of challenge?
	How do students support and interact with each other?
Purpose	What do students need to know or know how to do?
	How is it relevant to them? What do students understand about the purpose and the context?
	Are they making connections to prior learning and personal context?
Process	What are the learning pathways for students?
	How is the teacher sharing responsibility?
	How is the teacher building 21st century skills using content, strategies, questions, and tasks?
	In what stage of learning is each student?
	At what level are students thinking and working?
Understanding	What do students understand at this point in the lesson?
	How successful are they in the given tasks?
	How are they demonstrating understanding?
	How does the teacher monitor and adjust based on their understanding?

You can visit **resources.corwin.com/feedforward** to see how one leader uses this big picture frame as an evidence-collection template and tool

Strategy 9: Collect a balance of evidence with purpose

Focus your energy during an observation on the intentional collection of quantitative and qualitative evidence versus the recording of sporadic notes, writing of judgments, or scripting of the entire lesson word for word. We know many leaders have been trained to script every word. Yet the 2015 MET Project study reminds us that this evidence collection method is

> counterproductive. When all your attention is consumed by capturing every word, nothing is left to notice what people are doing. Untrained observers may [also] think evidence is whatever they write down during a lesson. It's not. Evidence is objective description of something observed. It makes no suggestion of quality. "Lesson objective clearly explained" is not evidence. (pp. 39, 41)

Now that you have reviewed Strategies 7 to 9 related to bias, let's shift our thinking toward *what to collect,* specifically during an observation and what we mean by a "balance of evidence" in RVL 1.B.

Stop and Think: What data do you usually capture, write down, or type during an observation? Why?

Identifying Types of Data

Observers often feel overwhelmed entering a classroom for an observation or during the middle of a lesson because of the pace and multitude of questions and answers, movements, and tasks occurring. Highly effective rooms are often moving at high speeds, with students working on different tasks in different spaces using different tools. It is important to remember a few suggestions that will lessen your feeling of concern about missing something:

- Understand the types of data you can and need to collect.

- Practice new strategies consistently and repeatedly.

- Refine and personalize evidence-collection strategies.

- Observe and debrief lessons with colleagues both informally and through your professional learning.

Quantitative and Qualitative Data

To successfully provide impactful feedback, it is critical for you to understand the types of evidence you should be collecting during an observation: quantitative and qualitative data.

Quantitative Data

Quantitative data comprise any evidence, such as tallies, number counts, or time stamps, that serves to help the observer calculate the frequency of something occurring. It is important to recognize that some quantifiable elements of instruction are immediately visible, allowing you to count *during an observation* (such as hands raised). While you may be tallying behaviors or determining duration of tasks during the lesson, ideally you will count those *after the observation* (such as number of questions asked).

The use of quantitative data can provide more than just a chronological series of events or list of numbers; it can play a part in the analysis of length or impact. In an example in the opening of this chapter, you might have noticed that the observer captured times when he swept the room looking at student behaviors and included numbers as percentages in the feedback statement. Perhaps this is something that you already do.

```
10:45 - 100% of students participate in turn-and-talk
```

This type of data collection is a good start and lays the foundation for the support of a claim about engagement, helping the teacher see if engagement was sustained throughout the observation and for how many students. Additional quantitative data can be provided as to how many pairs were thinking and talking at high levels, to extend a teacher's understanding beyond student participation:

```
Half of the partnerships were only providing one- to two-word
answers to the teacher's prompt.
```

Qualitative Data

Qualitative data include evidence such as quotes from the teacher or students, descriptive analysis of situations, materials, student work outcomes, or any evidence that "characterizes" activities or outcomes.

Details of what was seen and said not only increase objectivity but provide clear examples for a teacher to see what is happening during instruction. This type of data can be added to the previous example to further support a claim about levels of student discourse and engagement and to clearly show the teacher the impact of his or her actions, which will promote growth.

```
10:45 - 100% of students participate in turn-and-talk
```

Though students know to take turns and listen to one another, the discussion prompt, "turn and talk to a partner and tell them which of the two answers you chose," led to one-word answers based on the design of the question.

Notice these additional data open the door to talk about the cognitive demand of questions and the possible use of sentence stems to support students as they increase their depth of thinking and responses.

Understanding What to Collect

Now that you have organized your thinking about evidence into two categories, let's further explore what it is you can and should be collecting during a lesson. We start with an overview of possible quantitative and qualitative evidence available to you during an observation (see Table 3.4).

TABLE 3.4   TYPES OF EVIDENCE

Evidence Category	Quantitative	Qualitative
Student Actions	• # of boys/girls • # of hands raised • # of voices heard • # getting started/not getting started • # not finished/finished early • # waiting for a teacher (hand up, in line at a desk) • # of minutes students wait for the teacher • # of items/answers correct • # moving or not moving toward mastery	• Quotes of conversations with partners or within groups • Quotes of questions to teacher/each other • Quotes of responses to questions • Quotes of responses to observer questions • Quotes from students' ongoing work • Description of behaviors (e.g., compliant, starting work, how they transitioned, all engaged in group work) • Description of students' understanding/misunderstanding, success/lack of success
Teacher Actions	• # of students called on • # of times teacher calls on individual students • # of students helped, monitored, or provided feedback • # of times something is stated (objective, particular quote) • # of questions asked, # of types of questions asked • time stamps of start of new tasks, directions, shifts, mid-lesson teaching points (When did they occur?)	• Introduction/quotes to learning expectations, context, criteria, methods to self-assess • Directions given • Feedback statements/quotes/questions to students • Description/quotes of a shift or mid-lesson teaching point • Description of how students were grouped • Description of learning tasks, worksheets, activities • Description of methods of differentiation/personalization
Environment	• # of total students • # of groups, partnerships • # of minutes for a transition, clean up, setup, etc.	• Description of seating arrangement, supplies/resources, organization • Anchor, behavior, or organizer charts

Consider also relevant data outside of the classroom before or after an observation. Think about any important information you could possibly count/quantify or discover/describe that might be helpful. Some examples can be

TABLE 3.5	ADDITIONAL TYPES OF DATA
Quantitative Data	**Qualitative Data**
• # of English language learners • # of students with individualized education plans • # absent/# who are consistently absent • Length of class period • # of students not reading at level • # gifted	• Lesson plan • Context/location in the unit/curriculum • Teacher's guide descriptions • Language learners' acquisition levels • Needs/goals of students with individualized education plans or absent • Most recent assessment data/reading levels

found in Table 3.5 above. This additional data can only serve to deepen your analysis of how teachers are meeting students' needs.

It is important to note that the absence of evidence is evidence as well. Patton (2015) reminded us, "It can be important to note that something did not occur when the observer's basic knowledge of and experience suggests that the absence is noteworthy" (p. 295). For example, a lack of behavior issues could be a positive outcome, whereas a lack of differentiation, assessment, or a clear learning objective may point to an ineffective outcome. You may find you must record that something *has not occurred* or is missing to develop an accurate claim about practice or select the appropriate performance level.

> **Stop and Think:** Look through your instructional framework. When would it be necessary for you to note the absence of something during a lesson?

Pathways to Identifying Types of Data to Collect

Once you have an understanding of these basics of evidence collection, it is important to identify specific, critical evidence that is aligned to expected performance and outcomes, creating more purposeful and impactful feedback. We can use different pathways to accomplish this goal:

1. From the rubric language

2. As suggested by a program or curriculum

3. As it relates to targeted teacher instructional skills/student outcomes

As we work with administrators to develop a deeper understanding of the types of data, we typically have them begin with their rubric as we described in Chapter 2 (e.g., determine specific quantitative and qualitative data required of a specific attribute or indicator). We then add the lens of programs or instructional models in place in your region, district, or within your school. This ensures that teachers are supported within the context of the instructional models being deployed (e.g., Readers/Writers and/or Math Workshop). For example, what type of evidence might you collect during a minilesson that would be different from independent writing time? Beyond this and over time, and as leaders demonstrate increasing capacity and depth of understanding of the observed needs, we can then begin to support a deeper dive into identifying evidence types that relate directly to teacher, school, or district goals. For example, your district focus is assessment, so you would determine what evidence you need to collect on current use or lack of use, needs, and effectiveness of the use of assessments in classrooms. You can access detailed information on each of these pathways at **resources.corwin.com/feedforward**.

Regardless of the pathway you choose, your evidence collection should result in the following:

- A focus on the teaching *and* learning
- Coherence across district or system and personal goals and previous coaching
- Connections to your framework
- A big picture understanding of the lesson

Evidence Collection: The Basics

You may have noticed in the evidence tables in this chapter that you found examples you had never thought of collecting or just do not know how to collect. Through our thousands of classroom visits, we've come to recognize there are several general strategies for leaders of any grade level or content area to ensure they can collect that evidence. Remember, however, it is important as you move through this next section to consider how you can personalize and adapt the strategies and steps to your own needs.

Here are a few suggestions:

1. Don't fear talking to students while they are working. Choose your moments to move or engage with students at times when the teacher is not leading instruction or giving directions, or wait until you see students flipping a page or finishing a sentence. This does not have to be disruptive.

2. Talk to your teachers about observations. They are often intimidated or unhappy about your movement in their classrooms and your interaction with their students. For many who have been teaching over five years, there is a significant change in an observer's behaviors. Be transparent and share with them how your actions and interactions with students represent a shift from inspection to support for growth. They should, in turn, let students know visitors may stop and chat, listen, or read over their shoulders, and why.

Strategy 10: Place yourself where the learning is occurring

This strategy probably seems fairly obvious, and you are thinking, "Well, of course, I am where the learning is happening." However, we have seen time and time again when leaders are not in the same location as the actual learning, as sometimes it is spread out across a room, multiple rooms, or a building—resulting in missed important evidence. Even if you are observing a Socratic Circle, you will want to look over the speakers' shoulders to see what they are using for notes and what the peer circle and/or teacher is filling out for feedback to the participants. You are not where the learning is occurring if you are too far away to collect detailed evidence (e.g., seated in the back) while students are

- sitting on the carpet up front and engaging in turn-and-talks,

- working in groups or pairs all across the classroom,

- watching a teacher demonstrate a science experiment in the corner, or

- gathered around a teacher after directions to ask questions or at her desk for help.

Or consider when learning is in an authentic environment outside of the main classroom and students are outside taking care of animals, building a garden fence, learning to drive a tractor, examining an ecosystem, working in a darkroom, or traveling the school filming a video (all of which we have observed!).

Did you follow them?

Don't forget to keep your head up and stop scripting sometimes to determine who is where, what can be seen and heard, and where you need to be.

Strategy 11: Do what it takes to collect evidence

Very often, learning is occurring in multiple places within a single space. Therefore, we recommend that you do your best to stay mobile whenever possible. For example, if you cannot hear

teacher questions, student responses, student-to-student conversations, teacher feedback, teacher-to-student writing conferences, or small-group instruction—move! Remember, if you took our suggestion for making your work transparent to your teachers, they will know why you are close at hand.

If you cannot see

student work on screens, whiteboards, or desks; all partners or groups; mouths (think choral responses); thumbs up; facial expressions; posted objectives; or anchor charts—move!

Second, just because you have changed location doesn't mean you can easily record all that you are seeing or hearing. Think about your tools for efficiency.

1. We have found using both a laptop and a notepad to be the most effective in that the combination will allow you to quickly jump into hard-to-reach spots without trying to juggle a laptop, such as leaning in on turn-and-talks to capture quotes, navigating rows of high schoolers to look at student work, or climbing under tables with kindergarteners to listen to them read.

2. Add a phone for taking pictures, and you will be fully equipped. Stop trying to script everything and make technology work in your favor by taking pictures of student work, PowerPoint slides, posted charts, or objectives.

3. Ask students to share Google docs with you.

4. Unless you are a trained court reporter, capturing direct quotes and many details can be very challenging, so determine how you can use shorthand or abbreviations, such as T/S (teacher/student), TNT (turn-and-talk), or INC (incorrect response). Set locations in your notes for certain consistent evidence you need, like time stamps down the left side or an objective at the very top. When these spaces are blank, you will remember to collect that evidence.

5. Sketch a classroom layout or seating, or tally events, actions, or responses. This is so important that we created a strategy just for this suggestion: Strategy 13.

Strategy 12: Be comprehensive in your collection of evidence

We are not going to dictate how much evidence you should collect or how many quotes you should use in your feedback as examples, but remember that the end goal is to ensure teachers understand how and why you are making a claim about practice, how they are impacting their students, and how they can improve. Therefore, there are two key points to remember:

1. Your evidence collection should allow you to develop feedback about the teaching and learning of *most or nearly all students,* not just a few. Collecting comprehensive evidence is a considerable challenge for new observers or those new to moving around a room during an observation. Set goals for yourself, as this takes time to master. Can you visit 25 percent of the students in the room on your first week? Can you visit 50 percent in the next week?

2. Think about what you noticed in the key levers of the indicators on your rubric that require you to sweep the room to collect comprehensive evidence to accurately select a performance level. Based on the difference between ratings, notice in the indicator language in Figure 3.2 what an observer must be able to capture. (This is directly tied to our previous suggestion to align evidence collection to rubric language.)

FIGURE 3.2: PERFORMANCE LEVELS FOR COLLECTING EVIDENCE

Unsatisfactory	Progressing	Proficient	Exemplary
Less than **half** of the students can articulate: What they are learning, why it is important, or what mastery looks like	Focuses students at the beginning and throughout the lesson, so **most** of the students can articulate: What they are learning But, the teacher does not effectively convey the objective so half of the students cannot articulate: Why it is important or What mastery looks like	Focuses students at the beginning and throughout the lesson, by clearly stating and explaining to students: What they are learning Why it is important What mastery looks like, How to connect it to prior knowledge and their own lives Most students can demonstrate through their actions or comments that they understand each of the above.	Focuses students at the beginning and throughout the lesson so that **all or nearly all** students can clearly explain . . .

Source: Dallas Independent School District (2014)

Comprehensive evidence collection requires the use of Strategies 12 and 13 and a great deal of practice. Without this, leaders are unable to make accurate determinations of effectiveness, and coaching points will have limited impact on instruction for most students.

Strategy 13: Maximize the use of your notepad or tablet

Regardless of the tool you use, it is helpful to have the capability to tally, sketch, diagram, chart, or map what you are seeing and hearing, as these provide you with efficient means for capturing comprehensive evidence. There are countless ways an observer can utilize this strategy, and there are no right or wrong ways to use visuals for evidence collection. It is important to try these out, review the usefulness for your needs, refine, and retry.

To get you started, we provide a few examples of how to collect evidence in this section. Let's look at an example of tallying evidence using information from the sixth-grade math lesson you encountered in Chapter 2, where students had not finished Do Nows before the teacher went on.

Nearly half (8/20) of the students incorrectly completed the Do Now.

Five were not finished when the teacher put the answers on the board (six minutes of work time).

Notice how easily the observer can collect the necessary evidence in Figure 3.3.

FIGURE 3.3: EVIDENCE-COLLECTION METHOD 1

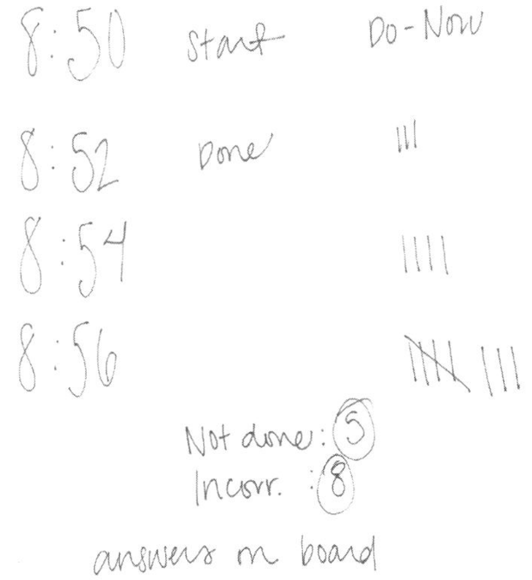

Another way to capture or visualize this same data could be through a map (see Figure 3.4), where a ✓ shows who has finished the Do Now correctly and a "O" represents those who have not finished.

Any amount of detail can be added to a map like the one below, such as the following:

- Whether the teacher stopped and checked on the student, perhaps adding a T next to the seat.

- Boys/girls or other populations or student need information at individual seats. If you know your students, you can add names as needed.

- Student answers/quick note of misunderstanding next to the seats of those who had incorrect answers.

FIGURE 3.4: EVIDENCE-COLLECTION METHOD 2

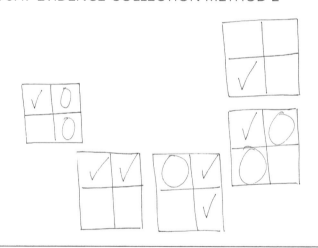

Though these types of visuals are very useful, an observer might want to remember which students have not finished and what the incorrect answers were to better analyze scaffolding and differentiation. One of our assistant principals in training shared that she now prints the class roster and uses it for notetaking during an observation.

Let's look at a more complex example of a map with additional detail from a fourth-grade social studies lesson to see what evidence a drawing can hold for you (see Figure 3.5). The students worked in pairs to locate key facts to summarize a piece of informational text by reading together and highlighting important information.

FIGURE 3.5: EVIDENCE-COLLECTION METHOD 3

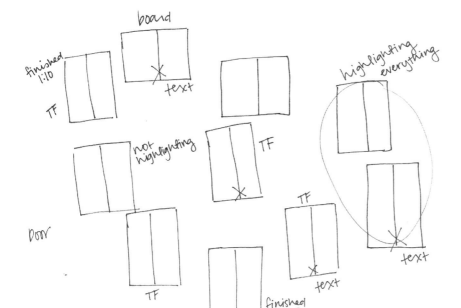

Notice the observer:

1. Added landmarks for bearing, such as the board, door, and a large carpet.

2. Used X to notate pairs who were unsuccessful.

3. Notated "text" when the level of the text was the issue. Off to the side, not visible here, the observer noted when one pair miscued 10 words in the first two paragraphs.

4. Noted "TF" for where the teacher visited and provided feedback.

5. Added additional qualitative data about behaviors observed, like the use of the highlighter, and quantitative data when students began finishing ahead of the others.

Observers can also add to this map evidence like the following:

- Quotes from students about the task, strategy, and content.

- Quotes from T-S next to the TF notation.

- How long those early finishers sat without direction, feedback, or another task.

- How long the teacher remained at each partnership she visited.

Notice how you can use a map to quickly count important elements, such as the following:

- How many partnerships struggled because of the level of the text (3).

- How many partnerships the teacher supported (4).

- How many needed support but failed to receive it (1).

- How many finished early (2).

Some of our leaders in training try out and find success with tools that allow for drawing and typing simultaneously, such as the Notability app or a tablet.

In all of the samples shared here, you might have noticed close attention was paid to what students were doing and understanding. Though teacher actions, such as when the teacher started and ended a Do Now and who/how many she supported with feedback, are included on the drawings, much of what can be captured includes evidence of student engagement and learning.

Stop and Think: Look back at the mapping examples and explanations for a moment. What type of feedback about teaching and learning could you provide a teacher using the evidence collected? How do the methods allow you to capture student evidence of engagement and learning efficiently?

Evidence Collection: Student Engagement and Learning

When we talk about identifying data to be collected, regardless of the type, the evidence should allow the observer to determine levels of student understanding and engagement, ensuring feedback focuses on the impact of the teacher on the learners.

Regardless of the amount of time you spend in an observation, and although you are merely taking a snapshot of instruction, you will be able to determine and convey an overall effectiveness of the instruction during that time because of the comprehensive evidence collected directly from students. Even within 10 minutes, a teacher should influence, impact, or affect learners in some way. Therefore, it is important to determine specifically what is happening and how. "Leaders can learn more about what students are learning and how well they are learning it when they look for what the students are actually doing to learn during the lesson . . . 'sitting in the student's seat' or 'taking the students'-eye view'" (Moss & Brookhart, 2015, p. 22).

Defining Engagement and Learning

During a lesson, you might walk over to students and see them typing on a Google Doc and think, "They're obviously engaged and learning." But how do you know this? What is the evidence that tells you this? To answer these questions and to collect appropriate data, an instructional leader must have a clear understanding of several key principles of instruction:

- How students construct an understanding of new learning

- The connection between engagement and learning

- The difference between engaged, on-task, or compliant

- Levels of engagement

- Methods and strategies that serve to engage students

Ideally, we recommend that you work with your leadership team and your teaching staff to build a common understanding of these principles of learning and engagement through the strategies recommended in Chapter 2.

To effectively shift the focus of feedback to teaching *and* learning, leaders need to be able to recognize what it, in fact, looks like when students are or are not engaged or successful in a learning task and to then collect specific evidence to support how the teacher is causing these observed results. You will encounter these ideas further in Chapter 4 as you build your capacity to analyze the evidence collected, and again in Chapter 5, as you will need to tap into your understanding of effective practices to determine a teacher's areas of strength and growth and necessary next steps.

The concept of how humans learn is a vastly complex topic. However, to provide you with jumping-off points, in this chapter we briefly dip into theory and definitions for your development of specific look-fors and related evidence-collection strategies.

> **Stop and Think:** What is your (and your teachers') understanding or definition of learning? How do you know if students are learning?

How Students Learn

Theory: If you are reading this book, you have probably taken at least one course in foundations of education or psychology and can easily recall names of pioneers in the field. Those early theories form the backbone of your work as an instructional leader and can help you recognize essential ingredients for learning. Table 3.6 offers a quick snapshot of how you might use what you know about learning theories to determine evidence that can be collected.

TABLE 3.6   EVIDENCE BASED ON LEARNING THEORY

Theory	Main Points	Potential Evidence (Effective)	Potential Evidence (Ineffective)
Social Constructivism (Dewey, Vygotsky)	Learner can construct new learning with others. Learner is working within his/her ZPD.*	Ss helping each other Groups collaborating Audible aha moments Erasing and correcting T small group or feedback to Ss	Heads down Partners/groups not helping/not able to help member
Cognitive Constructivism (Piaget)	Learner is doing the work inside his/her head to make connections.	T chunking the lesson or content, introduces lesson within broader context	Ss see task as isolated Ss not making connections Ss missing prior/essential skills
Behaviorism (Skinner)	Learner is a blank page.	Ss have repeated opportunity to apply T praise T/Ss using mnemonics	Full lesson is drill/rote tasks T/S reliance on tokens/rewards

*ZPD = zone of proximal development

Stages of Learning

Remember in Chapter 1 we discussed the quality of your time spent in classrooms? Even if you have small chunks of time to observe instruction, we want to help you maximize every opportunity. During busy days, you may not always arrive for the beginning of a lesson or remain until the end. Therefore, you may be dropping into the middle of students' learning progressions, so it is important to understand what is happening when you

HOW CAN YOU COLLECT EVIDENCE IN THE CLASSROOM TO IMPROVE FEEDBACK?

83

arrive. To make an accurate assessment of teacher effectiveness, you need to determine how the teacher and student actions/behaviors observed and evidence collected at that moment coincide with or reveal particular stages of learning. It is important to remember that students grappling or engaged in a good struggle is part of the learning process and does not necessarily point to ineffective instruction or inadequate scaffolding. Remember to limit your judgments and immediate conclusions until you have analyzed the evidence (further explored in Chapter 4).

Another method an observer can use involves the examination of the stages students move through to learn a new concept or skill. In Table 3.7, we provide an example of possible look-fors or behaviors during the different stages using a breakdown, such as the four advancing stages of learning (Haring, Lovitt, Eaton, & Hansen, 1978).

TABLE 3.7 EVIDENCE BASED ON LEARNING STAGES

Stages	Potential Teacher Actions	Potential Student Behaviors
Acquisition	modeling, thinking aloud	engaged and listening; observing the use of a new strategy or skill; examining exemplars, turn-and-talks
Fluency	"we do" task, drills	trying out a new strategy w/ teacher help; repeatedly practicing; showing they understand steps or directions, but may grapple or make mistakes, turn-and-talks
Generalization	"you do" or "you do together" tasks	independent or partner work using the strategy or practicing the skill, turn-and-talks
Adaptation	facilitating and monitoring a real-world application	engaged in group work to create or problem solve using the strategy in a new way; moving into automatic use, turn-and-talks

Stop and Think: Using what you understand so far in this chapter, what specific quantitative and qualitative evidence could you collect during each stage of learning? Does your rubric include an indicator or attribute related to instructional progression, scaffolding, or the sequence of a lesson (not just planning but execution) or an indicator measuring student movement toward a learning objective?

Some "Proficient" description examples that highlight progression of learning include the following:

"Use teaching strategies based on knowledge of students' physical, social and intellectual development and characteristics to improve student learning" (NSW Education Standards Authority, 2018).

"Most of the lesson components are organized and delivered to move students toward mastery of the objective" (Newark Public Schools, 2015).

Table 3.8 shows possible evidence you could collect when observing students during the acquisition stage and moving into the fluency stage. Notice if the evidence aligns to your related indicator(s):

TABLE 3.8   EVIDENCE DURING A LEARNING STAGE

Quantitative Evidence	Qualitative Evidence
# of minutes of the introduction # of Ss participating in assessment/# thumbs up/thumbs down* # Ss sharing brainstorm with partner before beginning work # of Ss' questions after directions	Description of the chunks of the introduction (e.g., connection to prior learning, statement of purpose, modeling) T quote of the prompt for thumbs up Ss' quotes of brainstorms T quotes for directions for group-work task Ss' quotes of questions before beginning

*Though the assessment evidence may tip into a different indicator, it provides evidence of student understanding before they begin the next task and is part of a lesson progression.

The Role of Engagement

Just because there is a logical progression of the lesson components, it is not an absolute guarantee that all students are moving through the learning stages toward application, transfer, and deep understanding. A key factor in their success is their level of engagement, as we know students who are not engaged at high levels will not readily advance in learning (Marzano, Pickering, & Heflebower, 2011). "Engagement for its own sake is just 'fun.' To enhance learning, students must be engaged in a cognitive verb" (Antonetti & Garver, 2015, p. 80).

Stop and Think: What is your (and your teachers') understanding or definition of engagement? Where is it addressed in your framework? Did you explore this as you moved through the strategies of Chapter 2?

For some, "engaged" is synonymous with "on-task." But are they really the same? Consider for a moment how students might exhibit very different example behaviors of the two, thus producing very different evidence if you are considering "engaged" to be something requiring higher intellectual demand—more than just following directions or complying with teacher requests. Notice how engagement is integrated in the sample component language in Figure 3.6.

FIGURE 3.6: ENGAGEMENT COMPONENT DESCRIPTION

Proficient

This technique results in active intellectual engagement by most students with important and challenging content and with teacher scaffolding to support that engagement . . . The lesson has a clearly defined structure, and the pacing of the lesson is appropriate, providing most students the time needed to be intellectually engaged.

Source: The Danielson Group (2013)

Think about what tools, research, or resources could help you better determine what engagement looks like in relation to your indicators, to better ascertain related available evidence during a lesson. There are a variety of tools to assist you in this work, but let's explore three possible resources. Though they overlap in some regard, together they help provide a comprehensive definition of engagement:

1. A selected taxonomy, like Bloom's or Webb's Depth of Knowledge

2. Phil Schlechty's five levels of engagement (2002)

   o Engagement (high attention and high commitment)

   o Strategic compliance (high attention and low commitment)

   o Ritual compliance (low attention and low commitment)

   o Retreatism (no attention and no commitment)

   o Rebellion (diverted attention and no commitment)

3. A threefold perspective of engagement:

   o Behavioral (your traditional on-task or participation)

   o Emotional (student ownership, dispositions, and connections)

   o Cognitive (rigor and complexity; Davis, Summers, & Miller, 2012)

Notice in Table 3.9 how potential evidence can be collected and aligned to the resource and framework language related to students' levels of engagement.

TABLE 3.9	EVIDENCE OF ENGAGEMENT		
Rubric Language (CSDE, 2014)	**Resource**	**Potential Quantitative Evidence**	**Potential Qualitative Evidence**
"critical thinking"	Taxonomy levels	# of questions asked/# of certain level questions asked # of questions or tasks requiring higher order thinking	Scripted quotes of T questions Scripted quotes of Ss' answers Description of learning task/Copy of Ss' work
"meaningful learning"	Schlechty's five levels	# of Ss engaged in critical thinking/# participating # of Ss who can make connections or see context to task/lesson	Scripted quotes of T introduction and connections/context Scripted quotes of Ss responses to O questions about connections
"purposeful discourse," "students take the lead"	Three types of engagement	# behavior issues # participating/risk-taking # talking in pairs/groups # asking questions	Description of T sharing ownership with Ss Description of Ss choices available Quotes of T promoting positive dispositions Quotes of Ss-created questions

Collecting Evidence From Students

There are various methods you can utilize to collect evidence from students of their understanding and engagement regardless of grade level or content area. We have organized what we've found to be the most effective methods into three core strategies that you can personalize.

Strategy 14: Listen to teaching and learning

Be attentive at all times not just for what the teacher is saying or not saying but what students are saying or not saying as well. Students' conversations, responses, and questions provide some of the richest evidence available during a lesson.

Strategy 15: View learning in action

Look over shoulders, read what students are reading or writing, look everywhere, and watch behaviors, body language, and actions carefully as you move around the room.

Strategy 16: Interact with learners

Engage with students about their learning and tasks. Ask questions and have a conversation that makes their thinking apparent to you.

TABLE 3.10 EVIDENCE COLLECTION METHODS

Strategies	To what?	When?	How?
Strategy 14: Listen	Ss' conversations	Turn-and-talks, group work, helping each other, Socratic-type discussion	Script what they are saying
	Ss' responses and questions to each other and/or T	After T asks questions After T sends them off to work independently	Script T questions <u>and</u> Ss answers Script Ss' comments and questions to each other or to T
	Ss' reading or sharing with group	Anytime it is occurring	Record anecdotal info/Ss quotes and Ss name or seat location
Strategy 15: View	Basic behaviors, body language, following directions	During routines and transitions During T-led During shared instruction	Describe Ss actions related to T directions Watch who raises hands or answers and count
	Level of completion, depth and quality of Ss work	At any point during an observation (e.g., during a Google Doc entry, while products are being designed like a PowerPoint presentation or while they are writing answers to questions)	Take a photo, copy down student answers
	T-assigned/ designed work	At any point during an observation (e.g., Do Now, worksheet requirements, lab analysis questions)	Take a photo, copy down questions or directions
Strategy 16: Interact	Ask questions	At any point when you will not be disruptive (e.g., transitions, independent work time)	Script your questions and their answers, track who you talk to
	Ask to see previous work, notes, or current resources	At any point when you will not be disruptive (e.g., independent or group work time)	Describe what they show you
	Ask the Ss to read their text, notes, vocab, worksheet, directions aloud	At any point when you will not be disruptive	Record anecdotal info/Ss quotes and Ss name or seat location

"Talking to students has made all the difference . . . . As we make the shift from teaching to learning, what could be more appropriate than looking at the classroom life and work through the eyes of a student?" (Antonetti & Garver, 2015, pp. 11, 16).

Table 3.10 on the previous page provides examples of methods associated with each strategy that you can use and make your own.

Interacting With Students

Asking students questions is one of the most powerful observation tools available to you, but this takes time for you to refine. Some questions you ask will not result in the evidence you seek or students will just be anxious or excited interacting with you. Just as when we were teaching, some questions can be preplanned and others will need to be crafted once you enter the classroom and the lesson evolves. In addition, you will need to determine what is appropriate for the grade level you observe. To get started, use your framework to help guide your questioning to elicit necessary evidence for feedback about the learning and thinking occurring. Look through your rubric and locate an indicator or attribute related to criteria or students' understanding of what mastery looks like. Earlier in the chapter, you came across this example from the Dallas Independent School District (2014) in the "Proficient" description:

> "Focuses students at the beginning and throughout the lesson, by clearly stating and explaining to students: What they are learning, why it is important, what mastery looks like, how to connect it to prior knowledge and their own lives. Most students can demonstrate through their actions or comments that they understand each of the above."

Think about what you could ask students to determine this. Here are some examples:

- What does mastery of today's learning objective look like? How do you know when you reach it?

- How are you using this [rubric/checklist/example] to help you in your work?

- What do you need to do to achieve level 4 on the writing rubric? What level are you working toward and why?

If we had observed only without interacting, we might have seen the tool on their desks but would have never understood how they were using it to self-assess

HOW CAN YOU COLLECT EVIDENCE IN THE CLASSROOM TO IMPROVE FEEDBACK?

89

and/or move forward—an important determination to promote teacher growth versus inspection. Remember, sometimes you only have valuable seconds to elicit critical evidence of student learning and thinking, so it is important to make each opportunity count with purposeful and targeted questioning.

Here is one last thought: Sometimes just watching students work or interact or simply listening to students talk instead of interrupting with a question is the better choice in the moment. Be discerning.

Stop and Think: If you are interacting with students during an observation, what do you tend to ask them?

With practice and refinement of your strategies, you will find you are more effective in evidence collection each time you return to a classroom.

Using a Balance of Evidence to Feed Forward

Once you have successfully collected a balance of comprehensive evidence from an observation, there are several important steps to execute:

- Organize and align your specific evidence to appropriate indicators to determine a performance level and begin to develop a claim (Chapter 2).

- Analyze the effectiveness of the lesson (Chapter 4) to make a claim about instructional practice and outcomes.

- Determine areas of strength and growth and next steps based on the evidence (Chapters 5 and 6).

When you develop feedback, the results from these steps will form the basis of the "connect" section of our Claim-Connect-Action thinking frame introduced in Chapter 2. Remember, the connect serves to support a claim, paint a picture of teacher impact on students, make clear connections to expected practice, and promote growth. You will explore explicit steps as to how to achieve these goals as you move through this book, but before we move on to Chapter 4, let's explore a nonexample to understand the importance of a clear connect section from a middle school social studies lesson. Students determined a stance and collected supporting ideas and evidence from three articles before the observer arrived. Students were preparing to engage in a debate through a structure called "Philosophical Chairs," using text evidence by discussing the value of the electoral college and whether it should be abolished. After the lesson, the observer created a claim about practice and outcomes from the "Developing" performance level of the framework in the sample attribute in Figure 3.7.

FIGURE 3.7: ATTRIBUTE LANGUAGE FOR CREATING THE CONNECT

	Below Standard	Developing	Proficient	Exemplary
Attributes				*In addition to the characteristics of* **Proficient**, *including one or more of the following:*
Strategies, tasks and questions	Includes tasks that do not lead students to construct new and meaningful learning and that focus primarily on low cognitive demand or recall of information.	Includes a combination of tasks and questions in an attempt to lead students to construct new learning, but are of low cognitive demand and/or recall of information with some opportunities for problem solving, critical thinking, and/or purposeful discourse or inquiry.	Employs differentiated strategies, tasks, and questions that cognitively engage students in constructing new and meaningful learning through appropriately integrated recall, problem solving, critical and creative thinking, purposeful discourse, and/or inquiry. At times, students take the lead and develop their own questions and problem-solving strategies.	Includes opportunities for students to work collaboratively to generate their own questions and problem-solving strategies, synthesize and communicate information.

Source: Common Core of Teaching (2014), Connecticut State Department of Education

Claim: The teacher included a combination of tasks and questions in an attempt to lead students to construct learning with some opportunities for critical thinking and purposeful discourse, but it resulted in discussions that were of low cognitive demand.

Connect: The articles were helpful resources for the topic. However, most students didn't understand enough about the electoral college, and many of their responses to each other were simple. They were rushed during the preparation before the discussion. "Philosophical Chairs" is challenging, so make sure students understand a topic before engaging in a debate with each other.

Stop and Think: Why is this sample considered a nonexample of clear and connected feedback that promotes growth? Based on what you have learned in this chapter, what is missing?

Remember, we want teachers to clearly understand how their practices represent a performance description (and if selecting a rating, how the rating is supported) and align against expected practice to answer "How am I going?" (RVL 1.A). We also want to use evidence to help a teacher process "Where am I going?" (promoting growth of RVL 1.B) as well. The information cited from the lesson should be specific so that the feedback statements are supported with detailed facts and examples. Let's look at the observer's improved feedback.

`Connect`:

[Connecting to the claim and supports the idea that the teacher did "attempt to lead students"]

`The topic of the electoral college was timely and highly relevant to the students in light of our current events. The articles were informative resources for the topic and allowed students an opportunity to synthesize information from multiple sources. Though "Philosophical Chairs" is a research-based strategy that allows students to engage in purposeful discourse, share multiple perspectives, and practice with using supporting evidence, students need time to read, take notes, process, and then organize for such a conversation.`

[Connecting to the claim and supports "low cognitive demand"]

`They shared with me that they only had seven minutes to read the articles (four students said they only read the first one) and then an additional seven minutes to prepare for the discussion. Six students had no notes taken, and when asked, five out of five could not explain to me how the electoral college worked. Once the discussion began, their statements revealed the limited depth of their understanding. Of the nine who spoke, comments included the following:`

> `S1: "I think the electoral college is bad because Trump won."`
>
> `S2: "It is bad because it makes no sense to have it."`
>
> `S3: "We have to keep it because it was in the Constitution."`
>
> `S4: "But it means our votes don't count in our small state."`

[Connecting to expected practice]

The number of resources and limited time to prepare allowed only half of the students an opportunity to critically think and understand the complexity of the popular vote versus the electoral vote to make informed decisions and support arguments about whether the college should remain.

> **Stop and Think:** How did the use of evidence improve the feedback in this sample?

Notice how there is a balance of specific quantitative and qualitative evidence that provides clear connections but also clear examples to help a teacher understand what was happening and how this compares to expected effective practice. This lays the foundation for next steps.

Final Thoughts

By now, you should be recognizing that the quality of your evidence collection directly impacts your ability to accurately make a claim and to promote growth in your feedback. Now, to determine the most impactful next steps and to continue to improve the connections between evidence you collect and the claims you make about practice, you must also learn skills and strategies that allow you to analyze the evidence collected to determine the effectiveness of the instruction. This is the direction we take in Chapter 4.

You tackled a great deal in this chapter—10 new strategies in fact! You have learned not only what to collect but how, upon which you will build quality feedback by accurately determining performance levels and creating framework-aligned statements. These observation skills included the following:

- Observe Objectively
- Identify Types of Data
- Collect Quantitative Data
- Collect Qualitative Data
- Collect Evidence of Student Engagement and Learning

Leading you to the following:

- Communicate Clear Connections

Through this chapter, you not only had the opportunity to develop your capacity with these observation skills but also to explore strategies to decrease your tendencies toward judgment or subjectivity while employing them. These strategies included the following:

- Develop an awareness.

- Observe with a wide lens.

- Purposefully collect a balance of evidence.

Once you understood what it was you were collecting, you utilized, practiced, and personalized the general evidence-collection strategies that supported you during the classroom observation:

- Place yourself where the learning is occurring.

- Do what it takes to collect the evidence.

- Be comprehensive in your evidence collection.

- Maximize the use of your tools.

Finally, you were provided an opportunity to examine three additional strategies that ensured you were able to gather evidence of engagement and learning:

- Listen to teaching and learning.

- View learning in action.

- Interact with learners.

Remember, the skills and strategies outlined in this chapter take time to master through practice. You are a new observer each time you step into a classroom because each lesson is different every day. Patton reminded us, "The first responsibility of the observer is to know what is happening, to see it, hear it, try to make sense of it. That is more important than getting the perfect note or quote" (Stake, 2004, p. 94).

Take the time to revisit this chapter's strategies over time and as needed, as Chapter 3 serves as the foundation for all of your work moving forward.

How can you determine effectiveness of instruction and a teacher's impact on learners?

4

Don't be fooled by the low number of strategies in this chapter (only three: #17–#19), as they represent some of the most mentally challenging steps. The work to determine a teacher's effectiveness and impact on students may be such a departure from what you have been doing but will become some of the most important work you will do.

We spend hours debriefing lessons together with leaders, framing their thinking and organizing evidence into cause-and-effect columns on a board. We practice in partners, building feedback statements that begin with frames such as, "Because the teacher . . ." or "As a result of . . ." so leaders can clearly convey these relationships in feedback.

From the field . . .
Feedback to teachers is much more powerful when the evaluator focuses on specific evidence regarding the interaction between teachers and students during an observation. The biggest challenge in this regard is to collect as

(Continued)

(Continued)

much or more data about what the students are doing during the observed lesson. The next hurdle is to then allow the collected information to guide the discussion about the <u>actual</u> achievement of student learning outcomes as opposed to the teacher's intended outcomes.

By doing this, I found that I could move the feedback discussion away from a summary of the lesson in terms of teacher practices to a richer more objective conversation about the cause and effect of chosen instructional strategies in the classroom and the subsequent result with students. Teachers have been much more engaged in post-observation discussions using this format because they are able to better understand the true impact of their instruction based on specific student feedback to me during the observation. As a result, the observation becomes a powerful coaching opportunity that allows a teacher to immediately pivot and change practice with his/her current group of students in the current year.

—Lisa Carter, Assistant Superintendent

As instructional leaders work to provide support and feedback that will change practices and impact student outcomes, the effort to truly *measure* teacher effectiveness remains a challenge. In Chapters 2 and 3, you explored the necessary first steps of defining and collecting evidence of effective instructional practice, recognizing that the framework provides you with this foundation. In this chapter, we introduce you to the next step of your journey toward becoming a highly impactful instructional leader.

Every day, coaches, evaluators, and administrators visit classrooms and have the rich opportunity to collect real-time data, review student work, and interact with students in the moment. Yet many instructional leaders do not recognize the necessity and/or have the capacity to then *analyze* the evidence they have collected to determine relationships between teacher actions and student learning. This often leads to a summary of events, as opposed to an analysis of effectiveness.

The third standard of effective evidence-based observation and feedback, RVL 1.C, is the focus of this chapter: *Making direct and explicit connections for a teacher, answering how he or she is impacting student engagement and thinking, conducting an examination of the teacher's level of success in moving students toward mastery of a learning target.* In this chapter, you will do the following:

- Recognize the need and goals for analysis of instructional practices.
- Develop strategies required to make the shift from previous coaching and feedback models.
- Understand impacts on engagement and learning based on five focus areas.

Skill Set for Determining Effectiveness

Remember in Chapter 1, we discussed the need to shift from a summary to an analysis. Let's take a close look at how we assess the quality of analysis in feedback using RVL 1.C on the ReVISION Learning Supervisory Continuum (see Figure 4.1 below).

FIGURE 4.1: RVL STANDARD 1.C

ReVISION Supervisory Continuum				
Domain 1: Evidence-Based Observation	**Beginning**	**Developing**	**Proficient**	**Exceptional**
C. Evidence cited in written feedback connects teacher action with student engagement and intended learning outcomes.	Evidence cited in written feedback provides little to no connection between teacher action and learning outcome or impact on students. Evidence cited in written feedback provides little to no connection between teaching practice and performance indicators.	Evidence cited in written feedback provides some connections between teacher action and learning outcome or impact on students but may remain too vague or unsupportive of claim.	Evidence cited in written feedback provides clear and explicit connections between teacher action and impact on student engagement and/or learning process and outcome in support of claim.	The detailed feedback strongly links observed teaching practice/teacher actions to expected student learning objectives, impact on student engagement, learning process, and outcomes.
	© 2018 ReVISION Learning Partnership, LLC All Rights Reserved			

To successfully shift from summarizing to analyzing in order to provide high-quality feedback and to meet the "Proficient or "Exceptional" performance levels in RVL 1.C, leaders must master the set of skills found in Table 4.1 on the next page.

You will notice that the most challenging skill required in this work involves an observer's ability to determine how a teacher is impacting the students or causing particular outcomes based on your collected evidence. Take a minute to review the common challenges you might face (see Table 4.2 on the next page).

TABLE 4.1	SKILL SET FOR RVL 1.C
Core Skills	**Description**
Determine Student Engagement Levels	Defining and using evidence to recognize levels of engagement
Determine Teacher Impact on Learning	Identifying factors that impact learning, understanding how students learn, and recognizing the teacher's role in student success based on the evidence
Determine Teacher Impact on Engagement	Identifying factors that impact student engagement and recognizing the teacher's role in student levels based on the evidence
Communicate Clear Connections	Citing evidence of overall teacher impact that clearly supports a claim about instruction and promotes growth

TABLE 4.2	RVL 1.C COMMON CHALLENGES

Listed evidence or narrative versus analysis

Lack of evidence to conduct an analysis

Lack of attention to student engagement/understanding/movement toward mastery

Using Your Evidence to Analyze Effectiveness

An instructional leader can develop a protocol or series of steps aligned to the essential skills in Table 4.1 to establish a process for analyzing evidence. The recommendations outlined in the rest of this chapter should serve as a guide, and though classroom examples are provided, it is important to remember that no two lessons are the same.

Let's look at an example of a comprehensive evidence-collection method in Figure 4.2 that provides an example of notes captured during an observation of a minilesson and independent work time of a second-grade Reader's Workshop lesson for determining character traits. This map allowed the observer to track and organize students' behaviors and actions, the type of books they were reading (NF = nonfiction), the use of resources, and the writing on their stickie notes.

Building on what you learned in Chapter 3, we will now utilize this map further to demonstrate how the observer can review the evidence to conduct an analysis of instructional effectiveness using three strategies.

FIGURE 4.2: EVIDENCE COLLECTION MAP

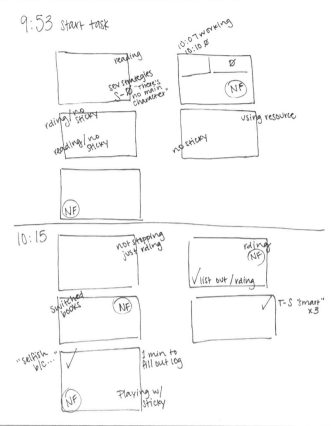

Strategy 17: Organize your evidence

Remember in Chapter 2, we talked about "tagging" evidence (noting as each piece relates to a specific indicator) as a good place to start. The next step is to work through the bits and pieces of evidence to begin developing an understanding of observed effectiveness that will lead you to create your claim about practice and outcomes. The observer should locate essential evidence that directly relates to student understanding, construction of new learning, and/or engagement. Notice what the observer collected and organized:

Ss left the carpet at 9:53. At 10:07, 10 min after the mini-lesson ended, 0/14 Ss were writing character traits on stickies.

2 were not working but looking at the others. 4 were reading but did not have stickies, 2 others were reading non-fiction books ("NF" on the map) and an additional

1 reading told the evaluator that there were no main characters so she could not complete the task.

1 Ss was using the resource list of possible character traits. T pulled a small group and was working with 4 Ss on a separate task.

At 10:15, T checking on all Ss. 1 more was using the resource list of possible character traits. 3 were reading non-fiction books and 1 had switched to a 2nd book (fiction) without recording anything.

Only 4 of 10 Ss polled could explain to the observer what a character trait was or how to determine traits. 2 Ss had listed a character trait (smart and selfish) and could explain to the observer how he/she supported the choice.

Note how the observer organized the evidence to arrive at a chronological snapshot of the critical teacher and student actions or behaviors.

Strategy 18: Ask questions about what you observed

Often leaders will stop here with the organization of evidence. The afore-mentioned list would then represent the feedback that would be provided to the teacher. However, it simply narrates witnessed events. Regardless of your rubric, to develop feedback that feeds forward and to move to a deep analysis that will result in an accurate claim/rating, instructional leaders need to next think about what was occurring during the lesson and *why it was occurring*. To do that, they must ask themselves questions, such as the following:

> *What was causing this to happen?*
>
> *What happened just before this evidence was recorded?*
>
> *How was the teacher in direct control of the outcomes?*
>
> *What was the expectation for what students should be doing? (Think beyond following directions.)*
>
> *Were they successful? Why were some successful and some not?*

As our observer reviews the evidence, taking into consideration the previously listed thinking questions and the expected student learning outcomes, an understanding of the effectiveness of the lesson and the teacher's impact emerges:

- The teacher followed the basic structure of Workshop with a minilesson (i.e., in appropriate duration, with a single targeted strategy, and modeling how to find traits from a story read together) and students set out to work with stickies and self-selected books from their leveled book bags.

- However, a majority of students did not understand the concept of character traits or characterization methods nor remember there was an available resource, a list of character traits.

- Students did not recognize that nonfiction books on sea life, occupations, or dinosaurs lack characters. (Though nonfiction may include characters, such as in a biography or narrative nonfiction, this was not the goal of the learning, nor did students have those books.)

Strategy 19: Determine causes of outcomes

The observer is recognizing that though there are strengths in the teacher's practices, the lesson did not set students up for success in determining character traits as they read. Though you may be drawing conclusions by answering the questions from Strategy 18—it is critical to purposefully take steps to determine clear causes of the observed outcomes. Remember from Chapter 3, the observer has to also consider the absence of evidence (i.e., a missing instructional step or an action that *did not* occur) as a potential part of the cause. Notice this is addressed in "Instruction *during* the Minilesson" in the following analysis. The observer made a determination of what did not occur based on what was needed for students to be successful:

Instruction During the Minilesson:

- The teacher did not build on prior learning regarding which books contain characters or the difference between fiction and nonfiction. She did not address how to determine traits through author's characterization methods.

- The teacher modeled using the book's pictures only. After closer analysis of the student responses on the carpet, it was clear they were guessing at emotions only, providing words as to how the character "felt" based on the illustrations or story events.

- The teacher did not clearly give directions as to which books to use. The intent was for students to make selections from the various works of fiction in their bags.

- Students were not reminded of nor did they know to use the resource of character trait words. There was no modeling of the use of that resource.

Small Group Instruction/Independent Work Time:

- The teacher immediately pulled a small group for support in an unrelated skill. Though this is often a suggested practice for differentiation, she did not monitor the other students at any point during the first 15 minutes of independent work to ensure everyone had the correct materials, understood the task, and was beginning to work successfully.

Stop and Think: Reflect on your own process of organizing evidence. What process do you use upon returning to your office with your notes? How similar is it to what we have outlined?

We know this is complex work, so be patient with yourself and recognize that the strategies and steps will take time and practice to master. Move on when you are ready to forge ahead into thinking about further using your evidence.

Understanding What We Are Analyzing

Observers struggle to know what specifically needs to be analyzed after visiting a classroom. Remember, recognizing what it is we need to analyze dictates what we need to collect during an observation. Let's revisit this sample feedback from Chapter 3:

```
10:36 - 100% students with eyes on teacher

10:42 - Students chorally respond "No" in response
to teacher question

10:43 - 100% of students with eyes on teacher

10:45 - 100% of students participate in turn and talk

10:52 - 100% of students with eyes on text reading
independently
```

Though the observer paid close attention to student actions, we have no information beyond these general behavioral observations. As we mentioned, instructional leaders must shift the focus for every observation to two central ideas around which feedback and analysis should revolve: advancing learning and levels of engagement.

Advancing Learning

The goal in classrooms is to always ensure students are advancing in their learning, understanding and applying new concepts, strategies and skills, or applying previously learned concepts in some way. With this in mind, leaders must determine the following:

1. *If* new learning is actually occurring

2. *What* the teacher has put in place for scaffolding and gradual release to build a pathway toward the new learning

3. *How* students are progressing toward mastery of a learning target

To arrive at accurate conclusions about the learners, observers can ask themselves these questions:

- Where are they in the progression toward the learning target?

- How are they making connections to previous learning and constructing the new learning? Is there a conceptual breakdown or gap causing an inability to build new learning?

- How are we asking them to use or apply their learning? Is the completion of the task demonstrating their understanding and aligned to the learning target?

- How are they set up for success to achieve higher levels? Is there a form of gradual release in place? Are they grappling or is it "too hard" or "too easy?"

> **Stop and Think:** Take a few minutes to revisit or reflect on what was discussed in Chapter 3 regarding learning theory and learning stages. What do we know about how students learn? What evidence do you need to collect to determine whether this is occurring?

Levels of Engagement

In Chapter 2, evidence that could be collected for engagement was explored by first defining terms like *cognitive* or *intellectual engagement.* The next step observers must take is to ascertain the level (or absence) of engagement while also determining what is causing this outcome. Remember, to analyze the level of engagement, leaders must always think beyond "on-task" toward the following:

- The depth of understanding or knowledge the tasks and questions require.

- How students are thinking, applying, and interacting around or with the concepts.

- What their conversations, responses, and questions reveal about the depth of their thinking and understanding.

- How students are connecting with the concepts or strategies as relevant, personal, and applicable outside of the context of the immediate lesson.

Did you notice in the earlier lesson example that the observer did not just determine how many were "working" (had a book selected or were reading) but *how* they were working?

Analyzing Engagement

From Chapter 3, we introduced Schlechty's (2002) levels of engagement for observable behaviors to provide a thinking frame for evidence collection. The next step is to utilize this concept of levels to analyze critical collected evidence to determine the cause of the outcomes.

Some Possible Causes for Level 1 (the lowest level of engagement or "Rebellion"):

Behaviors are often directly tied to the level of rigor or challenge of a given task or questions and can manifest from frustration:

- Learned habits of helplessness

- "Too hard" or "too easy" work or expectations

   - Limited differentiation or personalization and/or scaffolding so students are not working within their zone of proximal development (Vygotsky, 1978)

   - Limited resources available or lack of explicit instruction on how to persevere, use supports, or work independently

   - Not enough or too much time to complete tasks

Some Possible Causes for Levels 2, 3, and 4 ("Retreatism," "Ritual Compliance," or "Strategic Compliance"):

- Lack of clear daily purpose or criteria for learning
- Lack of relevance; lack of context within a unit, connection to previous learning, cross curricular, or real-world context
- Lack of authenticity in task or audience
- Teacher monitoring for task completion only

During and after a lesson, it is easy to make assumptions about levels of engagement. In the following example, notice that after an observer's initial judgment, he arrived at a different conclusion about engagement through analysis of specific evidence from a seventh-grade English language arts lesson about ethical actions:

Assumption: On first appearance, students are working in groups using technology. They are required to use text evidence and are analyzing the ethics of characters' actions against criteria/defining terms they have been given. This is the kickoff to a potentially highly effective lesson with high levels of engagement.

Reality: Students are seated in groups of four with one student designated as a "typist" and only one Chromebook on the table. Scripted student-student interactions reveal that at three of four tables, one student is leading the group and doing all of the talking while one is typing on the Google Doc and not participating. The others are just listening to the one who has taken the lead. The teacher visited each table to see if the document was set up.

(Engagement: one student at Level 5 [highest], one at Level 4, two at Level 3)

Analysis: The teacher was turning the responsibility of learning over to students by encouraging group work.

- However, he did not establish criteria for group roles or individual expectations and accountability up front, so there was no collaboration.
- There was opportunity to do this when the teacher visited each table, but he only determined if they had successfully set up the Google Doc (task oriented) versus how they were working through the task (learning oriented).
- The use of technology did not allow the others to follow the information being recorded nor did it allow them to view other groups' entries at the end.

Some Possible Causes for Schlechty's Level 5 "Engagement"

We should not only seek causes of *a lack* of engagement but also identify those teacher actions that serve to *increase* engagement in classrooms. Some contributing factors include the following:

- A clear daily purpose has been communicated and students can articulate the context, future applications, and personal relevance for the day's lesson or have their own daily goals.

- Students are provided opportunities to share in the learning and know how to work collaboratively with peers to construct new learning.

- Students are set up for success with resources through modeling, think-alouds, options for choices, and feedback reminders.

To change practice, promote reflection in teachers, and create positive outcomes for students, instructional leaders need to become more analytical about the cause-and-effect relationships occurring in a lesson.

Influences on Engagement and Learning

There are many factors that influence student achievement in the classroom. Some of these are not at all within a teacher's control, such as home life or developmental issues. For the purposes of this chapter, we focus on five main areas of instruction (see Figure 4.3) that fall within a teacher's range of control

FIGURE 4.3: FOCUS AREAS IMPACTING ENGAGEMENT

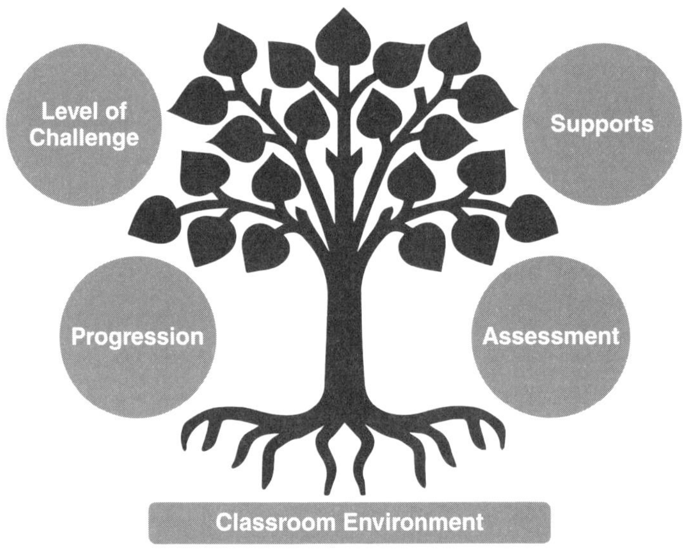

Source: RVL OnLine (2017)

and consistently and directly impact student engagement and understanding. Now more than ever, because of what our students are experiencing in and out of our classrooms that are not in our control, it is critical to provide them havens where they will feel successful, confident, and challenged, but supported. Creating and implementing lessons that lead to high levels of engagement and learning can achieve this. Leaders need to better understand what impacts engagement and learning to help teachers work toward these goals.

In each focus area explored ahead suggested observer questions have been provided. We also offer classroom examples, broken down into "What Was Happening" (or "Evidence") and "Potential Causes," to more clearly illustrate how to organize and utilize evidence to determine a teacher's impact on student outcomes and to help a teacher see these relationships.

Focus Area 1: The Classroom Environment

Stop and Think: How could a classroom environment positively or negatively impact learning and engagement?

Years ago research confirmed that there was a direct correlation between teachers' expectations that build student beliefs around self-efficacy and outcomes, which came to be known as the "Pygmalion Effect" (see Figure 4.4;

FIGURE 4.4: PYGMALION EFFECT

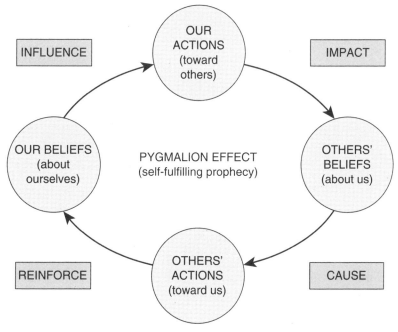

Source: Based on Rosenthal & Jacobsen (1968) and illustrated by Kirsten Nestor

Rosenthal & Jacobsen, 1968). Anyone who has taught or witnessed this first-hand can confirm that when a teacher creates a positive classroom climate of high expectations in which academic risks are supported, students will achieve at higher levels and become more independent thinkers and learners. Bandura (1989), through his extensive work, determined that "self-efficacy beliefs affect thought patterns that may be self-aiding or self-hindering" (p. 1175). Carol Dweck (2015), who began her research in the 1960s around learned helplessness, reaffirmed that students' mindsets—"how they perceive their abilities"—play a key role in their motivation and achievement and found that "if we changed students' mindsets, we can boost their achievement" (p. 20).

Suggested Focus-Area Questions for Observer Analysis:

- How has the teacher conveyed high expectations? How do the students respond to these?

- What are you hearing and seeing in students' interactions to demonstrate the teacher has or has not developed students' social skills and met developmental needs?

- Does the physical layout promote active learning? How are students utilizing the space?

- Is there a positive climate and culture where you observe students persevering, supporting one another, and taking risks? What is the teacher doing to promote this?

- Are there effective and efficient routines and transitions in place that students understand and execute?

When considering why students are or are not engaged or advancing in their learning, before pointing to a particular teaching strategy from an *instructional* indicator or domain of a framework, leaders must determine if a contributing cause is rooted in a *classroom environment* indicator or domain related to expectations and mindsets. Notice in the following sample "Proficient" description, to accurately select a performance level, analysis is required. (You might look to see if you have a similar attribute or indicator.)

> "Creates a learning environment in which most students are willing to take intellectual risks" (CSDE, 2014).

Notice that this indicator includes not only teacher actions ("creates a learning environment") but also the resulting impact on students ("are willing to take intellectual risks"). As a first step, leaders must determine how the teacher has created a space where students will try out ideas, speak up in front of others, challenge peers' perspectives, and/or offer constructive feedback to each other. For example, observers should review collected quotes of the teacher feedback:

Teacher 1:   T-"It's okay; let's give Brandon a minute to look through his notes to find it . . . he doesn't have it yet. [after waiting] . . . Do you want to 'phone a friend?'"

Teacher 2:   T-"Hurry, we are waiting." [S rushes to answer] "No, that's not right."

What effect does each type of feedback have on the student? On classmates? What if you then saw Brandon frown and put his head down? Wait time alone is a strategy that supports deeper thinking, and when coupled with positive feedback, it allows students to feel at ease with struggle, thus often resulting in an increased number of students taking risks. Table 4.3 provides an example of an observer's organization of evidence from a lesson and the possible causes for the outcomes.

TABLE 4.3 CAUSE AND EFFECT: ENVIRONMENT	
Evidence/What Was Happening	**Potential Environmental Causes**
• Not all Ss are raising hands or participating in turn and talks • The same 5 Ss are shouting out • 3-4 Ss don't question a quiet partner who just sits and waits during turn and talks	• It is the English language learners who are not raising hands, not yet ready to speak in front of the class • T does not have a protocol for hands or name sticks • There is no wait time • Ss have not been taught social strategies for turn and talk

Observers must be discerning, as the interconnectedness of instructional practice and classroom environment is subtle. Comprehensive evidence collection allows an observer to distinguish between the two. Potentially, the same outcomes in the table could also be caused by students not understanding new vocabulary or concepts. By analyzing student response attempts, questions, or incorrect responses; questioning them when they begin to work independently; and looking at student work in the moment, the observer can better determine root causes and long- and short-term action steps.

Focus Area 2: Level of Challenge

Stop and Think: How could the level of challenge within a lesson positively or negatively impact learning and engagement?

By now, we know teachers cannot successfully increase the level of challenge if foundational elements of a positive learning environment and mindsets for growth are missing. A second area of focus lies in determining if the level of challenge of the learning targets, tasks, and questions are appropriate for the learners.

Before moving too far ahead, it is important to consider what we mean by "level of challenge" to have a yardstick against which to measure or analyze "appropriateness." In our work, this "level of challenge" has become synonymous with level of rigor and high levels of engagement, or how students are being asked to use the learning. This chapter will scratch the surface of these ideas, so we encourage leaders to utilize our suggested resources as they provide the tools to further measure or define "level of challenge":

- Taxonomies, such as Marzano's (2000), a revised Bloom's (Anderson et al., 2001), or Webb's (1997) Depth of Knowledge framework

- Wagner's seven survival skills (2008) and Partnership for 21st Century Learning's (n.d.) skills for the "4 C's" (for the understanding of essential 21st century skills)

- Blackburn's seven myths about rigor (2012)

- Tovani's (2000) work on the concept of rigorous versus hard

Suggested Focus-Area Questions for Observer Analysis:

- What are students doing to *construct, apply,* or *use* the new learning? How are the teacher's choices of methods, strategies, questions, and tasks allowing this or preventing this?

- In which stage of learning are students? What would be appropriate challenge for that phase?

- What depth of knowledge must students utilize or apply when answering questions or tackling new tasks?

- Were there varying levels of the demand of the tasks? Was it necessary to build capacity using only recall or lower level questions during the observation or was the lesson predominantly requiring lower level thinking? Were students capable of going further?

- How does student behavior communicate whether the task is hard or rigorous?

- Are students working in their zone of proximal development? How do you know if this is occurring?

Observers may immediately recognize telltale signs of *inappropriate* levels of challenge, such as avoidance behaviors, or of *appropriate* levels, such as vocal "aha" moments. However, leaders often observe lessons that necessitate a closer review of subtle evidence, requiring an analysis of what has been collected related to the behaviors, conversations, and student work that was generated through the tasks.

Achieving this "appropriate level" in lesson planning and instruction has proven difficult for teachers. They have been asked to increase the challenge, align to Common Core State or new standards, utilize new curriculum, personalize instruction, and turn learning over to students for opportunities that promote good struggle or grappling with complex problems or text—and every day teachers are trying!

Yet leaders are experiencing the same levels of change. They have not been able to provide explicit and extensive support for teachers to learn how to execute these shifts toward increased rigor and higher expectations, nor how to ensure all students are successful in the work. Therefore, it is critical for leaders to learn to recognize the difference between that which is rigorous and that which is hard and to build teacher understanding and reflection. Cris Tovani (2000) reminded us, "hard hurts; rigor invigorates. Rigor invites engagement; hard repels it" (pp. 146–147).

Take a minute to look at two classroom examples. Consider whether the evidence points to tasks that are rigorous or ones that are hard.

Example 1—fourth-grade social studies (you encountered this lesson in a Chapter 3 map):

Ss are to work in pairs to locate key facts to summarize a piece of informational text. One partner reads aloud a section and has miscued 10 words in the first few paragraphs. The other partner is a stronger reader but does not assist or correct the miscues.

Example 2—fifth-grade math:

In groups of 3, Ss will apply the use of fractions in distances and travel by creating a hiker's guide. When asked by the observer, it was discovered in one group, 2 of the 3 Ss were missing foundational fraction understanding and did not know what a "key" for a map was, though one of the steps in the directions was to create a key. The 3rd S was doing all of the work for the group and the other 2 were just watching. The T had purposefully organized Ss into heterogeneous groups but was behind her desk during the group work.

Both classroom examples reveal that the task students were asked to complete met the criteria of "rigorous" in terms of alignment to standards. Each teacher was aware that some might struggle, placing stronger students with those who might find the task challenging. However, there were insurmountable obstacles in both tasks that rendered completion nearly impossible for some. When we put students in a position where they cannot overcome the challenges or obstacles, we have asked them to do something they cannot do, rendering the activity hard or impossible.

As suggested in Chapter 3, leaders must focus attention on evidence collection strategies to ensure a thorough analysis can be conducted of situations like these, using such data as scripted student–student conversations and teacher questions and feedback, photographed student work, and notes from interactions with students. Recognizing hard versus rigorous is a critical step, but it is directly connected to your ability to assess whether students are engaged at high levels and advancing in learning.

As previously recommended, leaders can utilize a foundational tool such as a taxonomy, classifying not only teacher-intended tasks and posed questions but student responses to more clearly discern the levels of cognitive engagement and depths of thinking. This takes time and requires a critical eye.

In Table 4.4, you will find an example of an observer's organization of evidence from an 11th-grade science lesson (not aligned to Next Generation Science Standards). The observer is considering levels of thinking or what we are asking students to do with their knowledge in all classrooms. In pairs, students researched alternative energy and then presented a PowerPoint presentation to the class.

TABLE 4.4	CAUSE AND EFFECT: LEVEL OF CHALLENGE OF TASK
Evidence/What Was Happening	**Potential Causes**
• Ss passively watched until the T said to presenters: "What should they write down?" Ss then copied what they were told to write. • 3 sets of presenters read from slides, I could not answer questions about the topic, though answers were on slides, I set mispronounced words/names on slides. • Ss were to create a "report" and were not given a purpose beyond "reporting" to classmates. (S-O "It's just to know.") • In creating the reports, Ss told the observer they used Wikipedia or the first sources they found when they Googled and copied and pasted information.	• Purpose was solely to create a report • No goals for presenters established beyond a list of required content on slides • No requirement for the listeners beyond copying notes • No "research" conducted or research guidelines offered

Analysis: Though the students were tasked with researching/using multiple sources, worked collaboratively, and were able to practice speaking and listening skills-all 21st century skills-the resulting level of thinking was low for the presenters and the audience. Creating a factual presentation does not represent a high level of Bloom's taxonomy, as students simply were reciting what had been copied onto a slide. Because the task was to "report," presenters included only facts and surface-level pros and cons. Because there was no task for the listeners beyond copying notes from slides or direction to use the information presented, audience members were compliant, either using recall or transcribing what was printed or stated. They did not need to evaluate, debate, or select one suitable alternative over another. Because students were not explicitly taught research skills, note-taking, and summarizing, they simply copied information from the Internet.

Let's look at Table 4.5 at very different evidence and outcomes from an eighth-grade social studies Socratic Circle that resulted in high levels of thinking and discourse.

TABLE 4.5 CAUSE AND EFFECT: LEVEL OF CHALLENGE OF THINKING

Evidence/What Was Happening	Potential Causes
• Ss were actively debating the cause of the economic crisis leading up to the Stock Market Crash of 1929 w/out T intervention or prompting. • Ss were using their notes and supported all answers with evidence or reasoning appropriate to each society member's perspective.	• Lesson/unit was designed around rigorous learning targets and high expectations. • Ss were given roles as different members of society and had to share from that person's perspective versus their own. • Ss had researched in teams primary documents and leveled informational texts to ensure accuracy. • T had been building Ss capacity to engage in Socratics through T-led, guided, and now independent practice.

Did you notice how the "What Was Happening" and "Potential Causes" sections differed from the previous table? By reviewing and referencing Webb's (1997) Depth of Knowledge framework, you could clearly explain to the teacher the cause-and-effect relationships that resulted in high levels of thinking. It is equally as important to ensure teachers hear when and why they are achieving effective outcomes.

Analysis: The teacher set rigorous expectations requiring students to use multiple texts and evidence and to sustain their own discussion, resulting in high engagement levels for all students. A debate is often classified as a Level 3 Depth of Knowledge task but tips into Level 4 when students must (and did) synthesize multiple sources. It is important to note that another cause lies in how the teacher set the students up for success. She carefully built student capacity to ensure they were able to work independently at higher levels-our next focus area.

Focus Area 3: Progression

Stop and Think: How could the progression of a lesson or unit positively or negatively impact learning and engagement?

Remember in Chapter 3, we drew your attention to how students learn and any indicators on your rubric related to progression, scaffolding, or the sequence of a lesson. The way in which a teacher designs and executes a lesson and unit progression to ensure success is one of the most critical and difficult elements of instruction. The effectiveness requires deep analysis by the observer. Let's review some related rubric examples to consider what it is an observer should be trying to determine for all lessons:

"Clearly presents instructional content in a logical and purposeful progression and at an appropriate level of challenge to advance learning of all students" (CSDE, 2014).

"Most of the lesson components are organized and delivered to move students toward mastery of the objective" (Newark Public Schools, 2015).

Notice that an instructional leader cannot simply list the lesson components and call it a day if the progression *appears* to make sense as logical. Indicators like these help us define a logical progression as one that (a) is at the appropriate level for all students and (b) advances students. Simply stated, if a logical progression is not followed, assigned tasks or questions asked can become too hard or too easy, and students will not move forward or be able to share in the responsibility.

Suggested Focus-Area Questions for Observer Analysis:

- Are the tasks aligned to the learning, providing a building block approach or pathway so you observe students constructing an understanding or moving toward meeting the target?

- How has the teacher offered opportunities for students to share in the responsibility of the learning? Are the students successful when working on their own?

- How is the teacher monitoring understanding to determine the next steps in a progression? What are students revealing about their readiness?

- How is instructional time impacting students' levels of engagement and understanding? Is the length of the introduction age-appropriate? Are students afforded enough time for tasks and higher levels of challenge? How do you know?

- How is the teacher using scaffolding, connection-making, and building of essential skills to ensure students can work at more challenging levels or with more challenging text/content? How do you know students are successful?

To be able to determine whether the progression is leading students to the desired outcomes, observers must review the student evidence. In this work, consider three key factors:

1. **Use of Time:** Remember from Chapter 3 that you might be capturing time stamps. You can then total the time spent on each component and analyze this against outcomes. Review developmental estimates for how long students should remain seated/focused on a single task (say, for an introduction) and suggestions from experts for strategies like a recommended length for a Reader's Workshop mini-lesson to allow for independent work time. Sometimes student behavior alone will help you recognize quite easily if time for a task or lesson was "too long" or "too short."

2. **Use of Scaffolding:** You want to analyze how the lesson has been "chunked" based on student outcomes. We can clearly assess whether a teacher is utilizing a suggested gradual release model, such as "I do it; We do it; You do it Together, and You do it alone" (Fisher & Frey, 2014). Observers can usually spot these chunks as they occur, but understanding the effectiveness of each of these practices can be more elusive.

3. **Integration of Skill-Building/Connection-Making:** Connected to the scaffolding, teachers must ensure that they are building capacity for students to work in their zone of proximal development, even in discovery learning. How are we allowing them to arrive at, conclude, or discover some new understanding? Observers also should pay close attention to a common possibility within the concept of connection-making—that there is something absent from the progression that has contributed to the observed outcomes.

Table 4.6 on the next page depicts an observer's thinking about a kindergarten lesson during which students were to sort events from a story by beginning, middle, and end. The teacher modeled and created a life-sized graphic organizer and involved every student during the introduction. However, the observer wanted to understand why half were struggling to sort on their own at their seats.

TABLE 4.6   CAUSE AND EFFECT: PROGRESSION

Evidence/What Was Happening	Potential Causes
• 25 min on the carpet • 6 min of independent seat time • 8/16 were unable to complete the task correctly (of the 8: 4 were sitting and told observer they didn't know how or what to do, 3 were seen going down an incorrect path and the T was helping 1)	• Well over the recommended carpet time for this age • Not enough time to apply • T never defined beginning, middle, and end • T modeled but did not think aloud as she sorted

Analysis: Through a quick assessment, the observer can clearly determine that 25 minutes is beyond a recommended introduction time for this age, and of course, six minutes was not enough time to apply a new strategy. The teacher shared responsibility and provided modeling and independent time, allowing students to sort on their own back at their seats with the same story. However, something was still missing in the progression, as evidenced by the lack of student success. If we do not build student capacity by addressing essential skills within the progression, they will not have success applying the new skills when we turn over the learning to them.

Remember the concept of hard versus rigorous? This task just became hard. It was not at the appropriate level of challenge to advance their learning. In the progression, the teacher actually missed defining "beginning," "middle," and "end." They practiced sorting, but she did not go so far as to explain how she knew where to place the card depicting the story event when she was modeling. The observer was able to arrive at this after asking five students—who could not accurately answer—how they knew where to place the events and what it meant to be "in the middle." It was also determined in this analysis that the teacher turned students loose to work on their own even though her monitoring revealed that not all understood how to sort correctly, which leads us to the fourth focus area: assessment.

Focus Area 4: Assessment Methods

Stop and Think: How could assessment and feedback within a lesson positively or negatively impact learning and engagement?

The process of analyzing assessment and feedback cycles allows a leader to engage in meaningful conversations with teachers to support growth in one of the most impactful areas of instructional practice—one when improved, results in exponential impacts on student outcomes. To provide feedback that advances learning, teachers must skillfully utilize checks for understanding, and as we know, "the most powerful single influence enhancing achievement is feedback" (Hattie & Timperley, 2007, p. 104).

As a necessary part of evaluation, to accurately select a performance level and develop a claim about practice, analysis is required to determine the effectiveness of the observed assessments conducted and feedback provided. Leaders cannot simply list assessment methods or determine whether there were checks in place. If you remember, the Dallas rubric sample from Chapter 2 included a "Progressing" description:

> Teacher "sometimes checks for academic understanding, but misses several key moments and/or mostly checks for understanding of directions" (Dallas Independent School District, 2014).

An observer must determine what are key moments throughout and also analyze the quality of the checks.

Suggested Focus-Area Questions for Observer Analysis:

- Is the teacher monitoring understanding, learning, and/or movement toward mastering an objective or only toward task completion?

- Is the assessment method measuring what it needs to measure and providing evidence/data for the teacher to use? Is the check truly serving as a "formative" assessment?

- What are the various checks telling us about student understanding and application?

- What is the teacher doing with the information? Were there missed opportunities for adjustments?

- What was the quality of the feedback?

- What are the impacts on students of the adjustments and/or feedback provided?

Completing an analysis of the assessment and feedback cycle is complex work. However, to give leaders a start down the road of this process, this section focuses on two key areas:

1. What the student evidence collected from the teacher's checks reveals about student understanding and engagement.

2. The effectiveness of the teacher's action or decision upon collecting that evidence.

Our Ongoing Assessment Thinking Map (see Figure 4.5 on the next page) provides an example of a frame to help leaders organize and analyze evidence after an observation. A completed map can be found at **resources.corwin .com/feedforward**.

FIGURE 4.5: ONGOING ASSESSMENT THINKING MAP

ONGOING ASSESSMENT THINKING MAP

When	What/How	Who?	What they said?	What it tells us?	What the teacher did about it?	Effectiveness of assessment or response?

Source: Courtesy of ReVISION

The circled columns above represent the analysis required.

A highly effective planning pathway utilizes a backward design approach with the end in mind. This requires teachers to think first about desired outcomes and then immediately consider what should be sought and utilized as evidence of understanding (Wiggins & McTighe, 2005).

What does the evidence from the checks reveal?

Consider an example from a sixth-grade English language arts lesson in Table 4.7. The learning target focused on students reviewing text features in informational books—recognizing the purpose of different types through a scavenger hunt so that on the following day, they could create appropriate text features for their own books. There were three observed checks for understanding near the end of the class, so the observer needed to consider the following:

- What is the teacher learning about their understanding and mastery of the learning target?

- How will/could she use the information supplied to make decisions for tomorrow's lesson?

When analyzing the assessment cycle of this lesson, consider whether checks are effectively being used to inform decision making.

TABLE 4.7 CAUSE AND EFFECT: ASSESSMENT EXAMPLE 1	
Evidence/What Was Happening	**Potential Causes**
Check 1: Group wrap up: T- Thumbs up or down: "Is everyone comfortable with text features?" Nearly all have thumbs up after 4 Ss looked around to see if peers had up or down before selecting.	Check 1: Not everyone put a thumb up, reliability of thumb method of assessing, use of a general question
Check 2: Group shares/T floated to listen: T directions- "Share with the other group something you learned today." 2 of 4 groups shared facts about the books' topics vs. about the text features.	Check 2: Unclear directions/ prompt not aligned to the learning target
Check 3: 3-2-1 exit slip: "Three things you learned in box 3, two things you find interesting about today's lesson, and one question you still have." 3 Ss were observed writing facts from their informational books.	Check 3: Unclear directions/ prompt not aligned to the learning target

Analysis: Though the teacher built in checks throughout and at the end of the lesson, they were not aligned to a specific learning target, and according to Marshall (2011), included "mediocre methods." Therefore, she was not collecting evidence of understanding from all students, nor can she plan or begin the next day with evidence of individual understanding. She does not know who is ready to create purposeful text features.

Was the teacher's decision/adjustment effective?

Every time a teacher leans over a student's shoulder, asks a question, and listens to a response, there is an opportunity to make a decision. Should the teacher:

a. Stop the whole class because many need some clarification, extension, or redirection?

b. Pull a small group or differentiate individually?

c. Provide individualized, specific, and actionable feedback?

First, observers should cite when any of these events do occur but also should notice and cite when any of this *needs to occur,* which requires analysis. Observers must help the teacher see how the shift, strategy, or action did or did not advance understanding. Three types of situations might arise to dictate *something* needs to change.

"If the evidence indicates:

1. Students are misunderstanding the instruction;

2. Students haven't 'gotten it at all' yet—that is, their pace of mastery is slower than anticipated; or

3. Students have already reached the level of understanding the lesson is aiming for and have none of the questions or confusion the teacher has anticipated and planned to address." (Popham, 2008, p. 49)

Teachers have many opportunities to provide not just an instructional shift but individual feedback when any of the aforementioned situations occur. Remember from Chapter 3 that when this is occurring, it is important to collect what the teacher said or did and which students received feedback, and it is imperative to then interact with those students in a way that provides evidence as to the effectiveness of that feedback, thinking: Did it move them forward?

Let's look at another classroom example in Table 4.8 to analyze the teacher's decision making based on assessments at the end of a minilesson. The fourth-grade social studies students were introduced to a new concept in their writing and research: determining an author's viewpoint and citing pros or cons of an issue before forming their own claim or stance. They practiced reading a short article on the carpet and were asked to add one point from the article to the "pro" or "con" column up front.

TABLE 4.8   CAUSE AND EFFECT: ASSESSMENT EXAMPLE 2

Evidence/What Was Happening	Potential Causes
Check 1: Ss began standing adding stickies and returned to their desks to begin work on their own topics.	Check 1: T did not read or count the stickies that were posted.
• 8 Ss did not add stickies and 1/2 of the ones posted were in the wrong column.	
• When asked by the observer, 6/6 Ss struggled to then define or show/give an example of "pros and cons."	
• [The observer read each stickie. The T did not review these before pulling a small group to work on a different task and Ss began working independently on their own research topics.]	
• 10 were observed struggling to complete the mirrored task on their own topics (filling out an organizer with two columns while reading a related article).	
Check 2 (missed opportunity to monitor): T pulled a small group and did not circulate.	Check 2: T did not check in or recognize students did not know how to complete the task or locate/determine pros or cons.

Analysis of Student Understanding: The teacher built in a check for understanding that could have provided her (and did) with immediate evidence of individual understanding. Not all students completed a stickie, and some of the ones posted were in the correct column. It became an ineffective formative assessment and also revealed an issue with the progression.

Analysis of Effectiveness of Teacher Decision: Because the teacher did not stop and address the missing stickies or misconceptions through a reteach or differentiation, students struggled on their own, so her decision was ineffective.

Analysis of Progression: Remember how closely related the idea of progression and an assessment cycle are when analyzing instruction. There was something missing in the lesson that caused students to place the stickies incorrectly. By speaking to students about why they put stickies in certain places, the observer was able to determine the misconception. This leads to a better understanding not just of the lesson components but potential needs of individual students.

Focus Area 5: Supports

Stop and Think: How could the level of support within a lesson positively or negatively impact learning and engagement?

This section—and final area of focus—connects with the previous four you have explored, but it specifically addresses the supports in place for students during a lesson. By now, you are recognizing that we cannot just provide teachers with a list of resources observed or supports in place or note that students were in fact working in groups, but the determination of

- how the supports are selected for or by students;

- how students are using the supports; and

- the effectiveness and impact of those supports on learning and engagement.

Consider where supports are addressed in your rubric, as they may appear in several indicators and how this sample "Skilled" description requires observer analysis:

The teacher supports the learning needs of students through a variety of strategies, materials, and/or pacing that make learning accessible and challenging for the group. Instructional materials and resources are aligned to the instructional purposes and are appropriate for students' learning styles and needs, actively engaging students. (Ohio Department of Education, 2015)

Notice in Table 4.9 the connections between this fifth focus area and the other four and how comprehensive analysis will always return you to the evidence you collected from students.

TABLE 4.9 CONNECTIONS TO FOCUS AREA 5

Focus Area	Example of Effective Practice/Outcomes Related to Supports
#1 Environment	Students are willing to use resources provided; they will persevere.
#2 Level of Challenge	Students are working within their zone of proximal development with the help of other students, the teacher, and/or resources.
#3 Progression	Students receive the appropriate support throughout the lesson to ensure success in a gradual release model.
#4 Assessment	Teachers use evidence of understanding and engagement to make decisions as to how best to support student needs.

As the concept of supports for students is a vast topic, in this section only an overview of a thinking process is presented. However, you will find that you consistently apply what you have learned in the previous focus areas when you are determining how a teacher is supporting students. The strategies can be applied to your analysis of any type of instructional support that is in place—or needs to be in place—during a lesson. (Think back to Popham's list in recognizing a need for a shift in Focus Area 4 and the progression of the lesson in Focus Area 3.)

Suggested Focus-Area Questions for Observer Analysis:

- Were some students struggling to answer, work, think, or discuss at expected higher levels? If so, why?
- Were some struggling with key concepts? If so, what specifically?
- Were some in need of extension or did some finish ahead of others?
- Could some jump into the task while others needed more support or review?
- How were different learning styles/multiple intelligences/varied modalities, readiness, or interests addressed?
- How did groupings/partnering/use of resources support the needs of the learners?
- How were students using peers and/or resources to construct an understanding?

Table 4.10 displays an observer's thinking about the effectiveness of the supports in place during a math resource room Algebra I lesson. Seven students were working in three stations.

TABLE 4.10	CAUSE AND EFFECT: SUPPORTS	
Evidence/What Was Happening		**Potential Causes**
• 3 Ss are looking at notes in ntbk. • Same work for all at each station; Stations 1 and 2: complete worksheets, 3: slips of paper for matching equations to words/Font too small for Ss to read. • No direct instruction observed/T only floated and addressed needs as she noticed. [Evidence to show supports are not effective]: • 5 Ss had incorrect answers on their papers; I said, "I'm confused." • I told the observer "It's easy" while just staring at it, but when T checked in, he did not know how to do it. • When asked by observer, Ss could not: make connections between the stations (though clearly related), define words in the objective (ex. substitution) or recognize how to use substitution to check answers when solving for variable. 1 Ss needed help from partner to solve 3 + x = 4. • After T spent 3 min w/ 2 boys struggling, they could not explain how to solve the problems.		• No direct instruction on concepts, vocabulary, or connections • No explanation of the station work • No differentiation/ personalization • Ss not understanding concepts • Notes not sufficient to help

Analysis: Though students were trying to use their notes and the teacher had partnered students, created stations, and was checking in and assisting as needed, the supports in place did not advance learning about the algebra concepts on the board. The observer spoke to five of the seven and revisited as they switched stations, and it was clear that they did not understand the concepts, based on their responses and incorrect work. Because there was no tailoring to students' needs, the act of floating was not going to meet individual learning needs nor ensure they could master the objective or even complete the worksheets correctly.

Meeting the needs of all students is challenging work for teachers, especially in this situation where students are missing many skills from earlier grades. It is important for teachers to learn to collect detailed evidence from students to ensure lessons are scaffolded at appropriate levels of challenge and to recognize which supports are of most benefit to the students. When the supports are successfully utilized, students are not only advancing in the day's learning but also developing growth mindsets and independence, along with skills to self-monitor and problem solve.

Final Thoughts

RVL 1.C is one of the most challenging standards of the ReVISION Learning Supervisory Continuum, yet it is one of the most critical. No longer can leaders provide a summary of events to support the teachers they serve. They must conduct a comprehensive analysis of the evidence collected during a lesson to determine teacher effectiveness—shifting the focus of feedback to teaching *and* learning.

In this chapter, you explored only three strategies to move you toward this goal but tackled the most complex steps in the work to support teachers through feedback:

1. Organize your evidence.

2. Ask questions.

3. Determine causes.

As you work to master the core skills required of standard RVL 1.C, to

- determine student engagement levels, and to

- determine teacher impact on learning and engagement,

you have begun the next step—using your analysis to define clear areas of strength and growth on which you and the teacher will build actionable next steps. You will find that through comprehensive analysis of the impact of instruction on the learners, the target areas for improved practice have begun to emerge. Remember, you can access support resources at **resources .corwin.com/feedforward.**

Chapter 5 will provide you with a set of strategies for our next standard—**RVL 1.D:** *"Feedback contains areas of strengths and areas of growth explicitly connected to the indicator and observed practices/evidence and are developed based on indicator language and the key levers between ratings."*

How can you determine a teacher's areas of instructional strength and growth?

As you and your teams consistently process evidence in the way we suggested in Chapter 4, suddenly clear areas of strength and growth that are rooted in the outcomes rise to the top with big red arrows. The aha moments are audible during our lesson debriefs when this occurs. Therefore, you will only encounter three strategies (#20–#22) that will help you refine, convey, and build reflection about those areas.

From the field . . .

I'm able to focus on something specific and actionable that feels relevant to the teacher. Too often the rubric has felt like an arbitrary outside entity that's separate and distinct from what's actually happening inside a teacher's room. Being able to increase my skills as a coach using the language of the rubric to connect to the instruction brings it to life, and allows the teacher to move forward in their thinking and practice. It gives us both something to ground

(Continued)

(Continued)

our conversation around. There may be other areas of a given lesson that need improvement or addressing, but if an evaluator starts discussing too much or doesn't find that explicit connection between what has been observed and what is being evaluated, that disconnect can create tension and confusion hindering future growth. Instead, I've been able to work with teachers to visualize the changes in their practice through those discussions of key points in the rubric. What elevates a certain strategy from good to great? What helps us create an action step that will deliver short-term progress for both teacher and students? By making those connections, I have found a greater sense of purpose in our discussions moving forward.

—Dr. Ruth Kidwell, English Department Chair

For an instructional leader to develop feedback after a lesson that feeds forward, it is critical to determine which of the teacher's methods, strategies, and actions (as they relate to the student outcomes) represent areas of strength and which represent areas of growth. This step forms the foundation to allow an observer to determine next steps that will be logical, attainable, and realistic for a teacher, while also promoting reflection. In this chapter, instructional leaders will be introduced to RVL 1.D: "*Feedback contains areas of strengths and areas of growth explicitly connected to the indicator and observed practices/evidence and are developed based on indicator language and the key levers between ratings.*" In this chapter, you will be introduced to strategies to help you

- define "areas of strength and areas of growth"; and

- refine your ability to recognize strengths and challenge areas as they relate to the learners, evidence collected, and your instructional framework.

You might notice as you read through this chapter that you move at a quicker pace through the skills and strategies, as this standard represents a culmination of your work through RVL 1 A, B, and C. As you apply the previously introduced 19 strategies, you may find the common challenges all but eliminated from your feedback (see Table 5.1).

TABLE 5.1 RVL 1.D COMMON CHALLENGES

- Not citing any strengths
- Only providing praise versus evidence-based strengths
- No clear determination as to whether practices were effective
- Unclear why/how actions, strategies, or outcomes reflect areas of strength or growth

Skill Set for Determining Areas of Strength and Growth

If you have worked through an analysis of your evidence as outlined in Chapter 4, you have actually completed a significant portion of the work in this process. The next step is to categorize your findings about the effectiveness of the lesson into areas of strength and growth for the teacher. Though our ultimate goal as instructional leaders is to promote teacher reflection about these areas, many times the teachers we coach require directive or guided feedback, as they are not ready or are unable to arrive at their own conclusions about the effectiveness of their lessons. Therefore, this chapter will provide strategies for explicitly identifying and citing areas of strength and growth, while Chapter 6 explores strategies to promote a teacher's ability to determine these through the use of reflective questions. Let's examine how we can measure associated skills and assess the quality of the feedback using standard RVL 1.D on the ReVISION Learning Supervisory Continuum (see Figure 5.1).

FIGURE 5.1: STANDARD RVL 1.D

ReVISION **Supervisory Continuum**				
Domain 1: Evidence-Based Observation	**Beginning**	**Developing**	**Proficient**	**Exceptional**
D. Feedback contains areas of strengths and areas of growth explicitly connected to the indicator and observed practices/ evidence and are developed based on indicator language and the key levers between ratings.	Clear areas for teacher growth have not been identified and/or areas of strength have not been recognized. They have little to do with observed lesson and teaching practice. The areas of strength and growth are not directly connected to evidence and/or indicator language. Key levers between ratings are not utilized for developing the areas of growth and areas of strength.	Some areas for teacher growth along with areas of strength have been identified. They are at least partially connected with observed lesson and teaching practice. The feedback for areas of strength and growth include some connections to the evidence and/or the indicator language. Key levers between ratings are addressed and sometimes connected and utilized for developing the areas of growth and areas of strength.	Clear areas for teacher growth along with areas of strength have often been identified and are often connected with observed lesson and teaching practice and the indicator language. Key levers between ratings are clearly connected to the areas of strength and growth and often utilized for developing specific feedback.	Feedback statements clearly articulate and define the areas of strength and areas of growth with specific data and evidence. They are clearly connected to the indicators and build on the key levers. Feedback provides explicit evidence that supports areas of growth across multiple indicators of the teacher performance rubric while reinforcing positive practice through articulation of effective teaching practice.

Notice the difference between the "Proficient" and "Exceptional" performance levels. To provide high-quality feedback that will result in improved practice and student outcomes, areas of growth and strength should be clear and rooted in evidence as well as the rubric. To achieve this, leaders must not only master the skills up to this point, related to RVL 1 A, B, and C, but also the additional set of skills found in Table 5.2.

TABLE 5.2	SKILL SET FOR RVL 1.D
Core Skills	**Description**
Recognize and Cite Research-Based Strategies	Identifying when an educator utilizes or neglects to utilize research-based strategies, building areas of growth and strength from this understanding, and citing this in feedback
Determine Performance Level	Utilizing the framework to determine areas of strength and growth
Determine Teacher's Impact on Learning and Engagement	Categorizing teacher effectiveness as areas of strength and areas of growth based on the teacher's impact on the learners

What Teachers Need to Know

As mentioned in Chapter 2, Hattie and Timperley (2007) established that high-quality feedback should allow a teacher to clearly answer three essential questions:

- Where am I going?

- How am I going?

- Where to next? (p. 86)

"Establishing meaningful, focused improvement goals requires a shared understanding of the present position in terms of student learning and teacher's teaching, the ideal destination, and the path between the two" (Frontier & Mielke, 2016, p. 107). So how do we do this successfully? Let's begin by clarifying terms you will encounter in this chapter.

An area of strength is considered an effective practice, or defined as any action that results in a positive impact on learners, such as increased or evident

- understanding of new concepts or strategies;

- levels of motivation, growth mindset, or engagement;

- shared responsibility for procedures and learning; and

- respectful relationships within the community of learners.

Whereas, **an area of growth** might reflect a potentially negative impact or a less-than-desired outcome, such as

- low engagement,

- limited success with procedural elements, and

- an inability of students to move forward in understanding.

This may also represent the "Where to next?" for a teacher after an effective lesson.

Just as we coach teachers to provide actionable feedback to students to advance toward a learning target, leaders must focus on providing teachers with feedback that will promote immediate action and advance their understanding of targeted practices. "Too often in education we spend time naming problems rather solving them. We talk about what's wrong at length instead of living in solutions" (Sackstein, 2016). This chapter will break down the process of *how* to put solutions into motion by identifying, organizing, and integrating clear areas of growth and strength into feedback.

> **Stop and Think:** How have you been helping a teacher answer "How am I going?" and "Where to next?"

Teachers Need Authentic Praise and Positives

"If you don't acknowledge progress, you lose people's trust." —Aguilar, 2013, p. 56

It is easy to jump right into dissecting ineffective practices in a lesson, processing solutions while you are still in the classroom instead of remaining present and objective. Maybe after you leave, your energy is focused on determining what needs to change, identifying what wasn't working, or noting those students who were not on task or doing what they needed to be doing—without ever recognizing a teacher's strengths and/or the practices that were positively impacting students in some way. It is as important for instructional leaders to refine the ability to recognize and cite those observed effective practices and to praise teachers for efforts and accomplishments for the following reasons:

- The positives serve as entry or jumping-off points for actionable next steps.

- This sends a message that feedback is about growth.

- The positives diminish a negative or corrective emphasis.

Ideally, leaders should *utilize evidence* to support positive statements and remember to praise a teacher for any of the following:

- Making an observed change from previous feedback or coaching.

- Exhibiting effort, risk-taking, or a growth mindset.

- Demonstrating baby-step improvements in a particular practice that still may not be meeting expectations.

Frontier and Mielke (2016) reminded us, "Appreciative feedback is essential because it helps others feel connected and valued. . . . [It] is the easiest to receive . . . and ensures that when giving coaching and evaluative feedback, those on the receiving end are willing to listen" (p. 97). Though we must often deliver news of ineffective lessons, many times the receiver of the feedback will focus on the low ratings or what he or she deems to be negative. "Negative feedback is more likely to be rejected as individuals seek to protect their egos and confirm their self-efficacy beliefs . . . [and] is more likely to be recalled inaccurately" (Lavigne & Good, 2015, p. 140). This is why it is so important to recognize and build on demonstrated strengths utilizing the strategies in this chapter.

Using Analysis

Remember, this is not an arbitrary process borne of opinion or what "seemed" to be occurring. To accurately and effectively determine these areas, observers can use their specific and comprehensive collected evidence (RVL 1.B) and thorough analysis of that evidence (RVL 1.C). Let's look at some examples that represent four different scenarios. Think about how the leaders are determining strengths and challenges from the observed lessons.

Scenario 1: Sometimes, areas of strength are immediately obvious to the observer while you are still present in the classroom:

- Upon arrival, all 6 groups are working independently and collaboratively using shared Google Calendars, Docs, and Slides, along with their notes and textbook to determine the focus area of their calculus final projects, and are planning the work timeline. The teacher monitors their conversations and plans, challenging students to increase the level of rigor of their proposed topics considering their audience.

- During the writing lesson, the 1st graders transition (without facilitation from the teacher) from the carpet to their seats and are working with required materials in under three minutes. They are working independently while the teacher pulls a small group to review writing foundations. Half at their seats are using texts as resources and 7/7 can explain to the observer what they are writing and why.

Scenario 2: Other times, you might find the areas of strength clearly emerge *after* reviewing collected evidence using strategies you learned in Chapter 4. We never want to be hasty in our judgments, so regardless of what you notice immediately and instinctually, it is important to collect detailed evidence to support what you are seeing. We not only want to notice the strengths but determine how and why they are occurring. Let's look at a few other examples:

- 16/20 students were mastering a rigorous learning target to utilize the new writing strategy because the teacher modeled the strategy through a think-aloud in the mini-lesson, showed mentor texts demonstrating the strategy, and connected and compared/contrasted it to previous strategies they had already been using.

- At each of the 5 tables, students were successfully facilitating their own group work advancing their learning because the teacher explicitly taught the use of the manipulatives before they began. Students shared that earlier in the year they were taught social and collaborative skills. Students shared this and could explain the rubric for group work expectations.

- In partners, nearly all students were using various available resources and helping each other to answer challenging questions about a text because the teacher promotes perseverance and independence and has taught students how to use the resources.

Notice the observer is thinking about *why* the evidence represents an effective practice or "strength" and how the teacher is causing these outcomes, communicating these connections with "because statements."

Stop and Think: How have you determined a teacher's areas of strengths after an observation?

Scenario 3: Or perhaps, thinking back to an observer's evidence you encountered in Chapter 2, the areas for growth may become immediately clear to you during a lesson:

- In the 6th grade math lesson, nearly half (8/20) of the students incorrectly completed the Do Now and 5 are not finished when the teacher put the answers on the board after 6 minutes of work time. The teacher checks to see that everyone copied down the correct answers but does not address the misunderstandings, going on with the day's lesson.

Scenario 4: However, again as with strengths, we do not want to simply cite areas of growth but determine how and why they are occurring as you review and analyze your evidence. Let's look again at some general examples from other lessons:

- When asked, 8/8 students had a surface understanding of the day's objective, task for the day, or why they were completing the task, because the teacher introduced the day's work in 3 minutes only, providing the directions for the task without communicating a specific learning target or context for the new learning. [Observer analyzed all of the student responses to determine this.]

- At each table during the Spanish lesson, there are 1-2 students who are not engaging in the group conversation to plan a skit using the new vocabulary because they can't see the Chromebook, only 2 have the list of vocabulary out, and one student is doing nearly all of the work. [immediately clear] However, when questioned, those not participating all had the same misunderstanding about their responsibilities in the group and at least 1 in every group was missing basic conjugation of common verbs and had no resources out, so they struggled to assist in writing lines.

- Half of the students are sitting waiting for the teacher to help because they either don't have their math notebooks and tools on their desks or know where in their notes to locate the necessary information. [immediately clear] [Upon investigation of evidence] 5 of the 8 students waiting had incomplete notes and could not explain to the observer the concepts they represented from previous days' lessons. They found the online resource "confusing."

Scenario 5: However, sometimes we need to analyze further because areas of growth are often just areas of strength in process (e.g., based on the time of year, developmental levels, or laying of foundations):

- Half the students do not know where to find the supplies or know the steps to start the science lab because this is the second lab of the year but the teacher is reminding students: of the posted protocols, to review the directions on their lab worksheet, and to use the labels on the containers. The teacher is working to promote independence and build student understanding of routines they will use all year.

> **Stop and Think:** Think about each scenario. Have you found yourself in any of these situations? Perhaps you noticed how the observer used quantitative and qualitative evidence to increase objectivity and clarity.

There are three key strategies observers can use to recognize what behaviors, actions, and dispositions represent areas of strength and growth based on an observed lesson, and you will notice they are grounded in your effective evidence collection:

- The overall effectiveness of the lesson in terms of engagement and learning

- The framework language, understanding how your district/region defines effective practice

- What you know about research-based strategies or program designs. Teachers need coaching that is rooted in the model or curriculum they are following. You might have observed a minilesson that was ineffective, but the teacher was reading the teacher's guide word for word, following the recommended instructional practice for this particular lesson. You will be challenged to recognize the root cause and next steps if you don't understand, say, the recommended structure of a minilesson along with how to differentiate within that model.

Strategies 20 through 22 are closely related and interconnected and do not require that you follow them sequentially. You might find you are executing these simultaneously as you use the strategies from Chapter 4, analyzing the teacher's impact on the learners. You might have noticed the observers in the previous examples were beginning to use these three recommended strategies.

Determining Areas of Strength and Growth

Strategy 20: Focus on the overall observed impact on student learning and engagement

Look for a moment again at the sixth-grade math lesson in Scenario 3. Did you notice that the attention was on student *mis*understanding? In the last chapter, you read many lesson analyses with attention to student evidence and outcomes. You will find that as you conduct a comprehensive analysis of effectiveness of the teacher's impact on the learners, you have already begun to clearly separate elements of the lesson into areas of strength and growth.

Let's think back to one of the first classroom examples from the last chapter—the second-grade English language arts lesson. Remember, we were working to determine the cause of the observed outcomes with focused attention on the learners, noting that students were not successfully recording character traits on their stickies. The observer had already started to determine what was effective or ineffective based on the number of students successfully attempting to use the strategy or appropriately following directions. Let's review the findings from that lesson now as potential areas of strength and growth:

> Areas of Strength: The teacher modeled during the minilesson and worked with a small group on a literacy skill. This is generally an effective practice because we know learners benefit from an "I do" step when learning new skills along with additional targeted support.

Remember, the observer noted that the teacher modeled using only the book's pictures yet wanted them to go beyond illustrations to use the author's characterization methods (dialogue, actions, emotions, thoughts, etc.) on their own. After a review of the student responses on the carpet and at their tables and through an analysis of what they understood about character traits, it was clear they were guessing at emotions, providing words as to how the character "felt" based on the illustrations or the story events. Emotions are important to follow in characters as they generally will change and are often clues to the character's traits and personality. However, this was Day 3 of a focus on characters, and second graders are able to discern between feelings and traits. So this starts to point to a potential area of growth based on what the learners were doing and saying.

> Areas of Growth: The teacher did not model the use of the strategy she wanted them to apply: to understand characters' personality traits (how they think, act, and feel) by using evidence or clues in the text. She did not walk them through a think-aloud for processing how to use the story clues to recognize traits. She did not help the learners make connections to prior learning (such as reviewing what a trait was and how it differs from feelings) or remind them of their resource list in their desks that they had been using for two days. We know this is a potential

```
area of growth because there were learners who were
not working at all, using incorrect text selections,
sitting without the necessary supplies, and who could
not explain traits on stickies.
```

Stop and Think: Look back at a feedback report you wrote or consider a coaching conversation you had with a teacher recently. How did those teacher's strengths relate to his or her impact on the students? Did you convey this?

Strategy 21: Use the instructional framework to recognize expectations

Look back at the first-grade example from Scenario 1 and independence in routines. Did you notice that the observer noted time of transitions? Most frameworks include an indicator that addresses the efficiency of routines, role of students, and use of instructional time (see Table 5.3), which helps an observer recognize expected practice.

TABLE 5.3   INDICATOR FOR EXPECTED PRACTICE

Proficient	Distinguished
There is little loss of instructional time due to effective classroom routines and procedures. The teacher's management of instructional groups and transitions, or handling of materials and supplies, or both, are consistently successful. With minimal guidance and prompting, students follow established classroom routines.	Instructional time is maximized due to efficient and seamless classroom routines and procedures. Students take initiative in the management of instructional groups and transitions, and/or the handling of materials and supplies. Routines are well understood and may be initiated by students.

Source: The Danielson Group (2013)

As mentioned in Chapter 1, and as you have surely noticed, most current instructional frameworks have consistently integrated student actions, behaviors, dispositions, and outcomes into the performance levels. Within these, you can find clear descriptions and look-fors of effective teacher practices, often along with the desired student outcomes. (Note: If your rubric does not include student outcomes, use what you know from research regarding what the ideal outcomes should be.) The indicators form the foundation for instructional areas of strength and serve as benchmarks for areas of growth.

Remember from Chapter 2 that to develop effective feedback, you are making claims about practice (that will represent/convey areas of growth and strength) utilizing the language from the framework. "To improve the quality of teaching, one must first have an understanding [of] what quality teaching is," and to effectively determine areas of strength and areas of growth, "school leaders need to understand the attributes of effective practice and the indicators of each level of performance" (McKay, 2013, p. 43).

Citing Areas of Strength and Growth

Areas of Strength

Let's look at a few other lesson examples of how to use the rubric to recognize areas of strength first.

FIGURE 5.2: INDICATOR EXAMPLE 1 FOR STRENGTH AND GROWTH AREAS

	Below Standard	Developing	Proficient	Exemplary
Attributes				*In addition to the characteristics of* **Proficient**, *including one or more of the following*:
Criteria for student success	Does not communicate criteria for success and/or opportunities for students to self-assess are rare.	Communicates general criteria for success and provides limited opportunities for students to self-assess.	Communicates specific criteria for success and provides multiple opportunities for students to self-assess.	Integrates student input in generating specific criteria for assignments.
Ongoing assessment of student learning	Assesses student learning with focus limited to task completion and/or compliance rather than student achievement of lesson purpose/objective.	Assesses student learning with focus on whole-class progress toward achievement of the intended instructional outcomes.	Assesses student learning with focus on eliciting evidence of learning at critical points in the lesson in order to monitor individual and group progress toward achievement of the intended instructional outcomes.	Promotes students' independent monitoring and self-assess, helping themselves or their peers to improve their learning.

Source: Common Core of Teaching (2014), Connecticut State Department of Education

After observing a high school chemistry lesson, the observer organized evidence and analyzed the teacher's impact, arriving at a conclusion about the effectiveness of the instruction. He recognizes that the practices and outcomes observed align with the "Proficient" description (see Figure 5.2 on the previous page), thus pointing to areas of strength.

> Claim: The teacher communicated specific criteria and provided multiple opportunities for students to self-assess.
>
> The teacher provided students with specific and clear criteria in the form of an electronic checklist for completing their lab reports. Because the teacher reviewed the checklist before they began working, referring back to it when he was providing feedback, all students were consistently observed assessing the quality and required elements of their final report against the checklist throughout the lesson, making adjustments, and altering their plans.

It is equally important to not just cite what was observed and its impact but to recognize that the teacher is building student capacity in some way. Leaders can use the framework "Proficient" and "Exemplary" descriptions to recognize those teacher practices or student behaviors that establish a foundation for a further targeted end goal—helping a teacher see how attainable these might be. Teachers receiving "Proficient" or "Effective" ratings want to know "What's next?" also. Consider supporting feedback from a seventh-grade writing lesson with the same rating/claim about criteria:

> In pairs, students were reading the opening of their own essays against an exemplar and writing rubric. It was evident in all 9 pairings that the teacher had built their capacity to share ideas, listen, and take turns, and to use tools to self-assess. They were successfully sharing with each other what they were noticing about their own work and one thing they might change to strengthen it. This is effectively building their capacity toward peer review/feedback.

Areas of Growth

Let's now build on what you learned in Chapter 2 about your rubric performance levels. You might recognize after you organize and analyze your evidence that the observed practices and outcomes do not align with the "Proficient" descriptions. This is the first step in determining an area of growth. The definitions and look-fors of less than effective practices are provided in the "Developing" or "Below Standard" rating descriptions on an instructional framework. In the next chapter, you will explore how to use the differences between the ratings (or the key levers) to help you build action steps. Let's look at an example of how to use the rubric to recognize areas of growth, thinking again about the sixth-grade math lesson from Scenario 3, looking this time at the second attribute for ongoing assessment (looking at Figure 5.2 again):

The observer cannot build a claim about practice from the "Proficient" rating.

```
Claim: The teacher assessed task completion rather
than student achievement and understanding.

The teacher moved forward with the lesson without
noting who was struggling or why, only ensuring that
students had copied the required information from
the board. Though warm-up activities are meant to be
brief, "Do Nows" can be used not to just activate
prior learning but to provide a teacher with evi-
dence of understanding of previous concepts before
beginning a new lesson. This allows her to make an
instructional decision about how to proceed. During
and after a Do Now are considered "critical points"
in a lesson that provide opportunities for a teacher
to monitor understanding of prerequisite skills.
Those struggling/not complete were observed strug-
gling on the guided partner problems later.
```

Stop and Think: Notice the integration of rubric language along with a Strategy 20 focus on the learners. But is ongoing assessment the only area of growth when you start to think about what was happening instructionally? What else should be considered?

Making Cross-Indicator Connections

If you look at the "Exceptional" description from our standard RVL 1.D (Figure 5.1) introduced at the beginning of the chapter, you will notice it includes that the leader "provides evidence that supports areas of growth across multiple indicators." We know nothing in a lesson exists in isolation, so leaders should strive to make explicit connections to other indicators or show teachers how one action or strategy impacts other aspects of instruction or outcomes.

This is supported by Bambrick-Santoyo's (2012) view that feedback should result in "action steps that drive improvement for the greatest number of aspects of the lesson at once" (p. 72). Sometimes in feedback, leaders will simply repeat the same suggested areas of growth for each indicator, which can be frustrating to a teacher. However, the observer can avoid this by focusing on the true intent of each indicator and aligning each area of growth and strength with the appropriate attribute or indicator. However, to then help a teacher see the interconnectedness of actions and impacts across the indicators, explicit connections can be made. Let's look at an example to make this clearer.

In the math lesson, the observer is thinking about assessment methods, but consider your work in Chapter 4 and the root cause of what was happening in this lesson. The observer has to dig further and question why so many students were unable to successfully complete problems that were in essence review from the day before. This potentially points to an issue in the progression and scaffolding in the previous and current lessons, the use of the previous day's evidence of understanding in planning, and potential differentiation that was needed.

To start down the path of making connections, the observer can add the following:

```
Without clearly determining who was struggling with
prerequisite skills and why, and then by not acting
on that information (i.e., providing them with nec-
essary support or reteaching), those students who did
not understand or correctly complete the Do Now prob-
lems were unable to construct an understanding of the
new concepts. This is directly related to the pro-
gression and differentiation indicators that support
construction of new learning.
```

To this point, we have helped the teacher see what was happening with the learners using the framework as the foundation.

Understanding Research-Based Strategies

Strategy 22: Use what you know about research-based strategies

We know there is plenty of research about the importance and impact of effective formative assessment during a lesson. Our next strategy addresses what you understand about research such as this, how you use this knowledge to determine areas of strength and growth, and finally, how you are building your teachers' understanding of the research through your feedback.

When we think about a lesson in terms of what the research says—what we know students need and what we do or do not see related to this—we begin to form the foundation of our feedback and next steps for the teacher. When you are developing feedback for growth, building a teacher's understanding of the related supporting research is critical, because this serves to increase the objectivity of your feedback and validate your conclusions while also promoting more purposeful planning and future reflection on the teacher's part. Generally, when research-based strategies or expected outcomes are observed in a classroom, they will be considered teacher strengths, as they result in desired actions, behaviors or dispositions, new learning, and/or high levels of engagement (or a teacher is moving in that direction). Think back to the second-grade English language arts example. The observer is aware of the structure of the workshop model and saw elements of the research-based strategies even though the teacher was not 100% successful.

What You Know

Let's start with what you do already know. You may already incorporate Strategy 22 in your observation and feedback work as an instructional leader. You also might be one who sits on the beach reading the best new education books every summer, follows thought leaders on Twitter, subscribes to well-respected journals, or attends professional learning sessions with your teams. (Remember, this was Cheryl and Christine's suggestion from Chapter 1.) You have also clocked many hours of schooling to increase your understanding of effective pedagogy, educational research, and theory to arrive at your position as an instructional leader. Therefore, when you are working through the steps outlined in Chapter 4—analyzing teacher effectiveness—you are tapping into your knowledge of research-based strategies. Let's start with a simple example and revisit evidence from two classrooms involving teacher feedback and the impact it can have on risk-taking:

Teacher 1:   T-"It's okay; let's give Brandon a minute to look through his notes to find it...he doesn't have it yet. [After waiting]...Do you want to 'phone a friend?'"

Teacher 2:   T-"Hurry, we are waiting." [S rushes to answer] "No, that's not right."

How did you know Teacher 1's practice was more effective than Teacher 2's beyond just watching the physical reaction of the student and your gut feeling?

Though you aligned Teacher 1's practice to an indicator and description that said, "Creates a learning environment in which most students are willing to take risks" (CSDE, 2014), what is the research behind this?

Remember, we mentioned that research confirmed direct correlations among teachers' expectations, student beliefs/self-efficacy, and student outcomes, and Costa and Kallick (2009) continued this work, affirming the power of teacher messaging through feedback to promote positive habits and mindsets as an impetus behind risk-taking. This information is important for you as a leader to know and understand and for teachers to always consider while planning and executing a lesson.

Let's walk through four steps to increase your understanding of research-based strategies.

Step 1: Identify what you don't know.

If you have a general understanding of the research, that is a good start. However, to effectively lead learning, it is critical to continue to build on what you know. Let's look at realistic expectations for instructional leaders. Ideally, you should be able to do the following:

- Recognize and connect research-based strategies to school and district/region goals.

- Recognize when research-based strategies are being utilized in instruction and are integrated into curriculum and program/models.

- Cite observed research-based strategies or an absence thereof.

- Explain to teachers why the strategies are important and the short- and long-range impact on students.

- Be able to make connections between the strategies and indicators on the district framework to explain *why* the practices in the higher ratings are effective.

Step 2: Focus on areas that impact learning and engagement. (Use Strategy 20.)

To start the process of assessing what it is you do not know, flip back to The Big Picture table in Chapter 2 (Table 2.3).

1. How many questions in the table can you comfortably answer after leaving a classroom?

2. How many questions can you explain to a teacher to affirm effective practice or support alternate strategies?

3. How many of these concepts do you integrate into your feedback to teachers currently?

"Although there are important distinctions in the social and learning needs that students have . . . there is a core of teacher instructional actions, dispositions, and beliefs that most, if not all students benefit from" (Lavigne & Good, 2015, p. 95).

> **Stop and Think:** You started with thinking about the chart, but what *truly* is the depth of your understanding of research-based strategies? Carefully consider the depth in the following areas. Use a system like a familiar self-assessment "Fist-to-5" (see Table 5.4) for this reflection and as you move through this chapter.

TABLE 5.4	SELF-ASSESSMENT
Fist	I don't understand at all.
1	I need help. I just have a very basic understanding.
2	I could use more practice, reading, and learning.
3	I understand pretty well and can communicate somewhat what I know.
4	I mostly understand and can communicate what I know easily.
5	I completely understand and can teach someone else.

Let's start with some basic overarching research-based strategies that we recommend every leader understands.

Overarching essentials include the following:

- Lesson and unit planning/curriculum and/or models in use.

- Development of specific and rigorous learning targets and learning criteria.

- Common Core State Standards/your new standards and 21st century skills (e.g., conceptual understanding in math, discipline-specific literacy strategies, new science standards, collaboration).

- An understanding of how to define, observe for, and measure engagement and learning (including understanding taxonomies to classify the level of thinking for tasks and questions).

Focus Area Essentials

You encountered five focus areas that impact learning and engagement in your analysis work in Chapter 4. Table 5.5 provides a framework and some suggestions to help you consider your own knowledge base in more targeted areas.

TABLE 5.5	RESEARCH FOCUS AREAS
Focus Areas	**Specific Practices to Understand**
Focus Area #1: Environment	Social, emotional, and developmental needs, student self-regulation mindsets and habits
Focus Area #2: Level of Challenge	Scaffolding, gradual release, zone of proximal development
Focus Area #3: Progression	Student-centered or student-driven instruction; essential skills for the 21st century/4 C's (e.g., learning to positively disagree to collaborate); use of technology
Focus Area #4: Assessment	Assessment and feedback cycles; design of rigorous assessments to apply new learning
Focus Area #5: Supports	Differentiation/personalization strategies

Step 3: Connect the research to the indicators on your framework. (Use Strategy 21.)

Remember, we mentioned that your framework is rooted in research.

- Take a breath and review your framework for a few minutes and think about your work from Chapter 2—the examination of the structure and organization of your rubric.

- Remember, overarching intents for indicators or attributes are the first clues as to how the designers integrated research-based strategies.

Stop and Think: Now look at the previous lists. Where/how are those instructional elements integrated into your framework? Skim your rubric's performance descriptions. How do they represent what we know about teaching and learning in the 21st century?

Step 4: Seek out resources.

You might have determined there are areas in which you gave yourself a fist or one to two fingers. That's okay! Think about a place to start and then set realistic expectations for your own learning with bite-sized goals. You can also prioritize focus areas based on the following:

- Current specific instructional needs in your classrooms.

- Team, grade level, school, and/or district/region goals.

It is important to remember that resources come in many shapes and sizes.

- Look for experts in your building. Your staff is your best source of information.

  ○ Learn about your teachers' areas of expertise, as they can become leaders in your building. Spend time in their classrooms and absorb as many exemplary practices as you can. Consider recording lessons to build a bank of exemplars for your teachers.

  ○ Coaches are highly trained in targeted areas. Go observe them while they are modeling practices, sit in on planning meetings with their teams, or ask them to mentor specific teachers.

  ○ Do you have a tech-support person? They are a wealth of information and eager to spread the joy of technology to anyone interested.

- Use the internet. Of course, be warned! If you Google "21st century skills," you will end up with 1.6 million results. Therefore, talk to colleagues and teachers about their favorite resources. Try to subscribe to an educational journal and informal blogs focused on targeted areas or practices. Consult known publisher sites and search by category for newest releases. Find quick hits of information through feeds with search engines like Twitter, video warehouse Teaching Channel, or information-rich sites like Edutopia or Edudemic (certainly to name just a few).

Stop and Think: What/who are the untapped resources in your building?

Using Research-Based Strategies in Feedback

Now that you have some strategies for increasing your knowledge base, let's get back to how we use this research to determine areas of strength and growth.

We return to an example from Chapter 4—the 11th-grade science lesson. As you revisit the evidence (see Table 5.6) and the observer's thinking, notice how areas of strength and areas of growth are clearly emerging. The observer is well-versed in the 4 C's (the district's goal) and wants to explicitly develop feedback around the related research-based strategies.

TABLE 5.6   CAUSE AND EFFECT: SCIENCE LESSON

Evidence/What Was Happening	Potential Causes
• Ss passively watched until T said to presenters: "What should they write down?" Ss then copied what they were told to write. • 3 sets of presenters read from slides, I could not answer questions about the topic, though answers were on slides, I set mispronounced words/names on slides. • Ss were to create a "report" and were not given a purpose beyond "reporting" to classmates. • In creating the reports, Ss told the observer they used Wikipedia or the first sources they found when they Googled and copied and pasted information. S-O "It's just to know."	• Purpose was solely to create a report • No goals for presenters established beyond a list of required content on slides • No requirement for the listeners beyond copying notes • No "research" conducted or research guidelines offered

The observer wants to be sure to recognize practices that demonstrate the veteran teacher's willingness to turn over learning to students, something they discussed in their last coaching session. She also wants to connect the related framework language in regard to the cognitive demand of the tasks, so she will integrate the language from the indicator in Figure 5.3 on the opposite page.

Based on the research and the indicator, the observer also wants to consider what strategies were and were not used (see Table 5.7).

TABLE 5.7   ANALYSIS OF OBSERVED RESEARCH-BASED STRATEGIES

Applied Research-Based Strategies	Missing Elements of Research-Based Strategies
• Integrating research into projects/use of a variety of sources beyond the textbook • Partner work for collaboration • Development of speaking and listening through presentations • Use of a relevant topic and choice of topics	• Direct instruction on how to research, search, use, and trust sites • Critical thinking in the design of the presentation or for the audience • Expectations for high school presenters • Rigorous use or application of new content

FIGURE 5.3: INDICATOR EXAMPLE 2 FOR STRENGTH AND GROWTH AREAS

	Below Standard	Developing	Proficient	Exemplary
Attributes				*In addition to the characteristics of* **Proficient**, *including one or more of the following*:
Strategies, tasks and questions	Includes tasks that do not lead students to construct new and meaningful learning and that focus primarily on low cognitive demand or recall of information.	Includes a combination of tasks and questions in an attempt to lead students to construct new learning, but are of low cognitive demand and/or recall of information with some opportunities for problem solving, critical thinking and/or purposeful discourse or inquiry.	Employs differentiated strategies, tasks, and questions that cognitively engage students in constructing new and meaningful learning through appropriately integrated recall, problem solving, critical and creative thinking, purposeful discourse and/or inquiry. At times, students take the lead and develop their own questions and problem-solving strategies.	Includes opportunities for students to work collaboratively to generate their own questions and problem-solving strategies, synthesize and communicate information.

Source: Common Core of Teaching (2014), Connecticut State Department of Education

Let's review the observer's annotated feedback in Figure 5.4 on page 148, pulling all of these ideas together. Consider the following:

- The way in which she integrates the absence and/or use of research-based strategies.

- The use of words like "though," "however," and "because" to connect the areas of strength and growth.

- A focus on a key area: level of challenge.

Stop and Think: Which of these feedback strategies do you already utilize and which would you like to try implementing next?

FIGURE 5.4: ANNOTATED FEEDBACK SAMPLE

The students were tasked with researching, using multiple sources, worked collaboratively, and were able to practice speaking and listening skills – all 21st century skills. Though they were offered choice within a current relevant issue, the resulting level of thinking or cognitive demand was low for the presenters and the audience members. Creating a factual presentation does not represent a high level of Bloom's, as they simply were reciting what had been copied onto a slide. Because the task was to "report," presenters included only facts and surface level pros and cons. Because there was no task for the listeners beyond copying notes from slided or direction to use the information presented, audience members were complaint, either using recall or transcribing what was printed or stated.

They did not need to evaluate, debate, or select one suitable alternative over another as an overarching purpose of the presentation and research.

Because students were not explicitly taught research skills, they simply copied information from the internet onto their slides.

> Citing effective research-based practices and areas of strength

> Citing challenges and areas of growth based on research-based strategies and

> Helping the teacher see examples of research-based strategies

> Connecting to an indicator about progression/scaffolding as a cause of the outcome

Pulling It All Together

Let's look at feedback developed after an instructional leader observed a sixth-grade English language arts lesson. The leader had been working with this teacher on progression of her lessons, focusing on how she introduced the learning objective and target strategy, helped students make connections, and modeled in the first 10 to 15 minutes. More than half of the students in this class are reading below grade level, and six of those students are English language learners. During the observation, students were reading a nonfiction text about the cause and impact of the Chicago Fire and were going to be locating and note-taking "important information" as they read. Ultimately, students struggled to comprehend the text and use the new strategy, so the leader wants to think about how to build on this teacher's strengths. Notice how the detailed evidence (RVL 1.B) is interlaced with cause-and-effect explanations (RVL 1.C). Read each section and determine how this observer used the three strategies outlined in this chapter to arrive at clear areas of growth and strength.

Feedback Sample (Overall areas of strength):

> Ms. R utilized an interactive read-aloud strategy
> with a complex grade-level nonfiction text in the
> lesson with an end task for students to write a sum-
> mary of what they read. Reading the text aloud pro-
> vided a model for fluency and also supported the
> struggling readers and English language learners as
> they followed along. She also included 5 turn and
> talks (stop and retell) for every 2 pages of text to
> allow students to share/gain knowledge with peers (in
> line with the suggested model), which can aid in com-
> prehension and maintain engagement in the reading.
> Building students' capacity to utilize during-reading
> strategies such as placing stickies on key points
> (stop and jot) is an effective practice to increase
> comprehension and promote self-monitoring.

Stop and Think: What did you notice about how the leader cited areas of strength?

Now read through the observer's analysis regarding three possible focus areas and what he knows about research-based strategies.

Focus Area: Progression

Claim: The progression of the lesson to include the introduction/
prereading, the during-reading process, and after-reading step
were each missing key components.

Connect:

> **Before Reading:** Explicitly discussing and modeling
> how to locate "important information" to create a
> summary did not occur (T mentioned she had shown them
> how with a video the other day). This resulted in
> 5 students with 1 stickie in the section, and 2 with
> more than 2 stickies with single words written
> (9:29). Only 2 students pointed back to the text in
> turn-and-talk #1 (this pair was not observed doing
> so again, nor was anyone else), and pairs never ref-
> erenced where they had placed the stickies.

During: At no time before or during the reading was the complex vocabulary addressed, which contributed to a lack of understanding. There were over 10 challenging words in this section (e.g., amplify, lamenting, scapegoat, scorn, diatribe). One student asked if he could get out a dictionary and he looked up "culprit" on his own—a keyword, as the section was about myths around who the "culprit" was in starting the fire.

After: Students were not provided time to discuss or reread before starting the individual summaries. Ss were unable to accurately summarize the text. As students began to write the summary, the observer questioned the pairs (P) using a quote from the last line of the text: "How did the fire change the city?" Students demonstrated a lack of understanding/nor did they use text-based answers [text talked about socioeconomic impacts]:

1. P1: The city was happy and calm and then everybody was depressed. The fire brought them together. It changed them because it was devastating and sad.

2. P2: They will start getting along more. They know they will have each other.

3. P2: They noticed it was a bad idea to make it out of wood.

4. P3: It destroyed the city. They have to rebuild it. It is different because of the fire. (observer: "How?" S-the memories, the people)

5. P4: They had to build things and be more careful. Everything wouldn't be the same—how would they build again if there was no money.

Focus Area: Level of Challenge The teacher did not ask any text-dependent questions, clarify vocabulary, or allow students to preview for challenging words/use the context. The story also became more challenging beyond details of the fire starting, which caused the quality of the turn-and-talks (1 minute timed on the clock for each) to diminish (often just guessing). This demonstrated a decreasing understanding of the text as the "story" of the impact of the fire on society was explored beginning around 9:25, with ideas that eluded students, such as "sweeping generalizations" "a public-relations campaign developed" and the fire as a "friend of the poor man." (Evidence: Turn-and-talk #1-3: Nearly all could share facts about the start of the fire and the myths that were generated. P1: "They thought the firefighters started the fire." P2: "It was a big lie because . . . ."

However, turn-and-talk #4-5: limited literal facts cited, 50% of students not sharing, conversations were shorter so 4 pairs were sitting waiting—"They were sad.")

Focus Area: Assessment The teacher did not monitor the fact that students were not using the stickies, were not talking to each other/quality of the conversation, or that they did not understand. Therefore, she was not providing feedback or stopping the reading at any point to address the diminishing understanding.

> **Stop and Think**: How did the observer use the three new strategies?

Did you notice the following?

1. **Attention to Learners:** collected and cited evidence and analysis of engagement, participation in turn-and-talks, on-task/completing stickies, content of the stickies, student comprehension of the text, and student understanding of the vocabulary

2. **The Rubric:** attention to indicator language related to a logical progression, attention to cognitive engagement and ability to construct understanding of how to use the strategy and assessment and feedback/adjustments

3. **Research-Based Strategies:** observed use of complex nonfiction text, integration of metacognitive strategies, interactive read-aloud of complex text, and integration of social learning opportunities

Final Thoughts

This is all important information to share with a teacher, but it would certainly leave him or her overwhelmed and potentially running for the hills if we tried to tackle all of this at once. According to Bambrick-Santoyo (2012), "Principals using a traditional observation and feedback model feel—rightly— that they have limited opportunities to share all of the feedback they come up with," often resulting in action-step overload (p. 70). Your next stop on this journey moves you into Chapter 6: completing your feedback, the determination of high-leverage coaching points, and the development of action steps and reflective questions—ensuring your feedback feeds forward as a learning tool that promotes growth.

If you remember from the RVL 1.D description, instructional leaders need to ensure a teacher understands clear areas of growth and strength directly connected to the observed lesson and evidence, teacher practice, and the rubric indicator language. The three core strategies you encountered refine your ability to do this, analyzing

1. the overall effectiveness of the lesson;

2. the framework language and understanding how your district/region defines effective practice; and

3. what you know about research-based strategies or program designs, such as Workshop Model or publisher programs.

As you work to master the core skills of RVL 1.D—determining the teacher's impact on learning and engagement, determining performance levels, and recognizing and citing research-based strategies—you are ready to consider potential next steps for the teacher and work to build reflective practice in Chapter 6 tackling RVL 1.E and RVL 1.F, our final standards. Remember, you can access support resources at **resources.corwin.com/feedforward.**

How can your feedback feed forward?

In our trainings, leaders share immediate concerns when first introduced to the RVL standards and our expectation to develop "feedback that feeds forward":

"That kind of processing and writing takes too much time."

"This isn't realistic."

"Teachers won't read all of that feedback."

Other leaders struggle:

"I am not sure what the right next step should be."

But one new leader surveyed summed it up: "More effective feedback makes more effective teachers." Developing effective feedback is no simple feat, as evidenced by the nine new strategies you will encounter in this chapter (#23–#31). However, after only one day of training, leaders return to us saying the following, attributing the use of the feedback frame as the key: "We had such a great conversation!" "I was able to support and explain my ratings so clearly." "My conversations were so different."

> **From the field . . .**
>
> *Out of all my work and professional development, one area stands out as having the greatest impact on my ability to provide meaningful and effective feedback to teachers. As "Claim, Connect, Action" became more clear to me, I began to feel its profound impact on* all *teachers and not just the professionals who had an area that fell in the "developing" range. First, I must mention that Claim, Connect, Action acted as a magnet which drew me into the language of our instructional framework. In order to make claims and connections, I found myself truly analyzing the language within the framework's indicators in order to better articulate to my teachers what I had observed during my observations. I felt myself becoming more clear and precise, I knew my messaging was more consistent, and I was taking advantage of opportunities to educate my teachers about the framework and the powerful connections to their teaching practices.*
>
> —Jeff Wallowitz, Principal

Look how far you have come on your journey as an instructional leader! You have worked through 18 skills and 22 strategies to learn to do the following:

- *Observe and collect evidence:* Collect and utilize a balance of specific evidence aligned to an instructional framework to support growth (Chapters 2 & 3).

- *Analyze evidence:* Determine teacher effectiveness and impact on learners (Chapter 4).

- *Provide written feedback:* Determine and cite areas of strength and growth (Chapter 5).

In this chapter, you will round out the third competency of providing written feedback through examination of RVL 1.E and RVL 1.F, the final standards of the ReVISION Learning Supervisory Continuum. The standards and skills you have learned to this point now form the foundation that will allow you to move toward determining logical, attainable, and realistic next steps for a teacher, ensuring your feedback serves as an objective learning tool.

In this chapter you will

- build an awareness of subjectivity in your feedback and strategies to overcome bias; and

- explore strategies to develop personalized next steps and reflective questions using your evidence and analysis.

Building on the ideas introduced in Chapter 3 regarding subjectivity in our practice, it is important to remember that observers enter a classroom with varying perspectives, opinions, emotional states, reactions, and/or preconceived notions, which are then often conveyed in feedback. This chapter explores several potential biases that emerge in written or verbal feedback and offers strategies to overcome or avoid these sometimes subconscious habits, focusing first on developing capacity around RVL 1.E: *Using evidence-based and nonjudgmental statements in feedback to teachers.* Then you will learn to bring all of the strategies together around RVL 1.F to determine actionable next steps, resulting in feedback that will serve as a valuable resource for teachers.

Take a few minutes to review the performance levels of Indicator E of the ReVISION Learning Supervisory Continuum (see Figure 6.1).

FIGURE 6.1: RVL STANDARD 1.E

ReVISION Supervisory Continuum				
Domain 1: Evidence-Based Observation	**Beginning**	**Developing**	**Proficient**	**Exceptional**
E. Evidence cited is objectively stated and without opinion.	Evidence cited about teaching practice is judgmental and based on opinions. Little to no objective evidence has been identified.	Some evidence cited is objective but the majority is not. Summary and subjective opinions dominate.	Most evidence is nonjudgmental and the majority of data collected is evidence-based including such things as quotes from teacher and/or students, statements showing evidence from assessments or student work, tallies, or other non-judgmental statements that link situations/moments in the class to effective teaching practice or student learning outcomes.	Nearly all evidence is nonjudgmental and data collected is evidence-based including such things as quotes from teacher and/or students, statements showing evidence from assessments or student work, tallies, or other non-judgmental statements that link situations/moments in the class to effective teaching practice or student learning outcomes.
			© 2018 ReVISION Learning Partnership, LLC All Rights Reserved	

After reviewing the "Beginning" and "Developing" descriptions and considering what you have learned so far, think about why a summary of an observed lesson might be construed as subjective. Notice some common challenges that arise for instructional leaders in relation to RVL 1.E in Table 6.1. Receivers can view subjective feedback as meaningless or as a personal attack, or they may not value the opinion of the leader—all of which can diminish trust.

TABLE 6.1	RVL 1.E COMMON CHALLENGES

- Use of words like *great, bad, good, excellent*
- Use of quantifiers without quantitative data, like *some, few, too long, too short*
- Summary of events (lacking evidence)
- Use of opinion statements or the words *seems* or *appears*

Skill Set for Developing Objective Feedback

While the skills you learned in Chapters 2 to 5 contribute to your success in this area, review the additional core skills required of RVL 1.E in Table 6.2.

TABLE 6.2	SKILL SET FOR RVL 1.E

Skills	Description
Analyze Objectively	Reflecting on one's expectations and biases and their influence on analysis and interpretation of evidence gathered during an observation
Review Feedback for Objectivity	Reflecting on detailed evidence collected from observation to ensure that feedback is objective

Bias in Feedback

In Chapter 3, you encountered strategies to build your awareness of any biases you might bring into an observation; however, we also need to think about our practices while preparing feedback reports and organizing thoughts for a post-observation meeting. We have found that there are five common areas that invite subjectivity: **Time, Quantity, Quality, Appearance,** and **Clarity**. In Table 6.3, review examples of each, and in the right-hand column find samples of related thinking questions that can serve to increase objectivity through a deeper analysis of evidence. (You might find that these can also lead you to realize you are lacking necessary evidence, which should provide opportunity for you to reflect and consider how to capture that data next time.)

TABLE 6.3	AREAS OF SUBJECTIVITY	
Lesson Element	**Examples**	**Questions You Can Ask Yourself**
Time	"The transitions took too long." "Students didn't have enough time to work."	How long were the transitions? How much time did students have? How do you know it wasn't enough?
Quantity	"Some never raised their hands." "A lot of students shared with their partners."	How many students raised their hands or shared with partners?
Quality	"That was an excellent organizer." "Your small group lesson didn't go well."	What made it excellent? Why didn't it go well?
Appearance	"I like the way your room looks." "The use of space doesn't work."	Does the room represent a productive learning space? If so, how? How does the physical layout affect students?
Clarity	"The minilesson was confusing." "The directions were clear."	Did it confuse students or only the observer? How many were confused? (How many were clear?) How do you know?

Let's look at an excerpt of subjective feedback that you encountered in Chapter 3 to see how opinions or biases can be manifested in written feedback. Remember, this was developed after an instructional leader observed a portion of a seventh-grade social studies lesson. This excerpt addresses **Time, Quality, Clarity,** and **Quantity**. See if you can catch each one.

The articles were helpful resources for the topic. However, most students didn't understand enough about the electoral college and many of their responses to each other were simple. They were rushed during the preparation before the discussion. "Philosophical Chairs" is challenging, so make sure students understand a topic before engaging in a debate with each other.

Stop and Think: Why would this sample be deemed subjective?

Now take a few minutes to review the finished product. Though the second example may take more time on the part of the observer, consider how the teacher might respond to this type of feedback. (For an explicit think-aloud as to how the observer used the strategies to increase objectivity, visit **resources.corwin .com/feedforward.**)

Feedback Sample

The topic of the electoral college was timely and highly
relevant to the students in light of our current events. The
articles were informative resources for the topic and allowed
students an opportunity to synthesize information from multiple sources. Though "Philosophical Chairs" is a research-
based strategy that allows students to engage in purposeful
discourse, share multiple perspectives, and practice using
supporting evidence, students need time to read, take notes,
process, and then organize for such a conversation. They
shared with me that they only had 7 minutes to read the articles (4 students said they only read the first one) and then
an additional 7 minutes to prepare for the discussion. 6 students had no notes taken, and when asked 5/5 could not explain
to me how the electoral college worked. Once the discussion
began, their statements revealed the limited depth of their
understanding. 7/7 who spoke provided comments like:

S1: "I think the electoral college is bad because Trump won."

S2: "It is bad because it makes no sense to have it."

S3: "We have to keep it because it was in the Constitution."

S4: "But it means our votes don't count in our small state."

The resources and limited time to prepare did not allow
half of the students an opportunity to critically think and
understand the complexity of the popular vote versus the
electoral vote to make informed decisions and support arguments about whether the college should remain.

Increasing Objectivity

Notice the use of language and what might be missing from the first feedback
sample. In this case, the observer actually had the evidence in her notes to
support her statements. During the students' exchange, the observer noted
that all comments demonstrated low-level thinking of a complex issue versus
analysis and evaluation utilizing the resources and text evidence: S1, "I think
the electoral college is bad because Trump won"; S2, "The way a president gets
elected doesn't work." The leader analyzed the three resources provided to the
students; she just did not include any of this information in the feedback.
Therefore, the teacher is receiving a subjective summary of the events. In no
way does this help him understand why the related indicator was rated
"Developing," which can be deemed arbitrary, or how to make a change.

To help avoid subjectivity pitfalls, instructional leaders can use the following thinking questions while preparing feedback:

- Is your bias, judgment, or opinion creeping in?

- Are you summarizing or listing?

- Are you using specific evidence to support your statements?

- Are you only focused on the teacher actions?

What do you notice from the excerpt based on these questions?

When we use words like *helpful,* we are conveying an opinion. How do you know the resources were helpful? Who were they helping and how? What were the content and format? For example, each resource was considered a complex text, and the format/text structure varied across the three articles.

This forces us to think about how students are interacting with the text and their literacy needs in a content area. Look closely! If students have been taught the essential steps and expectations for debating (determining stance, locating supporting evidence, participating in student–student interaction), often the choice and use of texts are possible causes for outcomes such as an ineffective debate.

Let's explore five specific strategies to help increase the objectivity of your feedback related to the RVL standards you have already learned.

Strategy 23: Use framework language to develop claims about practice (Chapter 2, RVL 1.A).

The district/region or school has determined and outlined what effective practice looks like in your instructional framework. Remember to align statements to those principles using common language so ratings do not appear to be opinion.

Keep an eye out for language choices on your framework that prove hard to measure in areas such as time, quality, or quantity. Words like *most, consistently,* and *appropriate,* are mentioned in Chapter 2 as key levers. When these appear, it is important to work with your district/region and teams to arrive at a common understanding or interpretation of the meanings.

Stop and Think: Does your framework include these types of words? Did you identify these within "challenging phrases" from Chapter 2?

Strategy 24: Cite quantitative and qualitative data (Chapter 3, RVL 1.B).

Utilize a balance of evidence to support your claim and promote growth versus using general statements or one type of data.

Strategy 25: Incorporate the impact on the learners (Chapters 3 & 4, RVL 1.B & C).

Analyze and cite student work, responses, and questions versus only focusing on the teacher. Utilize other measurement tools like Common Core State Standards or taxonomies to determine levels of cognitive demand and interaction instead of guessing whether students are engaged in higher or lower order thinking.

Strategy 26: Move away from summarizing or listing (Chapter 4, RVL 1.C).

Though it takes more time, provide an analysis of effectiveness versus a summary of events.

Strategy 27: Incorporate evidence-based areas of growth and strength (Chapter 5, RVL 1.D).

Areas of growth and strength and next steps should not be your opinions; they should be based on collected evidence and the teacher's impact on the learning and engagement. You can also try to include how an alternate step would impact the learners in a different way versus providing a seemingly random general strategy or suggestion.

> **Stop and Think:** If you noticed, the observer originally included a suggestion: "Make sure students understand a topic before engaging in a debate with each other." But what does "make sure" mean? What could the teacher have done differently?

The observer's next step would be to consider specific next steps and reflective questions that would help the teacher develop an understanding of how to build student understanding of complex topics for discussions and debates.

Feedback to Feed Forward

The last portion of the chapter focuses on the development of next steps and the ability you have to create feedback that will serve as a valuable learning tool for teachers. Though this entire book has been dedicated to your practice of writing feedback, it is really about the processing and then the conveyance. Your use of the suggested strategies will result in a report a teacher can use as a resource and will also allow you to conduct a highly impactful feedback meeting. "Planning an effective post-observation conference is an area where instructional leaders can continuously improve and constantly learn to tweak our practice" (Clark & Duggins, 2016, p. 158).

FIGURE 6.2: RVL STANDARD 1.F

ReVISION Supervisory Continuum				
Domain 1: Evidence-Based Observation	**Beginning**	**Developing**	**Proficient**	**Exceptional**
F. Feedback report as written serves as a comprehensive learning tool containing clearly articulated evidence-based feedback and explicit connections.	Supervisor does not demonstrate written skills that effectively communicate important findings from the observation. The feedback report is not written in full sentences and cannot stand alone as a learning tool. There are no explicit connections, details, and/or clearly articulated actionable steps.	The written report is sometimes unclear or nonspecific and does not always effectively communicate important findings from the observation. Full sentences are sometimes not used in the written report to communicate the feedback. There are some explicit connections, details, and/or clearly articulated actionable steps in the written report.	The written report is clear and specific. All of the feedback is written in full sentences. The written report includes some questions that invite reflective practice when appropriate. The written report contains explicit connections, details, and/or clearly articulated actionable steps. Portions of the report can serve as a learning tool.	Written communication is clear and concise providing supportive areas for development and new learning that can be identified by the teacher. The written report includes questions that promote reflective practice and problem solving when appropriate. The written report contains explicit connections, specific examples and details, and actionable steps for a teacher ensuring the entire feedback report is a comprehensive learning tool.
© 2018 ReVISION Learning Partnership, LLC All Rights Reserved				

Take a few moments to review RVL 1.F. of the Supervisory Continuum (see Figure 6.2 on the previous page). As you master the skills and strategies of this first domain of the Supervisory Continuum, you can begin thinking about Domain 2 and six additional standards for effective *verbal* feedback. Now that we have arrived at the last of the indicators in Domain 1, notice how all of the strategies and standards you have explored in this book culminate in a final standard.

> **Stop and Think:** Have you ever visited a classroom after providing feedback and next steps and nothing has changed? Why do you think this is?

Skill Set for Developing Feedback as a Learning Tool

You might have been sure you provided solutions, so let's start with a list of common challenges to see if any could have contributed. Notice how items listed as common challenges in Table 6.4 can diminish the value and objectivity of feedback provided to teachers (RVL 1.E).

TABLE 6.4   RVL 1.F COMMON CHALLENGES

- Providing bulleted points or listed evidence without sentences
- Providing unclear connections, ratings, and/or analysis
- Providing a summary report versus a tool for learning or reflection
- Providing *only* general suggestions (e.g., "You need to differentiate.")
- Misaligning action steps or missing an explicit cross-indicator connection (e.g., making an assessment suggestion when focused on an indicator for engagement)
- Recommending action steps that are not rooted in the evidence/or are subjective
- Recommending action steps that are not built on the language from the indicator and/or key lever between ratings (related to RVL 1.D)
- Providing action steps that are not actionable (scaffolded, meeting a teacher where he or she is) or high leverage
- Providing reflective feedback when more directive feedback would have been appropriate

Beyond the core skills outlined for RVL 1.A–E, let's look at additional skills related to this final indicator in Table 6.5.

TABLE 6.5	SKILL SET FOR RVL 1.F
Core Skills	**Description**
Build on Instructional Strengths	Utilizing determined strengths as entry points or building blocks in designing goals and next steps for teachers
Scaffold Next Steps	Building actionable next steps that reside within a teacher's zone of proximal development while also using the key levers of an instructional framework
Compose a Feedback Report	Creating a report that clearly makes an evidence-supported claim about instructional practice and provides actionable next steps for educators
Develop Reflection Questions	Writing questions that are directly related to observed classroom practices and generate reflective practice for the observed teacher

Defining "Actionable" Next Steps

"Picking the right area of focus only gets you part of the way there." —Bambrick-Santoyo, 2012, p. 75

If you noticed in RVL 1.F, "feedback should contain clearly articulated actionable next steps." This establishes an expectation beyond RVL 1.D (citing areas of growth). Later in this chapter, we venture into *collaborative* determination of action steps, but let's start with feedback you are developing for those teachers who require far more support or directive next steps. "Actionable feedback means not only identifying what needs improvement, but also offering a plan of action to make the necessary improvement possible. . . . Actionable feedback is where the solutions begin" (Sackstein, 2016). If we try to further define "actionable," we might simply say it means a teacher can take action or is capable of carrying out the action.

Determining action steps, in essence, is the practice of setting a pathway toward goals. Instructional leaders can follow three general recommendations related to what we know about goal setting to develop a clear idea of *actionable next steps*.

1. **Remind yourself of Goal-Setting 101.** Remember, "If you don't know where you are going, any road will get you there" (Frontier & Mielke, 2016, p. 107).

   Goal = A destination

   Objectives = What you need to accomplish to reach this destination

   Action Steps = What you need to do to meet objectives

2. **Use set criteria.** Most of us are familiar with the goal-setting acronym SMART (Doran, 1981), and you may have used this in your classroom. Over the years, the letters have taken on different meanings, so for the purposes of this chapter, apply what you best remember or what is most suitable:

- Specific/Sensible
- Measurable/Meaningful
- Attainable/Achievable
- Realistic/Reasonable/Relevant
- Time-Bound/Timely

We can apply this criteria to the design of action steps. Though you may have used these with your students, let's review each one through the lens of your role as a teacher of teachers.

Specific

"When action steps are fuzzy, teachers must figure them out on their own" (Bambrick-Santoyo, 2012, p. 75). The rubric language is a good place to start in determining areas of growth, but the practices and outcomes may be too general or broad. If you only reiterated what is printed in the "effective"/"proficient" description, the teacher might struggle to improve practice. Teachers benefit from examples of alternate specific action steps within the context of the observed lesson. However, leaders should ensure that the steps are not so specific that the teacher is unsure how or unable to implement changes in future lessons.

Measurable

Measurements of effectiveness should always be based on student outcomes. Leaders can help teachers see how next steps might impact students in a different way using research from Chapter 5 and the cause-and-effect thinking from Chapter 4. The framework provides one set of criteria against which the practices and outcomes can be measured as well. Beyond this, you and the teacher may set goals and determine next steps targeting a particular group of students, and you may find you need more specific ways to measure the impact on those students.

Meaningful

"We will commit to learning when we believe that the objectives are realistic, and important for our personal and professional needs" (Aguilar, 2013, p. 56).

We know that students engage at higher levels when learning is relevant to them, which is a critical element for adult learning as well.

Attainable

Be cognizant of Barber's research and the dynamic between challenge and support (Chapter 1) and what you know about the zone of proximal development (Vygotsky, 1978) to ensure your next steps are attainable for your teachers. Remember, the zone of proximal development is that sweet spot between what is known/what someone knows how to do and what is not known/what is not known how to do where growth will occur because there is support—the task or ask is neither too hard nor too easy. Just as in classrooms, we need to determine where this zone lies for teachers in the various aspects of instruction, as it will change or vary based on the area of focus. Leaders must always take heed as support and challenge will look different for everyone.

Realistic/Relevant

"We learn best when we can focus on one piece of feedback at a time" (Bambrick-Santoyo, 2012, p. 70). Asking a teacher to try to change too many practices at once is unrealistic. Your instructional framework provides "realistic" expectations, but this does not mean that next steps built from those are immediately attainable for a teacher. For some, this is like signing up for a ballroom dancing competition while stomping on toes during the basic box step. Next steps become realistic if leaders are utilizing a gradual-release model to scaffold support and consider the time and effort that will be required to make the change. Teachers also need to see relevance for their students and for themselves in the changes you are asking them to make.

Timely/Time-Bound

Bambrick-Santoyo (2012) reminded us of attainable next steps and realistic timelines: "The next challenge is making sure it is bite-sized: teachers can accomplish it in one week . . . multiple small changes, though, implemented week after week, add up to extraordinary change" (p. 75). In thinking again about the classroom where you observed no change, is it also possible the teacher just didn't expect you would come back again until the next formal evaluation? Remember from Chapter 1, Cheryl and Christine's teachers know they are returning. Instructional leaders who truly support growth do the following:

- Set a target date and put it in their calendars for their next step. This creates urgency for teachers and lets them know you are investing in them. Remember, some will require smaller chunks of your time for shorter durations while others will require more frequent support throughout the year (just as with students). You might observe again, attend a meeting with the grade-level team, or review lesson plans.

- Set short- and long-term timelines for/with the teacher. What is a realistic step within the week? What is something the teacher can work on over the next 30 to 90 days?

Stop and Think: What about that classroom where nothing has changed since your last coaching session? Did you set realistic and relevant goals? Or perhaps the time frame in which you expected change was not realistic?

3. **Don't forget adult learning theory.** "For those of us guiding adults in learning, it means we have more to work with—more starting points, and perhaps, more to undo. It means we don't meet our learners as a blank slate . . . we have to accept that people are where they currently are" (Aguilar, 2013, p. 55). The rest of this chapter will provide strategies to help build your capacity to determine actionable next steps for your adult learners—your teachers.

Developing Action Steps

There are four strategies instructional leaders can utilize to develop action steps for teachers who require more support or directive coaching. Under each you will see how the strategy connects to the SMART criteria and integrates adult learning principles. These are built here as somewhat linear, but by no means must be followed sequentially.

Stop and Think: What steps have you been taking to determine actionable next steps?

Strategy 28: Determine an accurate root cause

SMART Connection: Specific, Realistic

Adult Learning Theory: Immediate Impact/Relevance

Though similar to Strategy 19, Determine Causes of Outcomes, the focus here is on determining a single, central cause from which you will develop coaching points and a pathway for improved instruction. Bambrick-Santoyo (2012) outlined "criteria for the right action step" and asked, "Does the action step address a root cause affecting student learning?" (p. 71). Leaders must use the skills from Chapter 4 to discern potential causes of the outcomes versus symptoms of instructional issues and then work to arrive at a targeted entry point. Let's revisit our math lesson:

> In the 6th grade math lesson, nearly half (8/20) of the students incorrectly completed the Do Now and 5 are not finished when the teacher put the answers on the board after 6 minutes of work time. The teacher checks to see that everyone copied down the correct answers but does not address the misunderstandings going on with the day's lesson.

The observer asks herself,

> *Why are so many struggling with review material? What did yesterday's lesson look like? Where are yesterday's assessments? Did the teacher realize they were not all finished? Why didn't anyone tell her they were not finished?*

Take a few minutes to review Table 6.6 to see how the observer aligned her supporting evidence and analysis to each focus area. She could address the immediate issue of the Do Now, but what else do we notice in the observer's analysis of the evidence?

TABLE 6.6   OBSERVER THINK-ALOUD

Potential Causes	Analysis of Evidence
Focus Area: Environment	Students don't take risks or feel comfortable saying they aren't finished or don't understand in front of their peers.
Focus Area: Level of Challenge	For a high percentage of students, this portion of the lesson was too challenging, as they did not understand the review concepts.
Focus Area: Progression	The teacher went on to begin a new lesson without reviewing the Do Now concepts or ensuring everyone was ready to move on.
Focus Area: Assessment	The teacher did not monitor their understanding during the work and the design of the questions may be an issue, as the questions were all word problems. Though they measure application, these allow for a variety of potential errors or misunderstanding.
Focus Area: Support	There was no differentiation in place, so those who did not understand were not supported in their work.

Once the observer has arrived here, the important question is, "Which next steps should the teacher take to improve her practice and student outcomes?" There is no one right answer. The instructional leader is starting to see that this teacher needs help with planning a lesson, differentiation, and assessment. Often, multiple pathways will allow a teacher to arrive at the same destination— improved practice and outcomes. An immediate cause of students struggling in the beginning of the new lesson on the guided practice problems is based on the fact that they did not understand the concepts on the Do Now. A short-term goal might be rooted in the design and use of the assessment methods, but long-term goals might be rooted in overall lesson design/progression and differentiation based on data. Instructional leaders can also determine which of the causes will have the greatest impact on other focus areas. For example, if the leader helps this teacher with reviewing work in the moment or examining artifacts after the fact to determine what students need, the teacher can begin to make adjustments to differentiate, and fewer students might be challenged when the teacher moves into guided or independent practice.

Though the observer is getting close to a root cause, she must utilize the other strategies outlined in this chapter to arrive at the best entry point for a teacher.

Strategy 29: Use key levers for next steps

SMART Connection: Measurable, Realistic

Adult Learning Theory: Understanding the Target/Goal and Reason Behind/For, Relevance

Once you have started to home in on a particular indicator or area of practice for focused improvement or a coaching objective, it is then important to align that with the instructional framework. We recommend that leaders develop clear and explicit next steps through the language in the performance levels, using the key levers between ratings. Remember, evaluation instruments are not only used for rating a lesson; they become valuable resources through which you will leverage growth, as they house realistic expectations for teacher actions and student outcomes. After an observation, you should look to the "Proficient"/"Effective" descriptions (or higher for those receiving an "Effective" rating). The language in Figure 6.3 provides an example for the sentence frame for your feedback.

From the math lesson again: The leader determined the teacher's action of moving on without reviewing students' work on the Do Now represents a

"Beginning" level. Looking at the indicator, a next step can be launched from the "Developing" level in that we want the teacher to focus on the achievement of instructional outcomes versus completion of the task, but ultimately, from the "Proficient" description, we want her to focus on individuals, not just the whole group.

FIGURE 6.3: INDICATOR FOR NEXT STEPS

	Below Standard	Developing	Proficient	Exemplary
Attributes				*In addition to the characteristics of* **Proficient,** *including one or more of the following*:
Criteria for student success	Does not communicate criteria for success and/or opportunities for students to self-assess are rare.	Communicates general criteria for success and provides limited opportunities for students to self-assess.	Communicates specific criteria for success and provides multiple opportunities for students to self-assess.	Integrates student input in generating specific criteria for assignments.
Ongoing assessment of student learning	Assesses student learning with focus limited to task completion and/or compliance rather than student achievement of lesson purpose/ objective.	Assesses student learning with focus on whole-class progress toward achievement of the intended instructional outcomes.	Assesses student learning with focus on eliciting evidence of learning at critical points in the lesson in order to monitor individual and group progress toward achievement of the intended instructional outcomes.	Promotes students' independent monitoring and self-assess, helping themselves or their peers to improve their learning.

Source: Common Core of Teaching (2014), Connecticut State Department of Education

Review the leader's feedback building from the key levers:

> It is important to collect *evidence of learning at critical points to monitor individual* readiness, not just *completion* of the task. Therefore, be sure to monitor whether all students are finished with the Do Now and determine what each student understands before posting answers.

Strategy 30: Use logic

SMART Connection: Timely/Time-Bound, Specific

Adult Learning Theory: Practical and Results-Oriented

The next strategy is to use logic to break down an objective or short-term goal into one to two action steps that can be accomplished within a week. Think: What makes sense in a sequential progression of learning for the teacher considering we want next steps to be bite-sized? The following is in regard to our math teacher:

1. We noticed she went behind her desk to organize materials while students completed the Do Now and then waited up front. A very logical next step for her would be to move around the room. This would also allow her to see who was not finished.

2. Instead of, or in conjunction with, moving to see if they had finished, she could poll students to see if they need additional time or use a Fist-5/Traffic Light-type method to see who needs help.

3. It is also logical that she address incorrect answers, but you have to think about what is attainable to determine her specific next step (thinking about what she will monitor and what she is capable of doing with that information).

A note: What if the teacher is teaching from a program like Bridges or Math in Focus? Logically, you should search for the critical resource the teacher is following (e.g., the teacher's guide for this lesson) and analyze the suggested design of the lessons before and after this one. For example, when the observer did this, she noticed the teacher did not use the suggested warm-up questions from the book, so this logically should be a part of the feedback and follow-up conversation. Leaders and teams can utilize the strategies in Chapter 2 to further unpack curriculum and programs for look-fors and to better understand the research-based practices, so these can be integrated into the coaching and next steps.

Making Connections to Other Indicators

Remember in Chapter 5, we recommended that leaders make explicit connections to other indicators to help a teacher see that aspects of teaching do not exist in isolation. Leaders should use logic to consider which next steps could have the greatest impact on other aspects of instruction. For example, if the teacher polls students about their understanding, she is not only collecting information but sharing responsibility and building their capacity to self-assess.

Strategy 31: Build on teachers' needs and strengths

SMART Connection: Realistic, Meaningful, Attainable

Adult Learning Theory: Building on Teachers' Previous Experiences, Relevance

Though leaders work through a complex process to arrive at prioritized next steps, ultimately, this fourth strategy will be the final driver: Can teachers accomplish (with support) what you are asking them to accomplish? The math teacher could stop and look at each student's work but not really recognize how their answers represent understanding or a lack thereof of the skills required to master the learning target—or then, what to do with the information.

Stop and Think: After reading the suggested strategies, how could you have supported one of your teachers differently who was struggling to make changes in instructional practices?

Get Past Your "Go-To's"

Our math teacher heard from a previous evaluator, "Use a Do Now," which is an effective strategy for activating prior learning and collecting evidence before starting a lesson. However, when this is all that is provided to a teacher in feedback, actions like this can be considered a "go-to" or "stock suggestion." Though the past evaluator might have been attentive to the framework and key levers, perhaps this is a general action step provided for all teachers in all situations regardless of the lesson or students' or teachers' needs. These can include "use a rubric" for establishing criteria, have students "turn-and-talk" to increase discourse, or use "exit slips" to measure understanding. This is not to say these are not effective practices. However, instructional leaders need to support teachers so they understand *why* they would use these strategies and *how they impact learning and engagement*. Teachers often get frustrated with stock suggestions as they try to apply them without really knowing why or how.

Our math teacher is applying the feedback "use a Do Now" to begin her lessons. The leader wants to recognize the teacher's willingness to try this strategy and will include it as an area of strength on which she will build. So what is a next step for the teacher that is attainable and within her zone of proximal development?

1. Logically, moving around the room to check on students' progress is very attainable.

   - Maybe at first, she just needs to determine who has incorrect answers. (If questions are open-ended, she could check whether answers are appropriate or supported.)

   - Or, does she need to start by asking some students to volunteer their answers or put work on the board, so she is at least getting a snapshot? Possibly checking in first with those students she knows struggled with this concept the day before would also provide valuable information.

   - She can monitor what students do and do not understand.

However, addressing incorrect answers by conducting an error analysis is a little more complex. The teacher has to determine conceptually or foundationally what it is students do or do not understand and then act on that. Think for a second about what a teacher can do when half the room is confused, taking the steps in attainable pieces:

   - Short-term goal: She could learn to shift. This is attainable when teachers know when, why, and how. Maybe this teacher—for a first shot at this—could stop the ball from rolling and have students review in their groups of four before posting answers herself.

   - Mid-range goal: Shift and allow some to go on, while others review.

   - Long-term goal: Eventually, she will use the data from the day before to avoid having to always make on-the-spot instructional decisions, possibly with differentiated Do Nows and tasks and preplanned small groups.

2. It's attainable for the teacher to share responsibility with the students in a few easy steps. She could remind students it is okay to speak up if they are not finished or have a question and poll them while they are working. (However, though students should learn to monitor their own understanding, if there is an issue with her lesson progressions, possibly half will continue to want more time or need help each day.)

Determining the Entry Point

To gain a clearer picture of teachers' needs, it is important to determine their knowledge (or skill and will), which is only gained through conversation and getting to know your teachers.

Let's look at four considerations based on our math teacher:

1. *The teacher is unsure* how to use the Do Nows to inform instruction.

2. *The teacher thinks he or she is effective,* as she is using the recommended strategy.

3. *The teacher does not recognize the value or purpose* of a Do Now; she is just doing it because she was told to stop reviewing homework for 15 minutes at the beginning of the lesson.

4. *The teacher does not want to implement these practices or is afraid* to try because she wants to follow her lesson plan and she likes to teach whole group with everyone working on the same tasks at the same time.

Supporting Teachers Within Their ZPD

Not only is it important to determine a teacher's mindset and skill set, but you must also determine how a teacher best learns and what support would be most effective for the teacher to meet a new challenge. Think about a new skill or hobby you learned and how you improved. Did you watch a video? Read a book? Did a coach or instructor model the skill? Or did you try it on your own with someone watching and giving suggestions? Though you are the instructional leader in the building, remember that you have a wide variety of resources available to you. Though you want to monitor the teacher's growth, what else can you provide, suggest, or utilize as support? For example,

-   Is a math coach available to model for the teacher?

-   Could the teacher benefit from visiting another classroom?

-   Is there a video, site, article, book, or professional learning online that would help?

-   Is this teacher open to recording herself to review with you?

-   Can the leader collaboratively plan with the teacher over the next few days/weeks? Can the coach, another teacher, or department chair do this?

-   Is this teacher's area of challenge consistent with a trend in your building? Can you design professional learning experiences to address it?

Think outside the box! For our math teacher, could the instructional leader or math coach review Do Nows from the week with her? They could practice together how to analyze work to recognize student errors and conceptual understanding. They could determine what the evidence is revealing and think about what actions the teacher could have taken in the moment and/or for the next lesson. What if the whole math team engaged in this work because everyone needs help with data-driven instruction?

Prioritizing Next Steps

Think about Goal-Setting 101 from earlier. We know we can't tackle too many goals or objectives at once. Ultimately, instructional leaders must prioritize and determine what the best bite-sized piece might be and what can be the "high-leverage" next steps. Remember, as mentioned in Chapter 5, Bambrick-Santoyo (2012) identified these as "action steps that drive improvement for the greatest number of aspects of the lesson at once" (p. 72), and Aguilar (2013) added that a focused coaching point "has the greatest potential for improving the experience and outcomes of students, particularly those who are struggling the most . . . and it would positively spill over into other areas" (p. 123). These should drive decision making as an instructional leader develops feedback. Instructional leaders can also do the following:

1. Align targeted areas for improvement and next steps with a teacher's student learning objectives and/or the teacher's professional learning goals.

2. Consider current areas of focus based on recent coaching and previous feedback.

Ultimately, your relationship with the teacher and what you know about him or her will guide you in making the best decision about how to move forward. This is why we all recognize that coaching and leadership are considered both a science *and* an art.

Developing Reflective Practices

"Adults want to be the origin of their own learning; they want to control certain aspects of it." —Aguilar, 2013, p. 56

Though the strategies provided throughout this book and the standards of the RVL Supervisory Continuum Domain 1 are focused on written feedback, the practice of developing effective questions is invaluable preparation not only for use in written feedback but in your post-observation conference as well. Some leaders choose to send selected questions to the teachers before the meeting, allowing time to process ahead versus responding on the spot. Regardless of how you expect to utilize questioning as a coaching strategy, just as when you were you in the classroom, it is important to plan targeted questions and expect you will be responding to the teacher and adjusting ongoing questions to probe or clarify in the moment as well. Using reflective questions is one of the easiest ways to share responsibility with a teacher for his or her growth, but it will require scaffolding based on what you know about each teacher.

Stop and Think: Did you notice in the "Proficient" description of standard RVL 1.F that feedback "includes use of questions that invite reflective practice *when appropriate*"? When would it be appropriate to use questions in feedback and when is this not necessarily appropriate?

Though we hope all teachers will have the ability to process the effectiveness of their own instruction, as teachers of teachers we must facilitate growth toward that goal.

When we show up to a coaching session, we navigate between letting the [teacher] direct the conversation where he needs it to go and steering the conversation toward the ends the client has determined. But in order to steer effectively (as we often need to do), we must have thought through the learning chunks [scaffolding for the teacher]. (Aguilar, 2013, p. 133)

Sometimes in rapid pursuit of the end goal, instructional leaders will provide feedback that is predominantly question based. However, not all teachers are ready for feedback that requires high levels of critical thinking and reflection. Think about these two scenarios that could occur with the math teacher:

Scenario 1: Observer: *"Which students were ready to move on to the new lesson and which were not?"*

"I don't know. I think most of them were ready."

Scenario 2: Observer: *"How can you create a Do Now that will provide you with the information you need before starting the lesson?"*

"Can you give me an example? I'm not sure what you mean."

Sometimes leaders then try to ask more questions to help lead a teacher down the path. However, if instructional leaders jump right into questions or pepper a teacher with many in a row without thinking more about a teacher's knowledge, values, and skill sets, the conversation can result in confusion, frustration, and little to no change in practice. Remember the skill/will questions for a leader to think about in Strategy 31? This teacher does not necessarily understand the value and purpose of an opening task like a Do Now, so she will need more guidance to arrive at alternate strategies. Remember also, "productive feedback requires a sharing process that produces a perception of low threat to self-esteem" (Lipton & Wellman, 2013b, p. 8), so even tone and wording can impact a teacher's efficacy and mindset. Be ready with suggestions, examples, supporting evidence, and more directive feedback if you are including reflective questions for a teacher.

Bambrick-Santoyo (2012), Lipton and Wellman (2013a), and Aguilar (2013) all provide excellent resources to help instructional leaders determine how to best meet teachers' needs. Table 6.7 displays their categorizations of varying teacher/leader roles that help you consider how you will use questions:

TABLE 6.7   COACHING APPROACHES

Bambrick-Santoyo	Aguilar	Lipton-Wellman
Level 4 Leader driven/Leader identifies problem when teacher cannot		**Calibrating** Conveying gaps between expected and observed practice
	Directive Shifting beliefs by interrupting "mental models" by confronting, informing, or prescribing	**Consulting** Clarifying expectations and offering suggestions
Level 3 Leader guided/ Leader shares evidence to help the teacher recognize problem		
Level 2 50% Teacher driven/ Teacher can identify with prompting questions	**Facilitative** Leader working together to guide the teacher serving as a catharsis, catalyst, or support	**Collaborating** Working together to analyze and come up with solutions
Level 1 Teacher driven/ Teacher identifies the problem	**Transformational** Coaching that goes beyond just changing behaviors, helping a teacher examine beliefs and a way of being along with system contexts	**Coaching** Facilitating reflection and problem solving

Leaders can then integrate questions as appropriate with evidence-based statements and suggestions. Take a look at Table 6.8 and notice how your questions might differ based on the teacher's needs:

TABLE 6.8   COACHING QUESTIONS

More Leader-Driven Feedback	Collaborative Feedback	More Teacher-Driven Feedback
Purpose: Check for Understanding How are you thinking you can utilize the Do Now or opening task now that we have reviewed the purpose and value of such an activity? What is one way from the list we talked about that you can determine whether students understand the Do Now problems?	**Purpose: Promote Collaborative Work/ Gradual Release to Apply** What are some ways we can come up with to address those situations that arise when some students understand a Do Now and others don't?	**Purpose: Promote Application, Problem Solving, and Goal Setting** How can you anticipate who might struggle on a day's Do Now? What can you proactively build into your lesson knowing this?

Similar to the idea of considering coaching stances and teachers' needs, if you are using Marzano's (2007) Classroom Observation Tool, throughout you will find indicator- and performance-aligned questions that are targeted and impactful. For example, for a "Beginning" rating related to engagement strategies, a question includes the following: "How can you use response rate techniques to maintain student engagement through questioning processes?"

Developing Reflective Questions

"We learn by thinking about what we are doing. Reflection is a key component of learning." —McKay, 2013, p. 47

Have you ever asked a teacher in a meeting, "How do you think the lesson went?," which resulted in a 15-minute discussion about three specific students' issues, yet you only had 30 minutes to meet and you wanted to work with the teacher on the level of challenge of the tasks? Or, have you tried, "If you could change one thing, what would it be?," which resulted in, "It went well. I wouldn't change anything," though you are holding a list of ineffective practices? Remember, "the purpose of reflection is to build the teacher's capacity to engage in an ongoing internal dialogue that results in purposeful action to improve professional practice" (Frontier & Mielke, 2016, p. 119), and these types of questions won't always help the leader or teacher arrive at that goal. We have created a list of six specific suggestions you could use in isolation or concurrently (as you notice, they may overlap) to get you started in drafting reflective questions, along with some examples from our math teacher's lesson. (Always be ready with your own evidence and error analysis.)

- **Build targeted questions around your selected area of focus.** Though the path may change with the teacher's answers, this is the best way to guide a teacher's thinking and maximize meeting time. "How was the Do Now connected to the day's lesson?" "Why do you think students struggled during the guided practice?" "What misunderstandings did the Do Nows reveal?"

- **Use open-ended questions.** "What did you notice during the guided practice of the new lesson?"

- **Use the rubric language.** "How did you monitor for individual understanding during the Do Now before you began the new lesson?"

- **Use the evidence.** "Half of the students had not finished and six had incorrect answers when you put the answers on the board after four minutes." "What is something you could have done before, or instead of, putting correct answers on the board?"

- **Build questions from the big picture (Chapters 2 & 3).**

  Purpose:

  "What did you want students to know how to do before you started the new lesson?"

  Understanding:

  "Who was ready to begin based on the Do Now?"

- **Use stems that promote reflection.** "**How could you have** monitored student understanding?" "**How did you plan** for this lesson based on how the students were doing in the last lesson?

There are many resources available that focus on effective feedback conversations that offer a variety of stems often specifically based on the needs of the teacher.

Pulling It All Together

We have focused a great deal on a math teacher who needed support with assessment and progression, common areas of need for many teachers. Let's revisit the sixth-grade English language arts lesson from Chapter 5 and the teacher who is also struggling with progression while using complex nonfiction text, another common area of need for teachers. If you remember, the lesson was focused on readers extracting key pieces of "important information" (onto stickies) from a text to create a summary of what was read through an interactive read-aloud. (Turn back if you need a quick refresher on the lesson.) The observer has been working with the teacher for several months on her introduction to lessons for new reading strategies and feels she is becoming more reflective about her impact on the students—and continues to improve in small increments. Let's jump back into the instructional leader's head as he tries to work through the strategies to determine the best next steps based on a comprehensive cause-and-effect analysis of the lesson.

Root Cause: The bottom line was that students did not understand the text by the end and were unable to create accurate summaries, so the question is, can the observer narrow this down to a central cause? The root of this lies in planning: purposefully reviewing the text before the lesson, determining what would make this text inaccessible for students, analyzing the complexity beyond Lexile, and preplanning questions—none of which the teacher did. He wants the teacher to think through the critical parts, or **progression,** of an interactive read-aloud to then determine what needs to be planned.

Key Levers: As the leader has been working with the teacher on the progression of the lesson, leveraging growth from the related indicator (see Figure 6.4) is best.

FIGURE 6.4: INDICATOR TO LEVERAGE GROWTH FOR PROGRESSION

	Below Standard	Developing	Proficient	Exemplary
Attributes				*In addition to the characteristics of* **Proficient**, *including one or more of the following:*
Content progression and level of challenge	Presents instructional content that lacks a logical progression; and/or level of challenge is at an inappropriate level to advance student learning.	Presents instructional content in a generally logical progression and/or at a somewhat appropriate level of challenge to advance student learning.	Clearly present instructional content in a logical and purposeful progression and at an appropriate level of challenge to advance learning of all students.	Challenges students to extend their learning beyond the lesson expectations and make cross-curricular connections.

Source: Common Core of Teaching (2014), Connecticut State Department of Education

The progression was generally logical, but it did not advance learning of all students. The leader will chunk the observed progression steps and compare those against the essential chunks of an interactive read-aloud and then talk through the purpose of each. He will also help the teacher see how the students were unable to cognitively engage at high levels through the engagement indicator (see Figure 6.5), pointing to the specific strategies and questions that should have been utilized in each chunk of the progression.

Zone of Proximal Development: This teacher has been teaching for 16 years and wants to improve, but she has struggled through the new curriculum and Common Core State Standard shifts. She has improved in setting a narrow focus of a single reading strategy for each lesson and in communicating that objective and the bigger context to students. Text complexity layers are newer to her and she is not sure how to analyze a text before a lesson. She is going through the motions (essentially, she follows a script) but doesn't quite see how to build a reader's capacity. She recognized at the end that the students' summaries were not at a high level, but she did not know why. The leader is probably going to adopt calibrating and consulting stances (Lipton & Wellman, 2013a) to continue to build her skills, but he does not want to overwhelm her. He wants to make sure she understands the goals of an inter-active read-aloud, to include the following: building vocabulary, teaching the reading process/metacognition in authentic ways, modeling fluency, and pro-viding transferable strategies for complex text. Through this model, we want students to enjoy and discuss reading, finding success with a high-level text, and together they can determine the next steps to ensure this is happening.

FIGURE 6.5: INDICATOR TO LEVERAGE GROWTH IN ENGAGEMENT

	Below Standard	Developing	Proficient	Exemplary
Attributes				*In addition to the characteristics of* **Proficient***, including one or more of the following*:
Strategies, tasks and questions	Includes tasks that do not lead students to construct new and meaningful learning and that focus primarily on low cognitive demand or recall of information.	Includes a combination of tasks and questions in an attempt to lead students to construct new learning, but are of low cognitive demand and/or recall of information with some opportunities for problem-solving, critical thinking and/ or purposeful discourse or inquiry.	Employs differentiated strategies, tasks and questions that cognitively engage students in constructing new and meaningful learning through appropriately integrated recall, problem solving, critical and creative thinking, purposeful discourse and/or inquiry. At times, students take the lead and develop their own questions and problem-solving strategies.	Includes opportunities for students to work collaboratively to generate their own questions and problem-solving strategies, synthesize and communicate information.

Source: Common Core of Teaching (2014), Connecticut State Department of Education

Logic: This teacher taught straight from the printed lesson. She told students what strategy they would use, built in timed turn-and-talks with stop and jots, and had them write a summary of what they read—so logically this lesson should have had positive outcomes. As it did not, the leader has to think, what comes next for this teacher? He thinks he needs to focus his feedback on the goals and structure of the interactive read-aloud method, as she did miss some critical essentials. That means that logically, there are steps needed in each portion of the read-aloud:

1. **Planning:** Preread the text for challenging vocabulary, complexity, and the development of preread and during-read questions.

2. **Preread:** Establish the deep understandings through connections. The teacher only addressed the day's objective and strategy but did not provide a review or activate previous strategies for reading complex text. Prediction can be used and vocabulary addressed.

3. **During Read:** Ask preplanned questions at critical points. The teacher systematically stopped after every two pages, but if she preread, she could determine if there was a turning point, a challenging shift, or an important place to pause. Address the challenging vocabulary throughout.

4. **After Read:** Students could have used further pair or group discussion before writing.

Logically, a step toward a longer term goal would be to set up the sixth-grade team to work with the literacy coach on analyzing text for levels of complexity beyond Lexile. Additionally, this teacher needs continued support in how to explicitly introduce a strategy through modeling and think-alouds.

- Let's look at the feedback in Table 6.9. Consider what action steps and possible questions are immediately within the teacher's reach with some assistance and notice how the leader is getting ready with some specific suggestions based on the observed lesson.

Goal: Strengthening the overall effectiveness of the interactive read-aloud to meet the goals of the process and improve students' abilities to understand text

Prioritized Objective: Prepare for the next read-aloud ahead of time to integrate preread and during-read metacognitive strategies to improve comprehension.

TABLE 6.9	ACTION STEP AND QUESTIONS SAMPLE
Action Step #1: Lesson Planning	It is important to preview a complex text during planning to: Locate challenging vocabulary or phrases (e.g., amplify, lamenting, gawk, public relations campaign) Write 1 question for each stopping point (of varying levels) to help clarify the text and extend thinking. Examples from this lesson could have been: What were the different stories that arose about the cause of the fire? How did the stories get started? Why were the firefighters blamed? Why did they need to start a public relations campaign? What is a public relations campaign? What happened that eliminated or did away with the possibility of the poor owning homes in the city again? What impact did the Depression have on the situation in Chicago? What was the Depression?
Action Step #2: Reading Strategies	Prereading: Though you introduced the objective, strategy, and tasks, try to include a preread strategy to help students comprehend complex text. They can predict before reading using questions they or you build from the title (e.g., Title is: "Myths and Realities." Questions could be: What is a myth and what is a reality? How could those be related to a large fire that started?). During reading: Though you included stop and jots/turn-and-talks to summarize that section, during reading, stop and ask your preplanned questions and listen to what students are saying. You may need to improvise and ask more questions to ensure they understand before you go on. After reading: Students were immediately directed to begin their summaries. Before this step, revisit the title and the predictions they made. You can also do this as they are reading (e.g., What were the myths and what were the realities? What caused the myths to become some people's realities?). Give them time in fours to square-and-compare and gain more perspectives.
Reflective Questions	**Open-ended:** "What strategies do students need when they are facing complex text?" "What are the goals of interactive read-alouds?" **Rubric:** "What varied leveled thinking questions could you have designed during planning for your stopping points to check for comprehension and to encourage critical thinking?" **Evidence:** The text grew more challenging for students on page #_ (around 9:25), when the author began talking about socioeconomic impacts of the fire . . . . Half of the students stopped sharing by the last two turn-and-talks. "What did you notice about the quality of their turn-and-talks as the text got harder?" **Big Picture:** "Which reading strategy did you want students to use during the read-aloud?" "Were they successfully using this? Why or why not?" "What were the deep understandings or important takeaways of this text based on the title?" "What did the summary reflect about the students' understanding of the text?" **Stems:** From my suggestions for steps during planning, **"What could you do** before the lesson to support your students with complex text during the read-aloud?" "Of the suggestions I made for the parts of the process, **which part do you want to focus on** this week?" **"What did you notice** about the students' summaries?"

Final Thoughts

You have now worked through all three core competencies, six standards, 21 core skills, and 31 strategies. Congratulations! You are on your way, leading learning by developing highly effective, objective feedback to feed forward. Be clear on where you and teachers are at this current place and time, where you are headed together, and how you will get there (your destination):

Goal: A destination

Objectives: What you need to accomplish to reach this destination

Action Steps: What you need to do to meet objectives

Hopefully by now, it is clear how the mastery of the aligned core skills in this chapter allows you to develop feedback that creates a deep level of understanding for teachers, when you do the following:

- Analyze objectively

- Review feedback for objectivity

- Build on instructional strengths

- Scaffold next steps

- Compose a feedback report

- Develop reflective questions

In this chapter, you explored five strategies for decreasing subjectivity that were directly tied to previous standards:

1. Use framework language.

2. Collect and cite a balance of evidence.

3. Focus on the learners.

4. Move away from summarizing.

5. Determine clear areas of strength and growth based on evidence.

These paved the way for you to then add four strategies to develop actionable next steps:

1. Determine a root cause.

2. Use key levers.

3. Use logic.

4. Build on the teacher's needs/strengths.

You wrapped up the chapter considering how to build reflective practices through a set of suggestions for developing questions for teachers after a lesson:

- Build around your selected areas of focus.

- Use open-ended questions.

- Use rubric language.

- Use the evidence.

- Build from the "big picture" idea.

- Use stems that promote reflection.

Remember, what you have encountered here are complex steps in the development of feedback that will serve as a learning tool that promotes growth. To master the skills and steps, the process takes teamwork and time. You can also access support resources at **resources.corwin.com/feedforward.** As you move into our last chapter, you will be provided with five approaches for collegial, embedded, and ongoing learning for you, your school, and your district/region—to continue this journey. We share case studies and examples to inspire and guide you in this work.

What professional learning builds your capacity to lead learning?

7

We have presented at international conferences, lectured in aspiring leaders' college classrooms, and provided single day workshops for administrators of all levels, and the same question arises time and again: "How do I get this type of training and support in my district?" This last chapter is for you to share with the decision makers and professional learning designers in your world (or maybe they have been reading along with us all along?). But it is important to remember it is a collective *and* individual journey. All of the leaders included in this book have committed to their own learning and that of their teachers, but they also continue to serve as valuable resources for colleagues.

From the field . . .

The work provided a road map complete with both the vision and nuts and bolts of how to get to a place we have never been as a learning organization. The keys to our success lie in the design of our professional learning: our

(Continued)

(Continued)

learning is scaffolded, providing a highly engaging structure, and reinforcing the strides we are making. Workshops provide the perfect blend of healthy perspective, new information, time for administrators to construct their thinking and reflect in a collaborative environment, and opportunities for concrete, pragmatic planning for implementation.

—Natalie Simpson, Assistant Director
of Human Resources

What's Next?

The question now becomes, "How do we ensure that you as a leader and aspiring leaders are provided the preparation and effective ongoing professional learning to practice and develop the skills necessary to provide feedback that feeds forward?" Described in Chapter 1, as new evaluation models were rolled out across the United States, assumptions were made about the readiness of administrators to deliver quality feedback to teachers in support of improved classroom practice. Hopefully, by reading this book and delving into each strategy, you have recognized that while many of these assumptions from Chapter 1 may have previously hindered your efforts to meaningfully support teachers, you now have solutions to help you improve your practice. This final chapter focuses on how you can continue the journey to build your capacity alongside your colleagues through ongoing professional learning in your school or district/region.

Throughout the book we have highlighted not only the complexity of the work to truly lead learning through observation and feedback but also the fact that you deserve and require ongoing, progressive, professional learning in support of this work. But what should that entail?

In this final chapter, we summarize what we know about effective professional learning designs that serve to support the necessary skills and strategies presented in Chapters 2 through 6. We provide overviews of several district designs that are grounded in the ReVISION Learning Continuum standards that support observation and high-quality teacher feedback. We outline methods and approaches taken by districts that shifted the practice of their leaders to the highest level of instructional leadership, bringing the six standards of high-quality feedback and observation to life to maximize professional growth. What is described in this chapter is not typical training for observers nationally or internationally, emphasizing the reason we have dedicated our last chapter to highlighting these best practices.

The Current Approach

Why, after years of implementing new evaluation models, are teachers and leaders still facing more challenge than ever and receiving limited or no support? Every day we work hand in hand with administrators who possess a transformational mindset and are unwilling to merely trudge through implementing policy that often accompanies a compliance mindset of checking boxes and completing forms. On their behalf, we have been seeking the answers to this pressing question and, better yet, the solutions.

Earlier studies, research, and literature prior to 2010 (the year Race to the Top was introduced) were seemingly ignored by policymakers that should now be reconsidered (Fullan, 2007, 2008; Glickman, 2008; Kersten & Israel, 2005) to help us understand why we have been unsuccessful in reaching the desired outcomes associated with educator supervision and evaluation.

Most of the studies examine the perceptions of teachers and principals regarding the implementation of existing models and should be used to provide insight and ongoing guidance to states, systems, and local districts/regions. In a 2017 survey and through focus groups conducted with State Teachers of the Year (STOYs) and STOY finalists from every part of the country, exemplary teachers recommended that decision makers

> do away with one-size-fits-all professional development in favor of a system focused on differentiated and individualized professional development opportunities, taking advantage of online self-paced study opportunities, watching/discussion videos of excellent teaching with colleagues, and collaborating with teachers who have similar interests and needs for professional growth. (Goe et al., 2017, p. 2)

These realistic and effective opportunities for teachers will only result from ongoing observation and feedback and a leader who is actively involved in the teaching and learning in a building.

Responses from those surveyed teachers drive our sense of urgency:

- Only 29 percent of respondents with recent classroom experience indicated that they received timely and relevant feedback that helps them meet the needs of students.

- Fewer than half of respondents (49%) indicated that their observers were well-trained in conducting classroom observations.

- Forty-four percent (44%) of respondents believed evaluators could meaningfully assess their teaching practice.

- Forty-six percent (46%) of respondents thought evaluators could provide useful feedback on their teaching practice. (Goe et al., 2017)

> **Stop and Think:** What would the survey results look like in your school? Do your teachers view you as an instructional leader? Remember, we mentioned that effective and highly effective teachers want to grow as well. How are you specifically supporting their growth and providing leadership opportunities?

Based on our time spent in classrooms and schools, we have also been able to draw conclusions directly from those in the field—decision makers and professional learning providers, leaders, and teachers—that have allowed us to determine two factors that significantly contribute to what the surveyed teachers revealed.

Quality Versus Quantity

1. **The Quality and Focus of Time:** We know that it is not that leaders are unwilling to visit classrooms or provide feedback but, instead, that the typical activities that consume their days simply do not allow the opportunity to do so. In the breakdown of a leader's schedule from Chapter 1, we addressed the issues surrounding the *allotment* of time dedicated to activities that impact teaching and learning and posed some solutions. However, it is equally as important to further investigate the *quality* of time spent, asking yourselves not just *if* you are engaging in those activities that impact teaching and learning but *how.* We know that *how* leaders are using the time in classrooms is directly related to the quality of feedback and depth of support they are able to provide teachers.

Consistently, we have found many leaders simply do not know how to do the following during an observation:

- Focus on the learning.

- Recognize whether learning is occurring.

- Determine the teacher's impact on the learning.

Upon returning to their office, they also lack the ability to organize and then analyze the evidence they did collect. Therefore, resulting feedback or coaching points are subjective and unsupported, offering no clear next steps for teachers. Though many leaders are making the effort to visit classrooms multiple times a week across an entire year, they are unable to effect change because of the quality and focus of the time spent on the work—thus the motivation behind this book.

2. **The Quality and Focus of the Training:** Logically, if leaders are lacking in requisite skills or unable to effect change, it points to an issue with the training and support they receive—a lack of explicit

and embedded professional learning for observers. Remember, most professional learning programs still focus on routine inspection of teacher practice and development of accuracy measurements almost exclusively. In other words, these "learning" models are often limited to inauthentic demonstrations of an observer's capacity to identify and rate the quality of instruction and may occur infrequently or inconsistently across a year or even throughout a leader's career.

Video-Based Training

Few, if any, professional learning approaches support observation practice through the lens of supervision or are in alignment with what we know about change leadership and effective educator evaluation. Instead, the typical approach to training for an evaluator has been the following:

Step 1: Watch a video and talk about instruction.

Step 2: Repeat the process a few times.

Step 3: Score a video on your own for a review of interrater agreement.

Left at that level, training will do little to improve teacher practice and student outcomes in our nation's schools (MET Project, 2015). It is important to note that video calibration can provide valuable formative data on which to build professional learning, and we are not saying these forms of training should be altogether abandoned. In support of video-based programs, these do offer the best and most logical place to start with a new observer. Ongoing reviews of practice with video, especially when leaders are viewing with teachers, can be highly effective. However, currently in most professional learning models, video-based training serves as a tool for a summative pass/fail approach.

Calibration

"Ongoing calibration" often involves one to two group walk-throughs or video-based exercises per year (or every three years, in some cases) to ensure interrater agreement and prevent drift. According to the California Teachers Association (2012), all evaluators should "have extensive training and regular calibration in all evaluation procedures and instruments. Essential to this process are training and continuous discussion between all of the parties involved" (p. 3). The association suggested quality professional learning for evaluators/observers should do the following:

- Help evaluators articulate rationale for why an employee earned a particular rating.

- Provide evaluators with more confidence in their ratings.

- Ensure more consistent evaluations of an educator's performance by identifying potential evaluator bias.

- Assure new evaluation processes will be implemented with fidelity and will increase confidence in defining the differentiation of performance levels.

Though some form of "ongoing calibration" is a requirement of ESSA, it has often only been about demonstrating "proficiency" (accurate scoring). Many do not realize that the idea of interrater agreement can be misleading if everyone is calibrated around low expectations. We must broaden the definition and goal of calibration beyond achieving "interrater agreement" to include the collegial development of the skills and understandings in this book. It is important to note, however, that "high-quality training doesn't come overnight. It's the result of multiple iterations and capacity building" (MET Project, 2015, p. 28). The core skills and strategies necessary to ensure effective observation and feedback introduced in Chapter 1 and built on throughout the book require a significant commitment from not only the individual leader but also the organizations that support that leader.

Essentials of Effective Professional Learning Design

"Leadership and learning are indispensable to each other." —John F. Kennedy

Ironically, if we evaluated most of the current training approaches based on the current effectiveness models applied to teachers, they would fail both in design and outcome, as an analysis of almost every state's data on educator evaluation demonstrates that these approaches have had little impact on teacher effectiveness.

We have established and present here four foundational design fundamentals for professional learning for instructional leaders. We have also integrated five of the seven Learning Forward Professional Learning Standards. The attention to those standards supported the development of many of the approaches outlined in this chapter so that learning remained the central purpose for observers and quality instruction was integrated. Not only does learning design result in improved observation and feedback practice of leaders, but it increases their capacity to become "advocates for and facilitators of effective professional learning" for teachers (Learning Forward, 2015). Remember, Cheryl and Christine from Chapter 1 use what they know from their ongoing classroom visits and the time spent with teachers to build more effective learning experiences for them.

Table 7.1 shows the alignment between the Learning Forward standards and training essentials we discovered for supporting improved observation and feedback.

TABLE 7.1	LEARNING FORWARD STANDARDS ALIGNMENT	
Learning Forward Professional Learning Standard	**Professional learning that increases educator effectiveness and results for all students . . .**	**Essentials require that leaders/coaches . . .**
Leadership	. . . requires skillful leaders who develop capacity, advocate, and create support systems for professional learning.	. . . are provided professional learning that solidifies the knowledge, skills, practices, and dispositions to ensure they can practice instructional leadership in their schools.
Implementation	. . . applies research on change and sustains support for implementation of professional learning for long-term change.	. . . identify strategies for communicating adaptive messages to teachers regarding the purpose of observation and feedback. . . . receive support that promotes growth from facilitators through targeted, supportive, and actionable feedback.
Learning Designs	. . . integrates theories, research, and models of human learning to achieve its intended outcomes.	. . . engage in live, authentic reviews of teacher practice and are encouraged to set their own learning goals according to baseline data and ongoing formative feedback. . . . engage in sessions that include high-quality instructional strategies and that employ technology as a solution to support adult learning.
Learning Communities	. . . occurs within learning communities committed to continuous improvement, collective responsibility, and goal alignment.	. . . work in collegial groups to support collective learning to develop high-quality feedback while generating more calibrated approaches to reviews of teacher practice.
Data	. . . uses a variety of sources and types of student, educator, and system data to plan, assess, and evaluate professional learning.	. . . are provided formative data (based on validated criteria of supervisory skills) to support their own learning, while allowing district/regional leadership to use the data to measure leader growth and to uncover implementation needs related to teacher practice across their district/region. . . . receive support from facilitators who use formative data to align their instruction with participants' needs.

Source: Adapted from Learning Forward (2015)

Regardless of the skills you seek to develop in your learners, any professional learning model must align itself to the following four learning design fundamentals:

Fundamental 1—Use standards: We know standards provide us with clear expectations and drive learning. In education, we have come to understand that the impact of expectations on outcomes and professional learning is no different. Not only should standards serve as a foundation for the design of effective professional learning (as has been well-established by organizations like Learning Forward) but also be utilized to assess proficiency, measure progress, build feedback, and leverage growth for those participating in the professional learning. To maximize growth, assessment and feedback cycles should be tied to clear and measurable standards while the overall design should align to what we know about the most effective practices (DuFour & Marzano, 2011; Learning Forward, 2015). The RVL Supervisory Continuum expectations for effective observation and feedback are examples of such standards.

Fundamental 2—Create goals and provide high-quality feedback cycles: We know that assessment and feedback are the foundation of any great classroom, yet few, if any, of the policies and guidelines established in educator evaluation training models include these elements. Professional learning designs must integrate for the learners instructional research-based practices that we know are effective in the classroom and lead to growth, such as the following:

- Measurable long- and short-term goals
- Personalized instruction based on needs
- An assessment and feedback cycle (based on clear criteria—Fundamental 1)

Many leaders with whom we work often comment that one of the most influential aspects of their professional learning was that it included personalized feedback on their feedback—something they had never experienced.

Fundamental 3—Apply adult learning approaches: Professional learning programming needs to be aligned with research-based strategies related to adult professional learning, such as the following:

- Embedded and ongoing learning experiences
- Opportunities for reflection to promote discovery
- Opportunities for self-assessment and goal-setting
- Relevant learning that can be immediately applied
- Building of collective self-efficacy

Fundamental 4—Incorporate transformation and change research:
We have already explored ideas from thought leaders on change, such as Barber, Fullan, and Hargreaves. DuFour and Marzano (2011) highlighted another important characteristic of change leadership. They make clear that no one person has the knowledge and skill to lead learning entirely on their own, showing that through quality collaboration, leaders can have a profound impact on student achievement. While the shift to becoming a highly effective instructional leader clearly requires collaboration and partnership with one another and with teachers, to do so necessitates *new* learning on the part of the instructional leader.

> **Stop and Think:** Have your professional learning experiences included these essentials/fundamentals? If so, how were they included?

Building a New Approach

Marzano and Toth (2013) suggested that a "logical conclusion from the information currently available is that there is much work to be done relative to gathering observational data about teachers' classroom pedagogical skills as a component of teacher evaluation" (p. 12). Additionally, this new learning in observational practice must translate to more effective feedback to drive improvement at the classroom, school, and district level.

Figure 7.1 on the next page identifies three drivers as part of an effective system that serves to support and monitor feedback processes in districts. This model emphasizes the necessity of both consistent training for coaches and principals and a shared instructional vision, highlighting these as key "District Drivers" that serve to ensure quality feedback to new teachers (Park, Takahashi, & White, 2014). Notice the principles can be applied to all teachers.

Throughout this book, we have provided guidance on how to deliver on the "Classroom Drivers." Through application of the strategies, you develop the capacity to

- build relational trust;
- address instructional frameworks, new teacher goals, and needs;
- use coaching and communication strategies appropriately;
- use data/evidence to support observations; and
- provide feedback that is clear and actionable.

FIGURE 7.1: KEY DRIVERS OF FEEDBACK

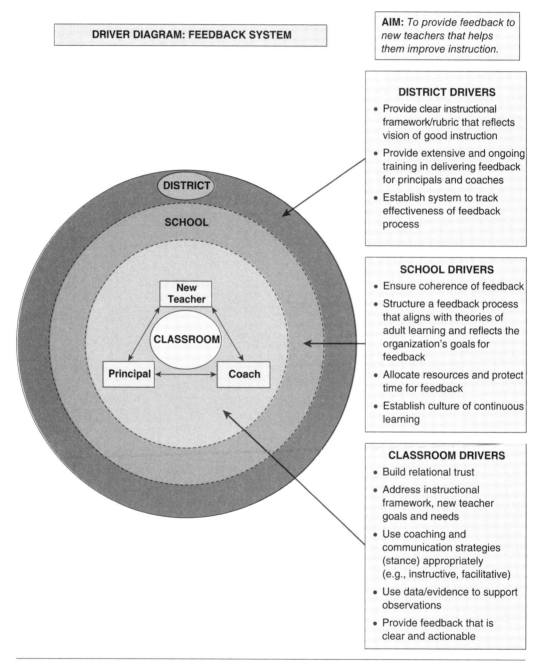

Source: Park, Takahashi, & White, 2014

The district/systems professional learning approaches described in this chapter were designed to ensure implementation of the Carnegie Foundation's "School" and "District Drivers," along with ReVISION Learning's six standards, as the foundations of effective design, implementation, and ongoing monitoring of quality observation and feedback practice. The highlighted districts continue to ensure that quality, ongoing feedback is delivered to all teachers by providing supportive and well-designed professional learning that

- uses standards to drive improvements in practice;

- allows for the creation of goals and incorporates high-quality feedback cycles;

- aligns with the principles of adult-learning theory; and

- incorporates our understanding of transformational change.

The designs presented in this chapter represent a commitment on the part of leadership teams to ensure that "extensive and ongoing training in delivering feedback" is provided to supervisors and coaches—a key "District Driver" outlined by the Carnegie Foundation (Park et al., 2014, p. 5). We have shared the approaches in hopes of supporting state, district, and school leaders in their efforts to shift the focus of educator evaluation to its original intent— examining teacher effectiveness and providing consistent and impactful teacher feedback to impact student learning.

Professional Learning Designs in Action

By understanding the research identifying the discrete skills associated with observation and feedback practice, we were able to design approaches to professional learning with districts that went beyond accuracy measures, supporting leader capacity to observe and collect evidence effectively and take action with that information to impact classroom practice. The districts highlighted in this chapter personalized the professional learning in a way that best suited their particular needs and culture, which ultimately also resulted in personalization for the participants. It is important to note that as you read through, careful consideration was given to the following:

1. Unique nature of the culture and climate

2. Readiness

3. Size

4. Current learning initiatives

Regardless of their differences, a unifying factor across the districts presented in this chapter is that they sought to make the fundamental shift in the focus and goals of evaluation practice.

By describing the work and impact of exceptional school leaders from several Connecticut districts, we hope to facilitate your assessment of current professional learning designs, informing you about initial steps you can take in your school/district/region. We show that not only did the leaders in these districts improve observation and feedback practices, but through a commitment to higher expectations for teaching and learning coupled with specific support, they also improved school/district culture.

The districts described in the remainder of this chapter took steps to ensure instructional leaders had access to the type of professional learning being highlighted by the MET Project, the Wallace Foundation, and organizations like Learning Forward. We sought to address the assumptions that resulted in limited capacity of instructional leaders to truly lead learning made by policymakers and professional learning designers outlined in Chapter 1. Through the designs created with our highlighted districts, five approaches for developing system-wide, high-quality, professional learning for observers and providers of teacher feedback emerged.

Approach 1: Evaluate how you are defining and assessing effective teaching and learning

> **Stop and Think:** You may have been ahead of the game or submitted a well-crafted rubric for Race to the Top, but have you revisited your evaluation system and instructional framework since 2010? How are you taking advantage of your newly found autonomy through the ESSA rewrite?

Approach 1 is considered a foundational step for districts/regions embarking on a path to make changes or improvements to policies, systems, and designs. "All evaluation tools must be research-based and regularly monitored for validity and reliability. Any evaluation system must be monitored and evaluated to ensure that it is working as intended and it remains consistent with its purpose" (California Teachers Association, 2012, p. 3). Continue to assess your system and framework each year, as you will inevitably learn lessons from the data being collected about the effectiveness of the system and the professional learning being provided. How teacher effectiveness should be measured has been greatly debated. Though we understand multiple measures are important, for the purposes here in our final chapter, we won't be wading into conversations about student learning objectives or value-added measures as part of the system. We recommend an examination of the instrument you are using to assess planning, establishment of classroom environment, professional responsibilities, and instruction as part of an overall evaluation of your current system.

Using the following guiding questions, you can begin to effectively evaluate (and potentially improve) your rubric:

- Do the descriptions in your "Proficient" and "Exemplary" performance levels match your expectations? Can they be used to promote growth?

- What are your data telling you? Are 98 percent of your teachers receiving high ratings? Is this accurate?

- Are teaching *and* learning integrated? Do descriptions only include teacher actions?

- Are the performance standards, indicators, attributes, and descriptions aligned to 21st century skills, desired instructional outcomes, and the district/region/state/national vision for student learning?

- Is the rubric usable and objective? Do the key levers between ratings progress logically? Are there numerous challenging phrases and quantitative measures that are either too general or too specific?

- How do indicators help teachers see the connection between professional practice/responsibility and instruction?

Our suggested requirements for this work include the following:

1. Teachers from varied grade levels, years of expertise, and content areas participate in this process.

2. The review team makes any changes with the teachers' input and support.

3. You begin this work months before your planned rollout. Determine how you will roll out and inform all stakeholders (board, parents, students) and then how you will initially train and provide ongoing support for all teachers and leaders.

This approach may be executed simultaneously or after steps suggested in Approach 2. For example, highlighted later, Regional School District 1 (RSD1) has worked to align its district-designed rubric to the vision of personalized learning for all students. RSD1 creates coherence by aligning instructional framework expectations directly to the expected vision it has for teaching and learning.

Approach 2: Create coherence by building comprehensive professional learning approaches

> **Stop and Think:** How is your professional learning aligned to district goals and teacher needs?

With the rapid and sometimes overwhelming influx of change in the past decade that flooded schools, leaders and teachers were often forced to focus on not only providing but clarifying and receiving necessary technical information. When will observations occur? How many will there be? Where do they get recorded? These questions needed to be answered to ensure that implementation could even happen. However, what was often neglected was the adaptive messaging (Heifetz & Linsky, 2009) or the "why" behind any of the new initiatives, requirements, and protocols. Everyone involved needs to understand the purpose and rationale behind all of these to effectively shift mindsets from buy-in to ownership—and they also need to see the interconnectedness. A first step on the path toward this is the creation of a shared vision of what teaching and learning could be and how the new initiatives, requirements, and protocols allowed the organization to arrive there.

By then seeking to apply a progressive, comprehensive, aligned professional learning design to a vision, you are able to create coherence among the many initiatives and systems that are being introduced. When we say "coherence," we mean a clear through-line that provides meaning and purpose to all the work and learning. However, as is often the case in complex organizations, not all members will recognize this through-line on their own. Professional learning should result in the following:

- a leader's ability to recognize his or her role and importance to the vision of the organization,

- but also improve his or her capacity to then communicate with teachers how they too connect to the purpose and goals (Hatch & Cunliffe, 2013).

Approach 2 outlines a deliberate approach to professional learning focused on ensuring alignment to the core instructional or strategic initiatives of an educational organization. Two Connecticut districts with whom we worked, Vernon and Brookfield Public Schools, designed a multiyear professional learning model to support confirmed needs associated with classroom practice in alignment with an instructional vision and/or a strategic school-improvement plan. Each district took slightly different approaches with consideration to their culture, climate, and personnel. However, both recognized that to make the types of changes needed at the classroom level, careful, collaborative, strategic planning would need to be reinforced by targeted leadership development that would ultimately result in focused teacher professional learning in the highest needs area.

Description:

Both districts in year 1:

- Engaged in a strategic-planning process.

- Engaged in an analysis of the current proficiency of instructional leadership skills (as defined through the RVL Supervisory Continuum and described in Chapters 2 through 6) to determine and gather baseline data regarding readiness.

- Examined and leveraged the collected baseline information about the RVL standards and skills to design targeted professional learning for their leaders.

Both districts in years 2 and 3:

- Continued to expand on support for leadership development related to the RVL standards and skills by engaging in three job-embedded, small-group, live classroom walk-throughs with a ReVISION Learning facilitator designed to calibrate observation and feedback practices against the standards for all evaluators in the district.

- Directly aligned all training across the district to the shared vision and began every training session with explicit connections to the strategic blueprints that articulated the vision.

Leaders collaboratively:

- Practiced collecting and analyzing evidence from classroom visits, refining their use of the skills outlined in Chapters 3 and 4.

- Determined the areas of strength and growth for teachers, increasing proficiency of skills outlined in Chapter 5.

- Submitted written feedback about a teacher after each visit, practicing the skill of producing unbiased feedback to support teacher learning, as outlined in Chapter 6.

Each leader then received individualized feedback about his or her submitted teacher feedback from a ReVISION facilitator.

- Vernon additionally required every leader to find time to observe a determined number of classrooms per week to ensure new learning was being transferred to classroom teachers.

- Vernon recognized that by simultaneously building teacher understanding of the expectations outlined in the framework, along with leader capacity, it could continue to communicate a cohesive and coherent message about teaching and learning at *all levels of the organization*. Vernon provided online coursework to teachers in key areas of teaching and learning, aligned to their instructional framework through three initial courses in year 2 and three additional courses in year 3.

- Vernon ensured that elementary school-based leaders engaged with their teachers in a combination of model lessons by grade level, along with training in observation and feedback through learning walks focused on the Math and Literacy Workshop models.

- Rockville High School "calibrated" department chairs and all teachers (87 total) around the learning purpose and scaffolding/progression indicator (a major need related to its goal to increase engagement). This not only deepened their understanding of effective practice and outcomes for their own growth but also built their capacity to serve as peer observers and valuable department team members. The groups participated in whole-school and then small-group half-day sessions to build understanding of indicators and related observation practices and then immediately practiced observing and deconstructing a lesson against defined expected practices.

FIGURE 7.2: CYCLE OF PLANNING AND PERFORMANCE IMPROVEMENT

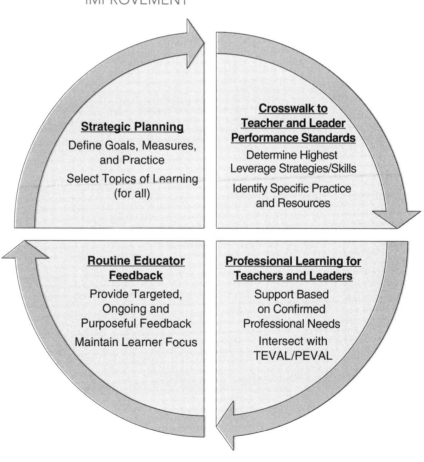

Source: Courtesy of ReVISION

Figure 7.2 provides an overview of the framework that guided the design of the professional learning programming. While each district engaged in this cycle with some customization and included agencies other than ReVISION Learning, the process outlined in our cycle shows each necessary step for full implementation of the types of comprehensive programming utilized by these districts.

Outcomes Toward Coherence:

- Each district designed an overarching strategic vision and plan on which all school improvement plans were then based and from which a coherent message was derived. Each strategic plan included a clear instructional vision that aligned to the instructional framework being used within the district.

- Each district demonstrated improvement over time in measured practice of evaluators in observation and feedback.

  o During the course of the first year, nearly 50 percent of the observers involved in the professional learning showed at least one full band of growth against the ReVISION Learning Continuum (see Figure 7.3 below).

  o During year 2, more than 80 percent of the participants moved at least one more band (see Figure 7.4). (What is important to note is that all but one met proficiency or beyond.)

FIGURE 7.3: EVALUATOR GROWTH 1

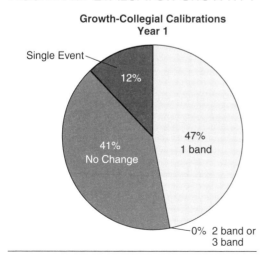

FIGURE 7.4: EVALUATOR GROWTH 2

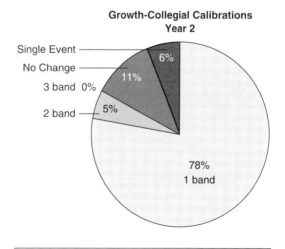

- Each district raised the leaders' levels of expectations and understanding of effective instruction.

  o The measurement of performance and practice directly tied to the teacher performance rubric showed significantly *reduced* ratings. While this may sound counterintuitive, as we do not expect to see declining teacher performance, what was actually occurring was an increased capacity on the part of leaders to recognize and analyze quality teaching practice and/or student behavior and outcomes against the district rubric.

The application of a more rigorous eye toward teacher practice and student outcomes led to lower, yet more accurate ratings. We know this more comprehensive evidence collection, understanding of research and teaching and learning, and more critical analysis will raise the levels of expectation (combating overinflation, as cited in Chapter 1). Ultimately, it will improve teacher effectiveness and job performance. However, it is critical to communicate with teachers as to what is occurring, as this can cause mistrust, confusion, and very difficult feedback conversations. Utilizing steps—like Rockville High School's training of teachers or New Milford's strategies from Chapter 2—simultaneously with leader training builds coherence and is a perfect example of finding the balance between challenge and support, ultimately building a culture for growth.

Approach 3: Build school cultures through focused, progressive, administrator team learning experiences

Stop and Think: Is your professional learning progressive in nature or is it a more wash-rinse-repeat method every year? How is your professional learning for leaders impacting your teachers and your school and district/region culture?

Canton Public School leaders embody a transformational mindset and understand the impact of leadership on an educational community. They engaged in an evaluation of their framework, moving to a new rubric with higher expectations of teaching *and* learning, as well as a multiyear model of professional learning, like that of Brookfield and Vernon, but they are in year 4 of a commitment to a progressive model of support for their leadership team. In the Canton Public Schools, department chairs, assistant principals, principals, the assistant superintendent, and the superintendent all learn together. Initially, the intent of professional learning was similar to that of Vernon and

Brookfield—to establish a coherent vision and align leadership practice accordingly. What became clear very early, however, was that through the professional learning design, Canton's leaders were not only creating coherence but also shifting the beliefs of teachers about instruction and the value of feedback.

Each year, leadership development focused on ensuring leaders had the capacity to engage in more purposeful and aligned conversations based on classroom observations. This in turn created a level of personalization for teachers, slowly shifting the perceptions they held about classroom observations and feedback. Over three years, leaders were provided access to a combination of workshops and similar job-embedded coaching (as outlined in Approach 2) that led to improved instructional leadership practice, especially related to teacher feedback and professional learning communities for teachers in support of targeted learning needs.

Description:

In year 1, Canton Public Schools:

- Designed a strategic vision and plan on which all school improvement plans were then based. Each strategic plan included a clear instructional vision that aligned to the instructional framework being used within the district.

- Calibrated district administrators as well as department chairs through workshops designed to provide direct instruction on key skills of observation and feedback, beyond simply rating teachers, and included the following:

  - Deconstructing the new district instructional rubric (Chapter 2).

  - Focusing on observer behaviors during a lesson and interacting with students (Chapter 3), which resulted in the greatest change.

  - Aligning student learning objectives to teaching in the classroom (Chapter 4).

  - Making learning in the classrooms student centered by understanding student ownership (Chapter 4).

- Practiced collecting and analyzing evidence through job-embedded coaching during live classroom visits (Chapter 2–6).

In years 2 and 3, the following took place in Canton Public Schools:

- Once leaders met proficiency against the RVL Continuum for observation and written feedback, the district continued to focus on leadership development by expanding its approach to feedback conversations and a second set of RVL standards.

- The district expanded its work with the team, designing its own learning experiences to include a partner-based model wherein two administrators observed a teacher and prepared written feedback collaboratively. The supervising leader engaged in a verbal feedback conference with the teacher while their partner and a ReVISION Learning facilitator observed. This allowed the administrator to receive comprehensive written feedback about his or her interaction with and support of the teacher. These feedback meetings were reviewed against a second set of standards for effective conversations, with attention to an alignment of the skills outlined in this book: the use of specific evidence to support a claim and promote growth, focused attention on the impact of the teacher on the learner, and clear connections and areas of growth and strength determined.

The superintendent and assistant superintendent even served as learning partners in the more recent step.

Outcomes Toward Improved Culture:

- The measured improvement in observation and feedback practice among administrators was clear, with 86 percent of the administrative team demonstrating "Proficiency" or "Exemplary" practice against the ReVISION Learning Continuum by year 2.

- The data collected at the end of year 3, showing teacher perceptions of the influence of the work, were most revealing. The representative data shown in Figure 7.5 from one of the district's schools reveal that teachers felt strongly supported by the feedback being provided (based on the approaches to classroom observation and feedback outlined in this book). Teachers' perceptions of the feedback and evaluation process changed. They began to value observation and feedback—improving culture, climate, and community and infusing trust in the supervisory relationship.

In 2016, we sent a teacher survey to 450 teachers in Canton and an additional district that received feedback from evaluators who had participated in professional learning to support observation and feedback practice. With a 28 percent response rate, the data were positive, showing over 80 percent of the teachers rated the feedback they received from their evaluator as "effective" or "highly effective"—with criteria such as, it provided clear claims about practice, identified areas of strength and development, was actionable, and demonstrated a clear connection between their teaching and student learning. (This is promising data after reading the STOY results!)

FIGURE 7.5: TEACHER PERCEPTION DATA

Canton High School

Q.37: How would you rate the overall effectiveness of the feedback at helping you as a teacher to identify your areas of development?

Very effective 24% — 16
Effective 61% — 41
Partially effective 15% — 10

Favorable: **85%**

Q.38: How would you rate the overall effectiveness of the feedback at providing actionable feedback to improve your practice?

Very effective 23% — 15
Effective 59% — 39
Partially effective 18% — 12

Favorable: **82%**

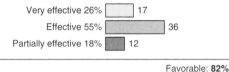

Q.39: How would you rate the overall effectiveness of the feedback in providing an understanding about how your practice impacted student learning during the observed lesson?

Very effective 26% — 17
Effective 55% — 36
Partially effective 18% — 12

Favorable: **82%**

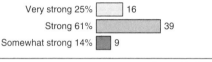

Q.40: How would you rate the overall effectiveness of the evidence providing in your observation feedback reports to support the claims about practice?

Very strong 25% — 16
Strong 61% — 39
Somewhat strong 14% — 9

Favorable: **86%**

Source: Canton Public Schools

Approach 4: Build internal capacity through training of the trainers to lead leaders

> **Stop and Think:** How are leaders supporting each other in your district?

Through Canton's partner structure, colleagues became valuable resources for each other. An important objective in all districts should revolve around creating internal capacity over time to provide ongoing support of peers within the district and to solidify the knowledge and application of the leaders' skills as participants in professional learning. A training-of-trainers model ensures that a district can execute scaffolded support for ongoing learning with necessary structures, practices, and policy to ensure a sustainable impact. After several Connecticut districts engaged in workshops or services in stages over several years, focused on building capacity in the three core competencies, the six standards, and the twenty-one core skills, they were able to move to a training of the trainer model and facilitate professional learning for their peers across the district.

Description:

In the 2016–2017 school year, Hartford and New Haven Public Schools, two of the largest districts in the state of Connecticut, each did the following:

- Participated in intensive, multiday/multidimensional training to develop a cadre of facilitators for the job-embedded model described in Strategies 2 and 3.

- Designed a customized professional learning program in alignment with our five learning design essentials that allowed the professional development to work to scale (given the large size of each district).

- Received coaching and support during the first year of implementation that allowed for real-time or group feedback, honing the skills of each facilitator.

  - In New Haven, the soon-to-be trainers observed and debriefed facilitated sessions to develop an understanding of the learning design, participants' needs, common levels of understanding, and skill proficiency. Based on the trends that emerged, they brainstormed district-level/systems needs and strategies for facilitation, preparing to implement the model independently.

Outcomes Toward Internal Capacity

As this was a more recent training, data about the outcomes of this professional learning approach are more anecdotal than other strategies, yet the surveys of the participating leaders still reveal a high level of impact:

- Greater acceptance and ownership among leaders due to the fact that their own peers were facilitating and could better contextualize the learning.

  - Q5: Please share any positive feedback from the sessions.

    "[Internal] Facilitator was excellent—small group allowed for everyone to participate and do so freely. Observing 'real' classrooms far superior to watching a video (often of questionable quality)."

- Greater awareness of the importance of instructional leadership practices over the managerial role that typically consumed a majority of large, urban district principals' schedules.

  - Q6: How can we improve the Observational Rounds sessions?

    "The session was perfect. It is just hard to leave our buildings for this work in addition to monthly Admin PL and cohort walkthroughs but please continue to provide more opportunities."

- Increase in confidence to implement associated skills of supervision and evaluation as outlined in Chapters 2 through 6

- Q7: How will this training affect your work as an evaluator this year?

  "It will help me refine and consistently practice the claim, connect, action aspect of the evaluation process."

  "This will encourage me to do a better job and provide me tools to confidently have those critical conversations."

  Additionally, the feedback from leader participants supported the need for an improved learning design.

- Reinforcement of the type of training needed to support effective observation practice.

  - Q5: Please share any positive feedback from the session.

    "Why did we not do this type of collaborative session sooner? So much better than those doggone videos."

Finally, feedback from teachers in Hartford Public Schools was gathered to understand the potential impact of the professional learning. Some feedback included the following:

> *"My evaluator offered feedback based on things that could be improved the next time. This feedback was very beneficial because the suggestions were things that I would not have thought of."*
>
> *"[Evaluator] . . . provided timely support and encouragement that my ideas are valid and worth pursuing and that they support the curriculum."*
>
> *"Informal observations throughout the school year, communication about current practice included strengths and areas of improvement via phone, text, email, etc. I was made aware of my strengths and areas of improvement and implemented suggestions that my evaluator had for me to help improve my practice."*

In 2017, West Hartford Public Schools began a training of trainers after five years of work to create its instructional framework, train teachers and administrators on the framework components, and calibrate its observers in applying the core competencies, standards, and skills. Seven selected leaders received training to build capacity around the RVL standards and engaged in guided practice sessions in pairs for new district leaders, while the team observed. This is the first step in a process of building a cadre of facilitators in the district to complete the professional learning from within.

Further research on the impact of training internal trainers to specifically support instructional leadership development within a district is an exciting and potentially powerful area of study. There is qualitative evidence that this model can and will impact the culture and climate of the district—shifting attitudes and beliefs about continuous professional learning and/or the purpose of leadership practice. While more needs to be understood about the influence these models have on the specific skills they intend to support, the initial outcomes are promising.

Approach 5: Measure professional learning using ReVISION Learning standards as benchmarks for professional growth.

> **Stop and Think:** How are your observation and feedback skills assessed and supported?

Approach 5 stands as an exemplar in professional learning, not necessarily because it is different from the other approaches taken to support improved observation and teacher feedback practices, but instead because of what it adds to a professional learning design.

RSD1 tied the performance of its instructional leaders to ongoing proficiency as measured by the six ReVISION Learning standards outlined in Chapters 2 through 6.

- Proficiency was a requirement. The standards were measured through participation in the same collaborative walk-throughs described in Strategies 2 and 3, along with more direct support/coaching so that administrators had the opportunity to receive differentiated and often personalized job-embedded coaching throughout the year, work with colleagues in small learning communities, and receive feedback from a facilitator about their own capacity to observe and provide teacher feedback. In taking this step, the leadership of RSD1 set clear expectations for administrators while ensuring targeted professional learning to support growth.

- Fourteen teacher leaders received extensive training in the instructional framework and observation to serve as complementary evaluators and engaged in "calibration" sessions throughout the year. They too needed to meet proficiency against the RVL standards before engaging in evaluations.

To extend the use of the RVL standards in a unique way, Hartford Public Schools, through implementation of the training-of-trainers model, used the standards for assessment and ongoing feedback as a benchmark for professional goals. To emphasize the importance of instructional leadership practice, the executive director of performance management (the person responsible for the evaluation of administrators and teachers throughout the district) designed his own performance goals in alignment with the six ReVISION Learning standards (see Table 7.2). In other words, his own performance measurement was directly tied to the leaders' improvements in application of observation and feedback practices.

TABLE 7.2	SAMPLE DISTRICT LEADER GOAL

SLO 1: Create a shared vision of excellent teaching and learning through observational feedback that is aligned to the CCT framework and is actionable.

Indicator 1: At least 90% of all HPS building level administrators will successfully complete two observational rounds that will focus on evidence, alignment, and actionable feedback. No baseline data available.

Indicator 2: At least 50% of all the second formal observations of non-tenured teachers who may be eligible for tenure at the close of the 2016-17 academic year will require a score of "Proficient" or higher on ReVISION Quality Feedback Continuum 1 F (Supervisory Continuum) "Feedback report as written serves as a comprehensive learning tool containing clearly articulated evidenced-based feedback and explicit connections." No baseline data available.

Indicator 3: TEVAL teacher survey administered in the spring of 2016 item Q7: How would you rate the overall quality of the observational feedback regarding the evidence, alignment to the evaluation rubric (FFT), and actionable recommendations will have a favorable increase of 5% (most or all feedback is . . .) from 64% in 2016 to at least 69% in 2017.

Though all five approaches have resulted directly in measurable outcomes for leaders and teachers, we are working to demonstrate how these improvements in educator effectiveness have impacted students.

Final Thoughts and Beyond

There is still much work to be done to support all instructional leaders.

"Even after high-quality initial training is in place, a school system may find as many as 40 percent of trainees still need additional support." —MET Project, 2015, p. 14

While we have seen tremendous success in shifting the practice of observation and feedback through our professional learning approaches, the work and the learning must continue for measurable effects to reach our teachers and students. Regardless of the selected approaches, professional learning to improve capacity to observe teachers must move beyond development and measurement of accuracy and provide progressive, personalized, and ongoing learning opportunities for all those who support teachers. If we wish to guarantee a quality teacher in every classroom for our students, then we must ensure that those teachers are provided with accurate and informative feedback that feeds forward toward improved student outcomes. Critically, the "professional learning that observer training affords is too important to be limited to administrators and others involved in formal evaluation; peer observers, instructional coaches, and classroom teachers need to know and be able to do what quality observation requires" (MET Project, 2015, p. 5). Districts/regions need to think about how professional learning can reach all those who impact teaching and learning in a building or system.

That was the fundamental purpose of this book: to provide a pathway and guidebook for all those who support teachers and seek to lead learning. This goal is one that we hope you call to mind time and again on your journey toward improved instructional leadership practice as you implement, personalize, and refine your processes and engage in this work.

The strategies and corresponding actions taken by the highlighted districts represent the type of adaptations needed to support instructional leaders as the landscape of teaching and learning continues to evolve. These districts understand (along with that which has been made clear in the MET Project study) that ongoing learning remains essential and that leaders need quality professional learning to develop and, most importantly, sustain key instructional leadership skills.

The route to teacher effectiveness and improved student outcomes is paved by shifting the mindset of administrators and teachers to ensure that instructional supervision and evaluation focus squarely on the engagement and learning of students in the classroom versus the inspection of teacher practice. No longer is it acceptable to have the complex world of teaching and learning measured two times per year or, even worse, every other year. No longer can we sustain our classrooms by providing a litany of what a teacher did or needs to do during a 45-minute lesson as the frame of our teacher feedback. Administrators and instructional coaches must—through routine interaction in classrooms, by incorporating the observation and feedback strategies outlined in this book, and through intentional and deliberate interaction with students to recognize engagement and learning—become partners with teachers in their journey to ensure learning for all students.

Your work to lead learning in your school and district/region will thrive through daily reminders of this noble purpose on behalf of the students we serve. We understand and promote the idea that you will need to go far beyond the policies and approaches of typical educator evaluation cycles to ensure teachers have the opportunity for growth.

Challenge yourself daily to do the following:

1. Embody transformative orientation versus compliance orientation in evaluative practice.

2. View yourself as a teacher of teachers.

3. Plan your teacher assessment design and make *learning* the focus.

4. Go beyond the policy—don't just do it right, do the right thing.

5. Plan for formative feedback and difficult conversations.

6. Define the coherence that exists—if you do not see it, start looking harder.

As you consider and/or form your own values and beliefs as an instructional leader and allow those to shape your day-to-day leadership practice, consider these six important practices and become the leader who creates an environment of trust, challenge, and ongoing support toward teacher effectiveness.

"It's not who I am underneath, but what I do that defines me." —Batman

What can you do to define yourself as a great instructional leader? Go feed forward and lead the learning!

Strategies List

Chapter 2

Strategy 1 • Understand the structure

Strategy 2 • Understand the connections

Strategy 3 • Understand the research

Strategy 4 • Identify challenging phrases

Strategy 5 • Identify key levers

Strategy 6 • Engage in the *behavioralization* process

Chapter 3

Strategy 7 • Develop an awareness

Strategy 8 • Observe with a wide lens

Strategy 9 • Collect a balance of evidence with purpose

Strategy 10 • Place yourself where the learning is occurring

Strategy 11 • Do what it takes to collect evidence

Strategy 12 • Be comprehensive in your collection of evidence

Strategy 13 • Maximize the use of your notepad or tablet

Strategy 14 • Listen to teaching and learning

Strategy 15 • View learning in action

Strategy 16 • Interact with learners

Chapter 4

Strategy 17 • Organize your evidence

Strategy 18 • Ask questions about what you observed

Strategy 19 • Determine causes of outcomes

Chapter 5

Strategy 20 • Focus on the overall observed impact on student learning and engagement

Strategy 21 • Use the instructional framework to recognize expectations

Strategy 22 • Use what you know about research-based strategies

Chapter 6

Strategy 23 • Use framework language to develop claims about practice

Strategy 24 • Cite quantitative and qualitative data

Strategy 25 • Incorporate the impact on the learners

Strategy 26 • Move away from summarizing or listing

Strategy 27 • Incorporate evidence-based areas of growth and strength

Strategy 28 • Determine an accurate root cause

Strategy 29 • Use key levers for next steps

Strategy 30 • Use logic

Strategy 31 • Build on teachers' needs and strengths

Tables and Figures List

Chapter 1

Figure 1.1 • Effects of Support and Challenge on Teachers

Table 1.1 • Core Assumption 1

Table 1.2 • Core Assumption 2

Table 1.3 • Core Assumption 3

Table 1.4 • ReVISION Learning (RVL) Guiding Principles

Figure 1.2 • Observation Checklist

Table 1.5 • RVL Skill Overview

Chapter 2

Figure 2.1 • RVL Standard 1.A

Table 2.1 • RVL 1.A Common Challenges

Table 2.2 • Skill Set for RVL 1.A

Figure 2.2 • Rubric at a Glance

Figure 2.3 • Rubric Design Example 1

Figure 2.4 • Rubric Design Example 2

Figure 2.5 • Examples of Research Language

Table 2.3 • The Big Picture

Table 2.4 • Indicator for Key Levers

Table 2.5 • Key Levers Annotation

Figure 2.6 • Annotated Rubrics

Chapter 3

Chapter 4

Chapter 5

Chapter 6

Chapter 7

References

Aguilar, E. (2013). *The art of coaching: Effective strategies for school transformation.* Hoboken, NJ: John Wiley & Sons.

Anderson, L. (Ed.), Krathwohl, D. (Ed.), Airasian, P. W., Cruikshank, K. A., Mayer, R. E., Pintrich, P. R., . . . Wittrock, M. C. (2001). *A taxonomy for learning, teaching, and assessing: A revision of Bloom's taxonomy of educational objectives* [Complete edition]. New York, NY: Longman.

Antonetti, J., & Garver, J. (2015). *17,000 classroom visits can't be wrong: Strategies that engage students, promote active learning and boost achievement.* Alexandria, VA: ASCD.

Archer, J., Cantrell, S., Holtzman, S., Joe, J., Tocci, C., & Wood, J. (2016). *Better feedback for better teaching: A practical guide for improving classroom observations.* San Francisco, CA: Bill & Melinda Gates Foundation/Jossey-Bass.

Bambrick-Santoyo, P. (2012). *Leverage leadership: A practical guide to building exceptional schools.* Hoboken, NJ: John Wiley & Sons.

Bandura, A. (1977). *Social learning theory.* Englewood Cliffs, NJ: Prentice Hall.

Bandura, A., (1989). Human agency in social cognitive theory. *American Psychologist, 44*(9), 1175–1184.

Barber, M., & Mourshed, M. (2007). How the world's best performing school systems come out on top. London, UK: McKinsey & Company. Retrieved from http://mckinseyonsociety.com/how-the-worlds-best-performing-schools-come-out-on-top/

Benson, B. (2016, September 1). Cognitive bias cheat sheet, simplified: Thinking is hard because of 4 universal conundrums [Blog post]. Retrieved from https://medium.com/thinking-is-hard/4-conundrums-of-intelligence-2ab78d90740f

Blackburn, B. (2012). *Rigor is not a 4-letter word.* New York, NY: Eye of Education.

Bravmann, S. L. (2004, March 17). Assessment's "fab four." *Education Week.* Retrieved from https://www.edweek.org/ew/articles/2004/03/17/27bravmann.h23.html

California Teachers Association. (2012). *Teacher evaluation framework.* Retrieved from https://www.cta.org/~/media/Documents/Issues%20%20Action/Teacher%20Quality/Teacher%20Evaluation%20Framework%204-23-15%20Final%20for%20website%20File.ashx

Cappello, M., & Moss, B. (Eds.). (2010). *Contemporary readings in literacy education.* Thousand Oaks, CA: SAGE.

Clark, S., & Duggins, A. (2016). *Using quality feedback to guide professional learning: A framework for instructional leaders.* Thousand Oaks, CA: Corwin.

Clotfelter, C. T., Ladd, H. F., & Vigdor, J. L. (2007). *How and why do teacher credentials matter for student achievement?* (CALDER Working Paper no. 2). Durham, NC: Sanford School of Public Policy, Duke University.

Colorado Department of Education. (2017). *Rubric for evaluating Colorado teachers*. Retrieved from https://www.cde.state.co.us/educatoreffectiveness/rubric-for-colorado-teachers

Connecticut State Department of Education (CSDE). (2014). *Common Core of teaching (CCT) rubric for effective teaching 2014* [Online pdf]. Retrieved from http://www.connecticutseed.org/wp-content/uploads/2014/05/CCT_Rubric_for_Effective_Teaching-May_2014.pdf

Connecticut State Department of Education (CSDE). (2017). *Regional School District 1 continuum of professional practice* [Online pdf]. Retrieved from http://www.region1schools.org/Uploads/Public/Documents/Staff/Special%20Education%20Teachers'%20Continuum%20(17-18).pdf

Costa, A. L., & Kallick, B. (2009). *Habits of mind across the curriculum*. Alexandria, VA: ASCD.

Costa, J., Sr. (2014). *Time sample study: Principals' work implementing the Connecticut system for educator evaluation and support*. Unpublished manuscript.

Dallas Independent School District. (2014). *Teacher performance rubric: Overview of domains and indicators* [Online pdf]. Retrieved from https://www.dallasisd.org/cms/lib/TX01001475/Centricity/Domain/8969/TEI%20Performance%20Rubric%202014%2004%2029.pdf

Danielson, C. (2007). *Enhancing professional practice: A framework for teaching* (2nd ed.). Alexandria, VA: ASCD.

The Danielson Group. (2013). *The framework*. Retrieved from https://www.danielsongroup.org/framework/

Davis, H. Summers, J., & Miller, L. (2012). *An interpersonal approach to classroom management strategies for improving student engagement*. Thousand Oaks, CA: Corwin.

Doran, G. T. (1981). There's a S.M.A.R.T. way to write management's goals and objectives. *Management Review, 70*(11), 35–36.

DuFour, R. (2002). Learning-centered principal. *Educational Leadership, 59*(8), 12–15.

DuFour, R., & Marzano, R. J. (2011). *Leaders of learning: How district, school, and classroom leaders improve student achievement*. Bloomington, IN: Solution Tree Press.

Dweck, C. (2006). *Mindset: The new psychology of success*. New York, NY: Random House.

Dweck, C. (2015, September 22). Carol Dweck revisits the "growth mindset." *Education Week, 35*(5), 20, 24. Retrieved from http://www.edweek.org/ew/articles/2015/09/23/carol-dweck-revisits-the-growth-mindset.html

Fisher, D., & Frey, N. (2008). *Better learning through structured teaching: A framework for the gradual release of responsibility*. Alexandria, VA: ASCD.

Fisher, D., & Frey, N. (2014). *Better learning through structured teaching* (2nd ed.). Alexandria, VA: ASCD.

Flath, B. (1989). The principal as instructional leader. *ATA Magazines, 69*(3), 19–22, 47–49.

Florida Department of Education. (n.d.). *Florida performance measurement system: Observation instrument* [Online pdf]. Retrieved from http://education.ucf.edu/clinicalexp/docs/FPMSForm.pdf

Frontier, T., & Mielke, P. (2016). *Making teachers better not bitter: Balancing evaluation, supervision, and reflection for professional growth*. Alexandria, VA: ASCD.

Fullan, M. (2007). *The new meaning of educational change* (4th ed.). New York, NY: Teachers College Press.

Fullan, M. (2008). *The six secrets of change: What the best leaders do to help their organiza-tions survive and thrive*. San Francisco, CA: Jossey-Bass.

Glickman, C. (2008). *Leadership for learning: How to help teachers succeed*. Alexandria, VA: ASCD.

Goddard, R. D., Hoy, W. K., & Hoy, A. W. (2000). Collective teacher efficacy: Its mean-ing, measure, and impact on student achievement. *American Educational Research Journal*, *37*(2), 479–507.

Goe, L., Wylie, E. C., Bosso, D., & Olson, D. (2017). State of the states' teacher evalua-tion and support systems: A perspective from exemplary teachers. Executive sum-mary. *ETS Research Report Series*, *2017*(1), 1–27. doi:10.1002/ets2.12156. Retrieved from https://www.ets.org/Media/Research/pdf/RR-17-30_Executive_Summary.pdf

Haring, N. G., Lovitt, T. C., Eaton, M. D., & Hansen, C. L. (1978). *The fourth R: Research in the classroom*. Columbus, OH: Charles E. Merrill.

Hargreaves, A., & Fullan, M. (2012). *Professional capital: Transforming teaching in every school*. New York, NY: Teachers College Press.

Hatch, M. J., & Cunliffe, A. L. (2013). *Organization theory: Modern, symbolic, and postmod-ern perspectives*. Cambridge, MA: Harvard University Press.

Hattie, J. (2009). *Visible learning: A synthesis of over 800 meta-analyses relating to achieve-ment*. New York, NY: Routledge.

Hattie, J. (2012). *Visible learning for teachers: Maximizing impact on learning*. New York, NY: Routledge.

Hattie, J., & Timperley, H. (2007). The power of feedback. *Review of Educational Research*, *77*(1), 81–112.

Heifetz, R., & Linsky, M. (2009). *The practice of adaptive leadership: Tools and tactics for changing your organization and the world*. Boston, MA, Cambridge Leadership Associates.

Horng, E. L., Klasik, D., & Loeb, S. (2009, November). Principal time-use and school effectiveness [Online pdf]. Retrieved from https://web.stanford.edu/~sloeb/papers/Principal%20Time-Use%20%28revised%29.pdf

Howard, J. (1992). Excerpts from getting smart: The social construction of intelligence [Online pdf]. Retrieved from https://www.efficacy.org/media/9600/gettingsmart jeffhoward.pdf

Kersten, T. A., & Israel, M. S. (2005). Teacher evaluation: Principals' insights and sugges-tions for improvement. *Planning and Changing*, *36*(1&2), 47–67. Retrieved from http://files.eric.ed.gov/fulltext/EJ737642.pdf

Killion, J. (2015). *The feedback process: Transforming feedback for professional learning*. Oxford, OH: Learning Forward.

Kraft, M. A., & Gilmour, A. F. (2017). Revisiting the widget effect: Teacher evaluation reforms and the distribution of teacher effectiveness. *Educational Researcher*, *46*(5), 234–249.

Lavigne, A., & Good, T. (2015). *Improving teaching through observation and feedback: Beyond state and federal mandates*. New York, NY: Routledge.

Lavigne, H. J., Shakman, K., Zweig, J., & Greller, S. L. (2016). *Principals' time, tasks, and professional development: An analysis of schools and staffing survey data* (REL 2017–201). Washington, DC: U.S. Department of Education, Institute of Education Sciences, National Center for Education Evaluation and Regional Assistance, Regional Educational Laboratory Northeast & Islands. Retrieved from http://ies .ed.gov/ncee/edlabs

Learning Forward. (2015). Standards for professional learning. Retrieved from https://learningforward.org/standards-for-professional-learning?_ga=2.60992364.1985290386.1506866610-459314610.1502539803

Learning Sciences Marzano Center. (2017). Marzano's focused teacher evaluation model. Retrieved from http://www.marzanocenter.com/Teacher-Evaluation/Focused-Model/

Leithwood, K., Seashore Louis, K., Anderson, S., & Wahlstrom, K. (2004). Review of research: How leadership influences student learning. Retrieved from http://www.wallacefoundation.org/knowledge-center/Documents/How-Leadership-Influences-Student-Learning.pdf

Lipton, L., & Wellman, B. (2013a). *Learning focused supervision: Developing professional expertise in standards-driven systems.* Charlotte, VT: MiraVia.

Lipton, L., & Wellman, B. (2013b). *The MiraVia learning-focused supervision model: Rationale and research.* Retrieved from https://www.nesacenter.org/uploaded/conferences/FLC/2014/handouts/Lynn_Sawyer_precon/Rationale_and_Research_Supporting_the_Need_for_Learning.pdf

Loveless, T. (2016, March 24). *Principals as instructional leaders: An international perspective.* Retrieved from https://www.brookings.edu/research/principals-as-instructional-leaders-an-international-perspective/

Marshall, K. (2011). *Teacher evaluation rubrics* [Online pdf]. Retrieved from http://usny.nysed.gov/rttt/teachers-leaders/practicerubrics/Docs/MarshallTeacherRubric.pdf

Marshall, K. (2013). *Rethinking teacher supervision and evaluation: How to work smart, build collaboration and close the achievement gap* (2nd ed.). San Francisco, CA: Jossey-Bass.

Marzano, R. (2000). *Designing a new taxonomy of educational objectives.* Thousand Oaks, CA: Corwin.

Marzano, R., Frontier, T., & Livingston, D. (2011): *Effective supervision: Supporting the art and science of teaching.* Alexandria, VA: ASCD

Marzano, R., Pickering, D., & Heflebower, T. (2011). *The highly engaged classroom: The classroom strategies series (generating high levels of student attention and engagement).* USA: Bloomington, IN: Marzano Research.

Marzano, R., & Toth, M. (2013). *Teacher evaluation that makes a difference: A new model for teacher growth and achievement.* Alexandria, VA: ASCD.

Marzano, R. J. (2007). *The art and science of teaching: A comprehensive framework for instruction.* Alexandria, VA: ASCD.

McKay, C. (2013). *You don't have to be bad to get better: A leader's guide to improving teacher quality.* Thousand Oaks, CA: Corwin.

MET Project. (2010). *Working with teachers to develop fair and reliable measures of effective teaching* [Online pdf]. Seattle, WA: Bill & Melinda Gates Foundation. Retrieved from https://docs.gatesfoundation.org/documents/met-framing-paper.pdf

MET Project. (2013). *Ensuring fair and reliable measures of effective teaching: Culminating findings from the MET's three-year study.* Seattle, WA: Bill & Melinda Gates Foundation. Retrieved from https://www.edweek.org/media/17teach-met1.pdf

MET Project. (2014). *Building trust in observations: A blueprint for improving systems to support great teaching.* Seattle, WA: Bill & Melinda Gates Foundation. Retrieved from http://k12education.gatesfoundation.org/resource/building-trust-in-observations-a-blueprint-for-improving-systems-to-support-great-teaching/

MET Project. (2015). *Seeing it clearly: Improving observer training for better feedback and better teaching.* Seattle, WA: Bill & Melinda Gates Foundation. Retrieved from http://k12education.gatesfoundation.org/resource/seeing-it-clearly-improving-observer-training-for-better-feedback-and-better-teaching/

Mielke, P., & Frontier, T. (2012). Keeping improvement in mind. *Educational Leadership*, *70*(3), 10–13.

Moss, C., & Brookhart, S. (2012). *Learning targets: Helping students aim for understanding in today's lesson*. Alexandria, VA: ASCD.

Moss, C. & Brookhart, S. (2015). *Formative classroom walkthroughs: How principals and teachers collaborate to raise student achievement*. Alexandria, VA: ASCD.

Moss, C., Brookhart, S., & Long, B. (2011). What students need to learn. Educational Leadership, *68*(6), 66–69. Retrieved from http://www.ascd.org/publications/educational-leadership/mar11/vol68/num06/Knowing-Your-Learning-Target.aspx

National SAM Innovation Project (NSIP). (2018). Retrieved from http://www.samsconnect.com/?page_id=2129

Newark Public Schools. (2015). *Framework for effective teaching* [Online pdf]. Retrieved from http://www.nps.k12.nj.us/wp-content/uploads/2014/08/NPSTeacherEvaluationGuidebook2014-15.pdf

NSW Education Standards Authority. (2018). *Australian professional standards for teachers* [Online pdf]. Retrieved from https://educationstandards.nsw.edu.au/wps/wcm/connect/8658b2fa-62d3-40ca-a8d9-02309a2c67a1/australian-professional-standards-teachers.pdf?MOD=AJPERES&CVID=

Ohio Department of Education. (2015). *Ohio teacher evaluation system* [Online pdf]. Retrieved from https://education.ohio.gov/getattachment/Topics/Teaching/Educator-Evaluation-System/Ohio-s-Teacher-Evaluation-System/Teacher-Performance-Ratings/OTES-Model-122315.pdf.aspx

Organisation for Economic Co-operation and Development (OECD). (2013). *Synergies for better learning: An international perspective on evaluation and assessment*. Retrieved from http://www.oecd.org/education/school/synergies-for-better-learning.htm

P21: Partnership for 21st Century Learning. (n.d.). Retrieved from http://www.p21.org/

Park, S., Takahashi, S., & White, T. (2014). Learning teaching (LT) program: Developing an effective teacher feedback system: 90-day cycle report [Online pdf]. Carnegie Foundation for the Advancement of Teaching. Retrieved from https://www.carnegiefoundation.org/wp-content/uploads/2013/08/CF_Feedback_90DC_2014.pdf

Patton, M.Q. (2015). *Qualitative research and evaluation methods* (4th ed.). Thousand Oaks, CA: SAGE.

Piaget, J. (1972). *The psychology of the child*. New York, NY: Basic Books.

Popham, W. J. (2008). *Transformative assessment in action*. Alexandria, VA: ASCD.

Popham W. J. (2013). *Evaluating America's teacher: Mission possible*. Thousand Oaks, CA: Corwin.

Rosen, R., & Parise, L. M. (2017). *Using evaluation systems for teacher improvement: Are school districts ready to meet new federal goals?* [Online pdf]. Retrieved from https://www.mdrc.org/sites/default/files/iPD_ESSA_Brief_2017.pdf

Rosenthal, R., & Jacobsen, L. (1968). *Pygmalion in the classroom: Teacher expectation and pupils' intellectual development*. New York, NY: Holt, Rinehart & Winston.

Sackstein, S. (2016, October 16). Actionable feedback is essential for growth [Blog]. *Education Week*. Retrieved from http://blogs.edweek.org/teachers/work_in_progress/2016/10/actionable_feedback_is_essenti.html

Schlechty, P. (2002). *Working on the work: An action plan for teachers, principals, and superintendents*. San Francisco, CA: Jossey-Bass.

Schmidt-Davis, J., & Bottoms, G. (2011). *Who's next? Let's stop gambling on school performance and plan for principal succession* [Online pdf]. Retrieved from http://www.sreb.org/sites/main/files/file-attachments/11v19_principal_succession_planning.pdf

Stake, R. E. (2004): *Standards-based and responsive evaluation*. Thousand Oaks, CA: SAGE.

Stiggins, R. (2007). Assessment through the student's eyes. *Educational Leadership*, *64*(8), 22–26.

Stiggins, R. J., & Chappuis, J. (2012). *An introduction to student-involved assessment for learning* (6th ed.). New York, NY: Pearson Education.

Stone, D., & Heen, S. (2014). *Thanks for the feedback: The science and art of receiving feedback well*. New York, NY: Viking.

Tovani, C. (2000). *I read it, but I don't get it: Comprehension strategies for adolescent readers*. Portland, ME: Stenhouse.

Tschannen-Moran, M., Woolfolk Hoy, A., & Hoy, W. K. (1998). Teacher efficacy: Its meaning and measure. *Review of Educational Research*, *68*(2), 202–248.

Vygotsky, L. (1978). *Mind and society*. Cambridge, MA: Harvard University Press.

Wagner, T. (2008). *Global achievement gap*. New York, NY: Basic Books.

Wagner, T. (2012). *Creating innovators*. New York, NY: Scribner.

Walker, T. (2013, March 25). How do high-performing nations evaluate teachers? Retrieved from http://neatoday.org/2013/03/25/how-do-high-performing-nations -evaluate-teachers/

Wallace Foundation. (2013). The school principal as leader: Guiding schools to better teaching and learning [Online pdf]. Retrieved from http://www.wallacefoundation .org/knowledge-center/Documents/The-School-Principal-as-Leader-Guiding -Schools-to-Better-Teaching-and-Learning-2nd-Ed.pdf

Webb, N. (1997). *Research monograph no. 6. Criteria for alignment of expectations and assessments in mathematics and science education*. Madison: Wisconsin Center for Education Research, University of Wisconsin–Madison.

Wiggins, G., & McTighe, J. (2005). *Understanding by design*. Alexandria, VA: ASCD.

Index

Note: Page numbers in *italic* refer to figures and tables.

CORWIN LEADERSHIP

Anthony Kim & Alexis Gonzales-Black

Designed to foster flexibility and continuous innovation, this resource expands cutting-edge management and organizational techniques to empower schools with the agility and responsiveness vital to their new environment.

Jonathan Eckert

Explore the collective and reflective approach to progress, process, and programs that will build conditions that lead to strong leadership and teaching, which will improve student outcomes.

PJ Caposey

Offering a fresh perspective on teacher evaluation, this book guides administrators to transform their school culture and evaluation process to improve teacher practice and, ultimately, student achievement.

Dwight L. Carter & Mark White

Through understanding the past and envisioning the future, the authors use practical exercises and real-life examples to draw the blueprint for adapting schools to the age of hyper-change.

Raymond L. Smith & Julie R. Smith

This solid, sustainable, and laser-sharp focus on instructional leadership strategies for coaching might just be your most impactful investment toward student achievement.

Simon T. Bailey & Marceta F. Reilly

This engaging resource provides a simple, sustainable framework that will help you move your school from mediocrity to brilliance.

Debbie Silver & Dedra Stafford

Equip educators to develop resilient and mindful learners primed for academic growth and personal success.

Peter Gamwell & Jane Daly

Discover a new perspective on how to nurture creativity, innovation, leadership, and engagement.

To order your copies, visit **corwin.com/leadership**

Leadership That Makes an Impact

Also Available

Steven Katz, Lisa Ain Dack, & John Malloy
Leverage the oppositional forces of top-down expectations and bottom-up experience to create an intelligent, responsive school.

Peter M. DeWitt
Centered on staff efficacy, these resources present discussion questions, vignettes, strategies, and action steps to improve school climate, leadership collaboration, and student growth.

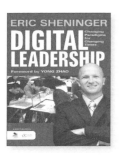

Eric Sheninger
Harness digital resources to create a new school culture, increase communication and student engagement, facilitate real-time professional growth, and access new opportunities for your school.

Michael Fullan, Joanne Quinn, & Joanne McEachen
Learn the right drivers to mobilize complex, coherent, whole-system change and transform learning for all students.

Russell J. Quaglia, Kristine Fox, Deborah Young, Michael J. Corso, & Lisa L. Lande
Listen to your school's voice to see how you can increase engagement, involvement, and academic motivation.

A SAGE Publishing Company

CORWIN HAS ONE MISSION: to enhance education through intentional professional learning.

We build long-term relationships with our authors, educators, clients, and associations who partner with us to develop and continuously improve the best evidence-based practices that establish and support lifelong learning.